Money capital in the theory of the firm

Money capital in the theory of the firm

A preliminary analysis

DOUGLAS VICKERS

University of Massachusetts

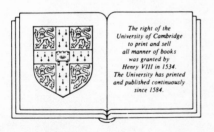

The right of the
University of Cambridge
to print and sell
all manner of books
was granted by
Henry VIII in 1534.
The University has printed
and published continuously
since 1584.

CAMBRIDGE UNIVERSITY PRESS

Cambridge
London   New York   New Rochelle
Melbourne   Sydney

Published by the Press Syndicate of the University of Cambridge
The Pitt Building, Trumpington Street, Cambridge CB2 1RP
32 East 57th Street, New York, NY 10022, USA
10 Stamford Road, Oakleigh, Melbourne 3166, Australia

First published 1987

Printed in the United States of America

Library of Congress Cataloging-in-Publication Data
Vickers, Douglas, 1924–
Money capital in the theory of the firm.
Bibliography: p.
1. Capital.   2. Business enterprises.   I. Title.
HB501.V515   987   658.1'52   86–23232

British Library Cataloguing in Publication Data
Vickers, Douglas
Money capital in the theory of the firm :
a preliminary analysis.
1. Working capital
I. Title
658.1'5244   HG4028.W65

ISBN 0 521 32841 1

Contents

v

PART II: The neoclassical tradition

Contents

PART III: Postclassical perspectives

Preface

The place of money capital in the theory of the firm is interdependent with the analysis of production, pricing, and capital investment. In this book I have examined those areas of economic theory that bear most directly on that analytical interdependence. In doing so, I have had principally in mind the needs of advanced students, including those who are making an initial approach to the subject at both undergraduate and graduate levels. I hope that my professional colleagues will be interested eavesdroppers, and that in those areas in which some novelty is proposed it might be thought that prospects exist for a meaningful reconstruction and new advances in the theory of the firm.

I have not set out, however, to construct a theory of the firm in its entirety. I have addressed the main issues of the relation between the firm's employment of real capital and money capital, and I have examined the linkage of those questions to the cost and availability of finance and relevant decision making in the firm. My perception of the needs of the student has determined the method and level of exposition. I have found, for example, that students have benefited from a reasonably painstaking exposition of the statistical foundations of probability theory and from a good degree of motivation for the mathematical development of such advanced topics as the utility function defined over stochastic arguments, the equilibrium theory of financial asset prices and yields, the cost of money capital, and investment decision criteria. A large number of more advanced treatments of these issues are referred to in the course of the argument and are noted in the list of references, but they are not all developed to the degree that might have been desirable if different objectives had been in view.

In the neoclassical tradition, the theory of the firm has not provided a rigorous working out of the analytical interrelations I have in view. As Boulding has lamented, the firm "as generally presented in the textbooks . . . is a strange bloodless creature." It is usually examined without any recognition of the place and significance of money capital. No serious attention has generally been given to sorting out the conceptual distinctions between, and the mutual dependence of, real capital and money capital. A lack of clarity exists as to the meaning and interpretation of capital as a factor of production whose cost may or may not be coordinate with that of factors of production in general. The need exists to reconsider the timeless, static, certainty or certainty-equivalent analysis of the firm to which our absorption with the general equilibrium apparatus has directed us.

The manner in which that need is addressed is indicated in more detail in the outline of the plan of the book in Chapter 1, which makes extensive prefatory observations unnecessary. After a preliminary sorting out of basic ideas and areas of analysis in the three chapters of Part I, I have arranged the main body of the work under the headings of "The neoclassical tradition" in Part II and "Postclassical perspectives" in Part III. The six chapters of Part II refurbish and expand the neoclassical theory of the firm in such a way as to approach, from that perspective, the possibility of an analytical integration of the kind I have referred to.

In Part III the argument is relieved of the weight of the conventional neoclassical assumptions. The chapters of that final part present an alternative view of the firm's pricing, production, investment, and financing interdependence in which, however, certain aspects of the preceding analysis are seen in a different guise and are accorded a different analytical significance. In the final chapter a new analysis is given of the firm's decision problems in the context of the uncertainties and ignorance in which economic action is bound. The neoclassical apparatus of the probability calculus and stochastic utility of Part II is replaced by potential surprise and a new Decision Index in Part III.

Parts of the book are unavoidably influenced by my previous writing on this subject, and that is referred to where appropriate. I am grateful to the University of Pennsylvania Press for permission to reproduce in amended form part of the argument contained in my *Financial Markets in the Capitalist Process*. My heavy indebtedness to the architects of the neoclassical theory will be clear from the chapters of Part II, and I have endeavored to make full acknowledgment to all those scholars whose work has formed my impressions and understanding in these areas. I am indebted also to those who have preceded me in the task of erecting a new and hopefully more satisfying and relevant body of theory, and I trust again that my acknowledgment of that debt will be clear in the argument of the book.

My thanks are due also to my colleagues, Professors Donald W. Katzner and Randall Bausor, with whom I have discussed many of the ideas contained in the book, and who gave me the benefit of their critical evaluation at earlier stages of the work. I absolve them, however, from responsibility for the blemishes that remain. I happily record my deepest thanks to Ann Hopkins, who undertook responsibility for the word processing and the production of the manuscript.

PART I

Theoretical issues and analytic motivation

CHAPTER 1

The firm in a monetary economy

Time, uncertainty, and money form an analytical triad that economic theory, if it aspires to realism and relevance, must take seriously into account. The historic, unidirectional flow of time carries with it the inescapable reality of uncertainty and the ignorance in which we are bound. Our analytical constructions that aim to explain the world must confront the influence, the ineluctabilities, with which the passing of time presses on our experience and understanding. Knowledge, it has been said, cannot be gained before its time (Lachmann, 1959, p. 73). Alfred Marshall, the architect of English neoclassical economics, cautioned that "we cannot foresee the future perfectly. The unexpected may happen" (1920, p. 347), and he pointed to the difficulties that arise, as a result, for economic decisions and action. Keynes's observation, when contemplating the impact of the future on economic behavior, that "we simply do not know" (1937, p. 185), recalls his well-known indictment of the classical economics and its attempt to evade the future by a probabilistic reductionism.

Many issues in the theory of the firm are brought into focus by these considerations. Terence Hutchison, whose work has provided luminous perspectives on economic thought, has seen these issues laced together in their interdependence. Noting that "uncertainty is present . . . in principle . . . with any piece of conduct in this world" (1960, p. 86), Hutchison observed with reference to the classical analysis based on its "Fundamental Assumption" of maximization that "the only way to make sense of most formulations of the Fundamental Assumption is to add the assumption of 'perfect expectations' " (p. 105). But perfect expectations, we shall argue at length, evade the real questions that claim our analytical attention.

If, in fact, uncertainty in economics could be escaped by allowing the assumption of perfect expectations to abolish the future, we would abolish also the third element of our analytical triad. There would in that case be no need for money. For there would then be no function for money to perform. Money, we shall see, is a time-and-uncertainty phenomenon. "An analysis of a world with any uncertainty in it," Hutchison has argued, "and particularly an analysis which takes into account the factor of money (which can be construed as a sign that uncertainty is present . . .), cannot start from the same assumption of 'sensible' or 'rational' conduct as that applicable in a world without uncer-

3

tainty, with which, consciously and explicitly or not, the bulk of pure economic theory from Ricardo onwards appears to have been concerned'' (1960, p. 88). Moreover, ''the assumption of a tendency towards equilibrium implies, on the usual definition, the assumption of a tendency towards perfect expectations . . . and the disappearance of money'' (1960, p. 107).

But the issues of time, uncertainty, and money have not adequately informed the theory of the firm in its received traditions. Notwithstanding the achievements of the Robinsonian–Chamberlinian revolution of the 1930s, the theory of the firm quickly accommodated to the timeless, static, competitive assumptions of the Walrasian equilibrium analysis (Robinson, 1969; Chamberlin, 1933).[1] A slightly fuller, but at this stage intentionally incomplete, consideration of some aspects of these questions will provide a basis for the argument of the following chapters.

Time

The theoretical problem of time is highlighted by the briefest look at the history of our subject. Marshall had insisted, at the high tide of neoclassicism, on ''the great importance of the element of time . . . the source of many of the greatest difficulties in economics'' (1920, pp. 347, 109). But his theory of the representative, or ''average,'' firm, though it was introduced in a context that took account of the evolution and decline of actual firms, served, as did Pigou's notion of the optimum or equilibrium size of the firm, as an intellectual construct designed to accommodate the realities of historic time to what was to become a timeless and static theory (see Robinson, 1969, pp. v–vi). Marshall had, of course, proposed the notion of economic equilibrium as analogous to ''the mechanical equilibrium of a stone hanging by an elastic string, or of a number of balls resting against one another in a basin'' (1920, p. 323), and he spoke of ''equilibrium price'' and ''equilibrium amount'' as these described possible market outcomes (p. 345). He went a good distance in accommodating his argument to the reality of the actual time span in which economic events transpired, and his conception of the short-run and the long-run period has become a familiar part of the analytical economist's tool kit (1920, p. 369f.).

But Marshall hoped that all of his arguments about equilibrium, along with his use of biological and mechanical analogies and ''all suggestions as to economic rest,'' could be seen as ''merely provisional, used only to illustrate

---

[1] Advances beyond the earlier static equilibrium theory, in the direction of intertemporal analyses, sequence models, and temporary equilibrium, can be inspected in Weintraub (1979). Weintraub observes, however, that while ''the path through [Walrasian] disequilibrium theory requires one to step through analytic time . . . 'real time' adjustment is badly handled in all these models'' (pp. 125, 127).

particular steps in the argument, and to be thrown aside when that is done''
(1920, p. 366). His cautions, however, were substantially ignored. The analogies absorbed the substance in the main body of economic analysis. The
Marshallian concern for the real and actual passing of time was transmuted in
the 1930s in the manner of Joan Robinson's influential *Economics of Imperfect Competition,* where she stated, in elevating the equilibrium theoretic tradition, that "the technique set out in this book is a technique for studying
equilibrium positions. No reference is made to the effects of the passage of
time'' (1969, p. 16). She did refer at a later time, in an admirable passage in
the second edition of her book, to her "shameless fudge" in having made an
"analysis which in reality consists of comparisons of static equilibrium positions . . . dressed up to appear to represent a process going on through time"
(p. vi).

Robinson's pathbreaking work in the theory of the firm, however, still in-
forms the traditional textbook treatments of the subject. She had directed attention away from the pervasive notion of perfect competition in economic
analysis to the notion of monopoly, or to the concept of the economic uniqueness of the firm. Commenting on the catalytic significance of Sraffa's famous
article of 1926 (Sraffa, 1926) and dissatisfied with the confusion in theory
stemming from "the logical priority of perfect competition," Robinson observed that "no sooner had Mr. Sraffa released the analysis of monopoly from
its uncomfortable pen in a chapter in the middle of the book than it immediately swallowed up the competitive analysis without the smallest effort. The
whole scheme of analysis, composed of just the same elements as before,
could now be arranged in a perfectly uniform manner, with no awkward cleavage
in the middle of the book" (Robinson, 1969, pp. 3–4). John Hicks, whose
Value and Capital in 1938 (Hicks, 1946) had substantially awakened English
economics to the Walrasian general equilibrium theory, has recently reflected
on this line of theoretical development by observing: "Why is it that the
theory of monopolistic competition, or imperfect competition, to which so
much attention was paid in the thirties, now looks so faded? Because it is
quite shockingly *out of time*" (1976, p. 149, italics in original).

Walras himself had recognized that time had to come into the picture. Consider the manner in which he specified his models of economic exchange and
production. "In *exchange,*" he said, "commodities do not undergo any change.
When a price is cried, and the effective demand and offer corresponding to
this price are not equal, another price is cried for which there is another corresponding demand and offer. In *production,* productive services are transformed into products. After certain prices for services have been cried and
certain quantities of products have been manufactured, if those prices and
quantities are not the equilibrium prices and quantities, it will be necessary
not only to cry new prices *but also to manufacture revised quantities of prod-*

ucts'' (1953, p. 242, italics added). In the italicized clauses, the realization of a process and a lapse of time emerges. "Production," Walras acknowledged, "requires a certain lapse of time." But the "complication" is immediately assumed away. "We shall resolve the . . . difficulty purely and simply by ignoring the time element at this point" (1953, p. 242). For Walras, there could be, in the economics of exchange, no false trading, or the consummation of transactions at other than equilibrium prices (see Hicks, 1946, p. 128), and in the production model there could be no false production. All bids and offers on all markets, and all tentative decisions, were understood to be notional so long as the search for the equilibrium price and quantity vectors continued, and transactions were effected only at the finally announced equilibrium prices (see Vickers, 1978, p. 14f.).

This structure of thought, from Robinson and Chamberlin through Hicks and the neo-Walrasians, has continued to influence the theory of the firm. It has failed to distinguish between what can be referred to as logical or analytic and real historic time. When the analysis has departed from the earlier assumptions of perfect expectations or certainty or certainty-equivalents, the future has generally been collapsed to the present by probability reduction methods. It has been imagined that although the future is unknown (and unknowable), nevertheless it is possible to assume, for decision purposes, that the future-dated variables in which we are interested can be described by subjectively assigned probability distributions and that the expected values of those variables can be unambiguously discounted to the present. By these methods, both uncertainty and the future are effectively abolished. True residual uncertainties have been metamorphosed to probabilistically reducible risks. We live, it is supposed, in risky conditions. But we know, or can assume that we know, the forms of the probability distributions that describe the possibilities ahead of us. In that strong assumption, we have effectively abolished ignorance. For we know, if that is the case, the general shape of things to come and we are no longer able to be surprised.

Progress is possible, we shall argue, if we recapture the sense of history and of historic time that gave credence to the earlier Marshallian analysis, and which has informed the work of Knight (1933), Keynes (1937), Robinson (1974), Shackle (1969, 1972, 1974, 1983), Hutchison (1937, 1978), Loasby (1976), Davidson (1978), Bausor (1982, 1984), Vickers (1981, 1983), and others. The relevance of time for the theory of the firm calls for analysis for several reasons:

1. The decision maker himself is locked in the process of actual time, with implications for his knowledge possibilities and his economic status and decision potential.

2. Production in the firm takes time, and cash outflows for the purchase of factor services occur before the completion of the firm's output and the inflow of sales revenues.
3. The firm's investment that structures the production process includes durable assets whose economic lives extend over more than a single operating time period.
4. The firm's investment in liquid assets, notably cash and marketable securities, is influenced by the intertemporal price of money or the rate of interest, as well as by the need to provide a refuge from the pressures of uncertainty and ignorance that real time involves.
5. As a means of raising money capital, the firm may borrow in the debt capital sector of the money capital market, and intertemporal valuations determine the cost and availability of such funds.
6. The firm's residual owners, the holders of its equity capital, receive its residual income after the payment of all costs of operation and interest on debt capital, and as the residual risk bearers they are vitally concerned with the intertemporal prospects of the firm and its income-generating ability over time (see Vickers, 1977, 1978, 1981, 1983, 1984, 1985b).

1   Real-time choice-decision point

To escape from the timelessness of earlier analysis, the breakthrough to a new logical construction must be made at one specific point. The significance of historic time enters economic analysis because the actual flow of it, and the unknowable expanse of it spread out ahead of us, impinge on the taking of decisions and the making of real-world choices. Historic time is significant because of the way in which it, or more precisely *our imaginative perception of the possibilities inherent in it,* determines what we do in our choice-decision moments and because of the way in which the passing of time qualifies our stance at successive decision points. The individual at his decision points in time does not choose between what exists or between probability distributions of what will exist, as though future possible outcomes are determined by a random generating device that churns out the results of replicable acts and experiments. Rather, choice creates history. Choice is between acts that hold out before them skeins of possible outcomes *constructed in the imagination of the person choosing,* skeins of imagined outcomes that are constrained to what the individual recognizes as possible. Expectations are thus subjective in the sense that they are highly personal and individual *imaginative constructions,* and in a given situation one individual will construct *imagined possibilities of outcomes* that do not occur, and could never have occurred, to other individuals (see Shackle, 1969, 1979; Vickers, 1986; Littlechild, 1979; O'Driscoll and Rizzo, 1985).

In his decision moment, the individual is perforce ignorant of the future, but he is able to conceive of "imagined possible outcomes" and assign to each of them a degree of "potential surprise." We refer to *potential* surprise because the decision maker can assign to possible future outcomes the degree of surprise he imagines *now* that he would experience *at a future date* if a contemplated event were to occur. He does this, in ways we shall consider more fully, because the decision he confronts is, in the general case, a "unique" decision. It is unique in the sense important for economics that the making of it precludes forever the possibility of its being made, or even contemplatable, again. In many areas of economic choice, decisions are what in this sense we call "self-destructive" decisions.

The decision to increase the amount of real capital employed in a firm, for example, along with the raising of money capital to finance that investment, must be regarded as a unique, nonreplicable decision. For the taking of it forever changes the firm from what it would have been if the decision to invest had not been made. Similarly, the annual rate of return on a firm's common stock cannot properly be considered a random variable that can be described by an assigned probability distribution. The firm that generated that rate of return this year was not the same firm, in many economic respects, that it was last year, or two years ago, or five years ago. Firms change their operating and financial structures, their product mix and input use, their market posture and penetration, and their technological orientation. Firms change, grow, decline, and die. The uniqueness of the decision maker's stance at his decision point in historic time, the uniqueness of his inheritance of endowment and environmental structures, and the uniqueness of his knowledge and epistemic status converge to determine the value he places on the actions he conceives to be possible and the choices that, as a result, he makes.

In the flow of time, knowledge is acquired by the decision maker. That knowledge cannot be unlearned in the sense that the individual can revert, after the lapse of time, to what he was and the position he was in, in every relevant epistemological sense, before. In their unfolding in time, successive decisions are, in their character and potential, unique, since situations, knowledge, and imagined possibilities change. We are therefore concerned with "an economics of movement and change, not in the sense of a mathematical dynamic system, in which time itself has been reduced to a serially dated variable, or in which equilibrium dynamic *paths* may simply have replaced equilibrium *states* without any basic reconstruction of the thought forms employed. Rather, I am interested in change in the sense of the next steps that, in more or less well understood situations, individuals might take to their best advantage" (Vickers, 1978, p. 21).

2   Production time period

The fact that production takes time raises the problem of financing the production process for the period between the hiring of factor inputs and the sale
of their product output. The firm accordingly faces a cash flow problem, and
this implies the need to obtain money capital in the required amounts and at a
satisfactory cost. The firm's production process and product mix, along with
its policies on marketing and market penetration, generate a demand for money.
Its optimum holding of cash depends on the rate of interest or, as we have
referred to it, the intertemporal valuation of money. This is so because the
debt incurred in raising the money capital to finance the firm's asset investment will have to be repaid at a later time, and the rate of interest associated
with it will depend on the spectrum of money market opportunity costs of
making that money capital available.

We shall keep in mind, however, not simply, or even mainly, the firm's
demand for money as such. In order to sustain its operations at any desired
level and structure, the firm will need to maintain an asset mix that is itself,
in some sense, optimal. Among its assets, the amount that is held as money,
or the proportion of the money capital available to the firm that is invested in
money balances, will depend on a number of complex considerations related
to the optimal use of the money capital market. This in turn will determine
the structure of the liabilities reported on the firm's balance sheet. For liabilities are employed to finance the acquisition of assets. The intertemporal costs
we have referred to can therefore be interpreted as the costs of raising, or
varying under designated circumstances, the liabilities to which the firm has
access. The costs of money capital will partly determine, also, the structure
of production and marketing processes that the firm undertakes, the timing of
its input and output, and the degree of real capital intensity it decides upon.

3   Real capital asset investment

The firm's decision regarding the real capital intensity of its production process implies the acquisition of fixed capital assets. In technical economic terms,
the firm's production function will be considered a flow–flow function, meaning thereby that the flow of attainable output depends functionally on the flow
of factor inputs. The input to the production function is not the *stock* of capital
assets actually held by the firm but the *flow* of services per period of time that
those assets provide. If, for example, it was technologically necessary or desirable for the firm to employ, during a designated time period, a specified
number of machine tool hours of a certain technological specification, that
flow of machine tool hours would properly be regarded as the input flow of
factor services. At the same time, an asset would appear on the firm's balance

sheet designated as the machine tool that provided the flow of services. But in the flow–flow production function, the machine tool is not the factor of production. If it were so regarded, we should be working not with a flow–flow production function but with a stock–flow function.

The question of time enters this capital usage problem in a number of ways. First, the durability of real capital assets again gives rise to the need to acquire money capital to finance the asset investment. Considerations of money capital sources and the distribution of available money capital over different possible asset mixes again come into view. Second, it may be desirable, under different possible conditions as to technology and the markets for real capital assets, to consider the optimum lives of the assets actually being used. The asset investment decision may confront a trade-off between an asset with a relatively short economically useful life that did not call for a high periodic maintenance expenditure to keep it in efficient operation and another asset, of comparable technological capacity, that had a longer economic life but required a larger periodic maintenance and servicing expenditure.

The capital asset investment decision depends critically on the level and stability of the future cash inflows that the asset is expected to generate and on the present discounted value of those cash flows. That present discounted value, or present capitalized value, will at times be referred to as the economic value of the asset. A relevant investment decision criterion will compare that economic value with the money capital outlay necessary to acquire the asset and bring it to operating or income-generating condition in the firm. Involved, therefore, is a discount factor (or rate of interest or cost of money capital) at which future possible cash flow magnitudes are reduced to present values. Alternatively, the future cash flows that an asset is expected to generate might be analyzed to determine the implicit rate of return they would provide on the money capital invested in the asset. Then that rate of return, which will be referred to under appropriate conditions as the marginal efficiency of investment, might be compared with the rate of interest or the cost of raising the necessary money capital. In either event, the intertemporal value of money, or the opportunity cost of money capital as determined by the complex of money capital market conditions, and the real-time dimension of the capital usage problem come prominently into view.

4   Liquid asset portfolio

An investment in money balances is required by the firm in order to enable it to pay flow costs of production and other maturing liabilities if the timing of cash inflows from the sale of products does not mesh precisely with the demands for cash outflows (see Davidson, 1965; Baumol, 1952; Miller and Orr, 1966; Brealey and Myers, 1984, p. 677). The demand for money is, however, a demand for a non-income-earning asset. The effective cost of investing in it must be interpreted as an opportunity cost measured by the income sacrificed by not allocating the firm's investable money capital to alternative asset forms that offer a comparable degree of risk. If, for example, an asset existed, such as a short-term government security, that promised a high degree of marketability and liquidity, it would conceivably make sense for the firm to hold a portion, probably a significant proportion, of its liquid asset requirements in such a form.

Investing liquidity in such income-earning assets, however, does involve a degree of risk, and a trade-off exists between expected rates of return on such assets and the risks they incur. In the case of short-term marketable securities, the so-called market or interest rate risk refers to the possibility that a rise in the general level of interest rates may occur during the time for which the asset is held, causing a decline in the asset's market value. In such an event, the holder of the asset will have incurred a capital loss. The firm might therefore be advised to hold liquidity in a diversified portfolio of marketable assets and not only, or even mainly, in cash (see the seminal paper, Tobin, 1958). The risks involved in such portfolio decisions have generally been assessed in terms of the dispersion of a subjectively assigned probability distribution of possible rates of return. This gives rise to what has become widely referred to as the risk–return trade-off in asset portfolio construction.

As a result of recent developments in the banking and financial sector, a wider range of income-earning liquid assets has become available. Firms are able to invest temporarily surplus cash in bank certificates of deposits, which may, under certain arrangements, be negotiable or saleable in the money market, thereby permitting access to cash funds at any time. Additionally, banks and other financial institutions are now permitted to pay interest rates on business firm deposits, and such rates, following the deregulation legislation of the early 1980s, are not subject to regulatory ceilings (see Vickers, 1985a).

The uncertainties inherent in the flow of time make the holding of liquid transactions balances necessary, and cash balances provide a cushion against unforeseen and unfavorable developments that would otherwise cause financial embarrassment or loss. The holding of money also provides a refuge from the pressures of uncertainty and ignorance that inhibit real economic activity. In this respect, it has potentially significant implications for the employment of real resources in the firm and in the economy. As Keynes has observed, "our desire to hold money as a store of wealth is a barometer of the degree of our distrust of our own calculations and conventions concerning the future. . . . The possession of actual money lulls our disquietude" (1937, p. 187). Money may be held when the uncertainties surrounding economic prospects make it desirable to defer the commitment of resources to real investment and the pursuit of real economic activities. To the extent that this is so, available real resources will not be utilized as fully as would otherwise be possible. The firm and the economy are in that case operating within, rather than on the boundary of, attainable production opportunity sets. In this sense, the firm's holding of money and liquidity is defensive. But it may also be offensive, in the sense that the holding of money imparts a degree of flexibility to the firm's production and factor use decisions, and may permit it to take advantage of previously uncontemplated investment opportunities.

5   *Debt capital financing*

The possibility of the firm's use of borrowed funds and the prospects of profit on the one hand and the risks and dangers of losses due to excessive indebtedness on the other have given rise to a distinguished literature in economic theory (see Kalecki, 1937; Copeland and Weston, 1983; Minsky, 1975). The economic significance of the firm's use of debt capital is due largely to the contractual nature of the arrangements entered into in connection with it. Loans are obtained by the firm from the debt capital sector of the money capital market, from both financial intermediaries and individual investors who purchase the debt securities as a means of allocating their savings funds. Certain kinds of loans, such as short-term commercial paper issued by corporations with undoubtedly high credit ratings and some short-term loans from financial institutions, may be unsecured. But in the general case, and certainly in the case of long-term corporate debt, the loans will be contractually secured. They may be secured against certain specific assets of the firm or by specifying the order of ranking of their claims against the general income-generating ability of the firm.

In exchange for money capital, the firm will issue debt certificates that specify (i) the length of time between the date of issue and the maturity date, or the date in the future on which the amount borrowed and described in the certificate will be repaid to the lender, and (ii) the rate of interest (stated on the face of the debt certificate and referred to as the "coupon rate") that the firm undertakes to pay each year on the amount of the loan. Additionally, the contract entered into between the borrowing firm and the trustees of the debt (or bond) issue will specify the nature of the rights of the debt holders in the event of the insolvency or dissolution of the firm. The debt holders, then, have what is referred to as a prior claim against the annual income and the assets of the firm. This means that the firm must pay the interest on the debt capital out of whatever income remains after paying operating costs, before any residual income can be paid to the common stockholders in the form of dividends. Moreover, in the event of the dissolution of the firm, the debt holders will have a claim against the liquidation value of the firm's assets before any distribution can be made to the equity holders.

Time and risk are interwoven in this nexus of contractual obligations. The lenders of debt capital will need to evaluate the prospective income-generating ability of the firm over the period of time for which the debt will be outstanding. They will be concerned with the level of the firm's earnings, the possible trend in earnings, and the stability of the income stream in the face of economic fluctuations. The greater the assessed or envisioned risk in the contemplated income stream, the greater will be, in general, the rate of return the lenders will require in order to induce them to hold the debt.

At the same time, the borrowing firm will make its own estimates of the likely level, trend, and stability of earnings and the proportion of its net operating income that will be absorbed by the contractual interest payment on the debt. If, as will generally be hoped, the rate of return earned on the money capital raised in the form of debt is greater than the rate of interest payable on the debt, the additional earnings will accrue to the residual owners, the common stockholders of the firm. In such an event, the stockholders are said to be realizing the benefit of favorable financial leverage. At the same time, however, the overall riskiness of the common stockholders' position may be increased by virtue of the additional fixed-cost financing sources (debt capital) employed in the firm.

6   Residual ownership investment in the firm

In the theory of the firm, a confusion and ambiguity frequently surrounds the treatment of capital as a factor of production. Most usually, the discussion of the factor combination problem considers capital as a factor coordinate in every analytical sense with, say, labor or other variable factors. Adequate attention is not always given to the "price" at which the capital factor is obtainable or to the manner in which its durability over time influences the specification of its cost. This analytical hiatus has stemmed from a failure to distinguish clearly between what we shall call real capital on the one hand and money capital on the other. Moreover, when that necessary distinction is established, a further question arises. In what sense, we can ask, is capital to be understood as a factor of production? Real capital, we have already said, is a factor of production. But we have indicated the sense in which, in a flow–flow conception of the production function, it is not the actual real capital assets held by the firm that enter the production function as arguments or are regarded as factors of production. The capital factor is described by the flow of services that those capital assets provide per period of operating time. Money capital, on the other hand, is not a factor of production. Money capital functions as a constraint in that it provides the purchasing power that gives the firm control over factors of production and necessary cooperating assets.

This distinction between real capital and money capital raises the question of the forms, and the possibly optimum forms, in which money capital should be raised and made available to the firm. The detailed and intricate possibilities that actually exist can be summarized in a twofold classification of (i) debt capital and (ii) equity, or residual ownership, capital.

The total equity capital employed in the firm derives from two sources. First, the sale of shares of common stock in the money capital market provides the initial infusion of funds to a firm and establishes it as a going concern. As the firm operates over time, it will distribute its residual income to the common stockholders, the providers of equity capital, in the form of dividends, or it may retain some or all of those earnings and use them to finance the expansion and development of the firm. In the latter case, the retained earnings nevertheless become the property of the equity owners, in the sense that their total stake in the firm is increased as a result. Many aspects of the relation between the firm and the money capital market have to do with the possible, or hoped for, increase in the market value of the shares of common stock that results from such a retention and reinvestment of earnings. An earlier and significant, but until recently a relatively neglected, literature in the theory of the firm wrestled with these highly important questions.[2]

Bringing together these sources of money capital, we shall incorporate into the theory of the firm what we shall call a money capital availability constraint. This will require a careful analysis of the possible form of that constraint, the degree to which debt and equity capital are combined to provide money capital, and the manner in which the constraint may be relaxed by introducing marginal units of either debt or equity capital to the firm. At the latter point, the question of the intertemporal value of money again becomes relevant. For the introduction of money capital involves a liability on the part of the firm to repay that money capital at a specified later date if it is debt capital or to service the equity capital by paying dividends at the end of each operating period or increasing the equity owners' claim on the firm if the residual earnings are retained. In either event, relaxing the money capital availability constraint raises the question of the effective economic cost of doing so. Entering the analysis, therefore, is the concept of the "full marginal cost of relaxing the money capital availability constraint." Its magnitude will be affected by the general level of interest rates in the money capital market, or the market's opportunity cost of supplying money capital to the firm, and by the evaluation of the risks involved as they are seen by the supply side of the money capital market.[3] That perception of risk will depend on the general

---

[2] See Buchanan (1940) and Williams (1965). Seminal work in the theory of the growth of the firm appeared in Penrose (1959), Baumol (1959), Marris (1964), and Gordon (1962). For significant earlier discussion of the integration between the production and the capital investment problems in the firm, which does not, however, take account of the financing question, see Smith (1959, 1961).

[3] On the question of the money capital availability constraint, see the early but neglected paper by Lange (1936). See also Gabor and Pearce (1952, 1958) and Vickers (1968, 1970).

estimate of the level, trend, and stability of the firm's future income and cash flow streams and on the existing debt-to-equity ratio, or the financing mix, in the firm's capital structure.

The question of risk enters in a unique way in connection with the availability and cost of equity capital. The equity holders are the residual owners of the firm, they receive the residual income after all operating costs and debt interest have been paid, and they are, among the providers of money capital, the residual risk bearers. They bear the final brunt not only of what has been termed the variability risk, or the risk of variability in the firm's income stream, but also of the default or bankruptcy risk. The latter arises from the possibility, however large or small it may be, that economic conditions or failures of management may make it impossible for the firm to meet its monetary obligations for the payment of operating costs and the interest on debt capital. In the event of the insolvency and dissolution of the firm, the claims that the debt holders and other creditors have against the assets of the firm rank ahead of the residual claims of the equity owners. For these reasons, the cost of equity capital will in general be somewhat higher than that of debt capital. This cost differential is an important factor in the determination of the firm's optimum use of money capital or its optimum financing mix.

Uncertainty

Our discussion of time has carried along with it at many points the question of uncertainty. We have distinguished risk on the one hand from true or residual uncertainty on the other. This is necessary because of the nature of our decision points in time and their economic environment. In economic decisions, we stand at a "solitary moment," locked in the "now" between a "dead yesterday" and an "unborn tomorrow" (see Shackle, 1969, p. 14f.; 1972, p. xi; 1970). The future is not only unknown. It is unknowable. Our task is that of corraling its prospects into imagined forms and shapes that permit us to choose courses of action that will lead us from where we stand to what we envision as preferred positions. We have observed that economic theory has generally come to terms with this question by assuming that the variables in whose future possible magnitudes we are interested can be interpreted as random variables describable by subjectively assigned probability distributions. The significant logical, or epistemological, question is whether meaning can properly attach to such a procedure and whether, therefore, the probability calculus is genuinely and meaningfully applicable for our purposes.

In his *Three Essays* a quarter of a century ago, Koopmans concluded that "our economic knowledge has not yet been carried to the point where it sheds light on the *core problem of the economic organization of society:* the problem of how to face and deal with uncertainty" (1957, p. 147, italics added). Sidney Weintraub had earlier wrestled with the fact that "uncertainty colors all economic behavior'' and that in the decisions of the firm ''uncertainty will color the choice'' in various ways (1949, pp. 339, 366). He was later to write of ''the operations of an economy in which anticipations dominate conduct, in which the expectations have an elusive vagueness, an unsureness, and thus an *uncertainty in decision making* that escapes model builders, who graft ill-fitting mathematical probability concepts onto essentially unique and non-repetitive events'' (1977, p. 4, italics added). But traditions became securely established, and by means of the assumption of perfect expectations, or that of the reduction of uncertainty to certainty-equivalents by the use of probability devices, more comfortable knowledge assumptions were embedded in the theory. By this means, uncertainty was reduced to risk, and the probability reductionism that was employed prepared the future magnitudes of variables for discounting to present values.

Uncertainty in its residual sense was abolished. Although decision makers do not know fully the outcomes that will result from their actions, they do, it was supposed, know the probability distributions of outcomes. But such an assignment of probability is, of course, an assumption of knowledge. Uncertainty, on the other hand, has to do essentially with ignorance and the absence of knowledge.

What, we can ask, are the conditions that must be satisfied in order to render probabilistic arguments usable and epistemologically efficient? Two possibilities exist. First, the events we have in view might be able to be regarded as outcomes resulting from a stable event-generating mechanism. They are then generated by ''the behavior of a system whose structure we can inspect, and from which we can deduce the relative frequency with which this answer or that will occur'' (Shackle, 1969, p. 53). Or second, the events may be conceived as the outcomes of genuinely and completely replicable experiments. In the first case we are dealing with a priori probabilities and in the second with *statistical* probabilities.

Unfortunately, the nature of decision situations in business and economic life, particularly in relation to production, investment, and financing decisions, are decidedly not the kind that permit the inspection of a stable structural system and the assignment of unarguable a priori probabilities. Nor, it would seem, is it possible to interpret probabilities in the economic context in the alternative or statistical sense. For the economic observations we make are most generally not the outcomes of repeatable experiments. They are what we referred to earlier as unique events, in the sense that the structure of forces determining them exists only once at a point on the passing continuum of time. Because that is so, the very uniqueness of economic events and decision situations precludes the treatment of relevant economic variables as distributional variables, or variables that are meaningfully describable by assigned probability distributions. John Hicks has recently cautioned us that ''the prob-

ability calculus, which is a powerful tool of discovery in the sciences, has
seemed to be carrying all before it in economics also. . . . It is my belief that
the relevance of these methods to economics should not be taken for granted"
(1979, p. xi, Ch.VIII). In the handling of the unique decision moments that
characterize economic life, "the probability calculus is useless; it does not
apply. We are left to use our judgment, making sense of what has happened
as best we can, in the manner of the historian . . . by all means let us plot the
points on a chart, and try to explain them; but it does not help in explaining
them to suppress their names. The probability calculus is no excuse for for-
getfulness" (Hicks, 1979, pp. 121–22. See also Davidson, 1978, Chs. 2
and 3).

The state of our subject so far as decision and choice under uncertainty is
concerned is clear, however, from the recent exposition and summary of the
theory by Hirshleifer and Riley, who define "the economics of uncertainty"
as encompassing "decisions made under fixed probability beliefs" (1979). In
the 150-item bibliography appended to their survey article, not a single reference appears to the conceptions of uncertainty we have just envisaged and
to which we drew attention previously in the work of Hutchison, Knight,
Shackle, Keynes, Loasby, Davidson, Bausor, and others. The conventional
probability theorizing has been consolidated firmly in the financial theory of
the firm. Mossin, for example, a principal contributor to the newer financial
theories, has crystallized the issue, as he sees it, as to "what the theory of
decision making under uncertainty is all about. . . . The theory deals with
choices among probability distributions. By choosing one action, we get one
probability distribution; by choosing another, we get another" (1973, p. 6,
italics in original. See also Vickers, 1978).

It may be rejoined that although in business and financial decision making
it is not possible to invoke probability in either an a priori or a relative frequency sense, it is nevertheless valid to employ probability in a *subjective*
sense and to work with subjectively assigned or "as if" probability distributions. This suggestion, however, appears wide of the mark, for it fails to
understand the meaning of the irreducible uncertainty with which real-world
economic decision making is actually confronted. For what, in that case, is
the basis in reason or fact for the postulation of probabilities? In short, where,
then, do the "probabilities" come from, and how is it possible to define
exhaustively the set of possible outcomes to which the probability assignments are to be made? Moreover, if we acknowledge the uniqueness of economic events and the nondistributional character of the variables describing
them, what meaning inheres in any attempt to take an average value of such
variables, an expected value for example, or to perform a mathematical manipulation to provide, for example, a variance or other measure of dispersion
of them? What meaning can be attached to the "variance" of unique mea-

sures of unique events or outcomes? We shall return to these questions in Chapter 12.

Money

The relevance for the theory of money of the issues of time and uncertainty follows from the fact that money is essentially a time-and-uncertainty phenomenon. In the absence of uncertainty, as in the neo-Walrasian theories of general equilibrium, all future-dated values can be unambiguously reduced to present values, markets can be assumed to exist for all commodities tradeable at all future possible dates, and in that event goods effectively exchange directly for goods. As Hahn has summed it up, "the Walrasian economy . . . is essentially one of barter," and in an economy described by the traditional general equilibrium theory "money can play no essential role" (1970, 1971. See also Davidson, 1978, pp. xiii, xiv).

Money, it has been said, is a link between the present and the future. It is also a link between the past and the present because we may carry into the present in money form part or all of the value of the resources we have decided to refrain from committing to active economic uses. In that notion lies the true function of money. It is a means of transporting purchasing power not only over space and distance but also over time. Money can serve as a store of value in the sense that when, in the presence of uncertainties, we are reluctant to commit our resources to investment in income-producing activities, we can take refuge in holding money. By holding money we are enabled to take refuge in deferred purchasing power. The holding of money is our speculation against our own lack of knowledge, precipitating a demand for money as "a substitute for knowledge" (Shackle, 1972, p. 216).

The same phenomena and pressures of uncertainty also influence our understanding of the medium-of-exchange function of money. Shackle has recognized the point. Granted that it is convenient to have on hand a store of general purchasing power to satisfy a transactions demand for money, an amount of money that is required "because we are not sure what we want to buy." Then "it is being kept because of uncertainty, a petty rather than a momentous kind of uncertainty, if you wish, but for the purposes of theory, of the *unity* of theory, this characterization is important" (Shackle, 1974, p. 62).

We shall examine in the following chapters the ways in which the exigencies of time and uncertainty provide congruent perspectives on the firm's demand for money balances and on its demand for, and investment of, money capital.

Plan of the book

The place of money capital in the theory of the firm follows from the interdependence between the firm's production, pricing, capital investment, and financing decisions. In the neoclassical or textbook theories of the firm, that interdependence has not been accorded a significant analytical priority. The "real" and the "financial" theories of the firm have enjoyed separate and substantially unrelated developments. Our task in Part II of the book, therefore, will be an examination of the ways in which the neoclassical traditions in the theory of the firm may be expanded to take account of the interdependence we have referred to. The chapters of Part II will therefore be essentially in the neoclassical tradition. Based on fairly standard assumptions regarding the structure of the single-product firm, Chapter 4 will present a model of production, money capital investment, and financing interrelations. In doing so, it is not presenting a "new" theory of the firm in a fundamental sense. Rather, it attempts to demonstrate the extent to which the received traditions may be employed to the best possible advantage to throw light on the money capital problem. An alternative construction, aligned with viewpoints that we shall term *postclassical* rather than *neoclassical,* will be developed in Part III.

The neoclassical tradition requires an understanding of the manner in which the probability calculus has been extensively employed to address the question of uncertainty or to abolish true uncertainty and replace it by probabilistically reducible risk. In Chapter 5 the foundations of probability analysis are laid, and the subject is developed in a self-contained fashion that is adequate for our present purposes. The foundations are thereby laid for the application of probability thought forms to financial asset choices and investment decisions and, in particular, to the question of the selection of optimum financial asset portfolios. The latter problem lies, in the neoclassical scheme of things, at the basis of the theory of the firm's cost of money capital.

Chapter 6 takes up the question of utility theory and the manner in which this underlies the neoclassical theory of choice. In conditions of risk, however, the theory of utility needs to be expanded and reconstructed to take account of the variability of the possible values of the objects of choice. We shall develop at that point, therefore, what we have termed stochastic utility, or the analysis of utility functions defined over stochastic or random possible outcomes. This again will contribute to the analysis of the financial asset portfolio problem, leading a stage further to the erection of the neoclassical or neo-Walrasian model of financial asset market prices and to the significance that that has for the firm's cost of money capital.

The remaining chapters of Part II then take up the cognate questions of the cost of money capital, the controversies surrounding it, and the alternative recommendations that competing viewpoints provide. A slightly fuller statement will be able to be made at that point regarding the neoclassical criteria for the choice of optimum-investment projects in the firm.

In Part III, with the building blocks and some of the superstructure of the neoclassical theory behind us, our attention will turn to alternative constructions. We shall develop in Part III, under the heading of what we have termed "Postclassical perspectives," two main lines of analysis. First, we shall suggest an alternative method of envisioning the interdependence between the production, pricing, investment, and financing decisions of the firm. This will require us to take account of the manner in which the oligopolistic firm, or what Eichner (1976) has expressively called the "megacorp," sets its selling price in such a way as to enable it to generate a cash flow that will contribute to the supply of money capital required for financing investment in the firm. The firm's selling price will be seen to be related to both its production costs and the mark-up necessary to produce the desired flow of internally generated funds. At the same time, interconnections will be seen to exist between the availability of internally generated funds and the supply of money capital, at variously specifiable costs, in the external money capital market.

Second, we shall examine more thoroughly in Part III the question of uncertainty, to which we have already referred in a preliminary fashion in this chapter. It will be possible there to set out more completely the manner in which the neoclassical reliance on the probability calculus and probability reduction methods can be replaced by an analysis of "potential surprise" defined over possible, rather than probable, outcomes. From this alternative perspective, a Decision Index for the guidance of investment decisions in the firm will be constructed.

It will become clear that the arguments of Part II, "The Neoclassical tradition," and Part III, "Postclassical perspectives," are not completely independent. Many of the building blocks and parts of the conceptual apparatus of Part II will be relevant, though frequently in quite different guises, to the basic thought forms and analytical constructions of Part III.

Preparatory to the development of the argument, the following two chapters of Part I will examine the basic questions of (i) the financial statements of the firm and the analytical perspectives that an understanding of them provides and (ii) the meaning and the relevance of the concept of economic value. In the neoclassical tradition, resting as it does on marginal optimization criteria and the maximization of attainable economic values, the problem of valuation is pervasive and stands at the core of the argument. In the last analysis, however, the economic values that can be generated by the firm's activity depend, in the presence of genuine uncertainty, on the rates of return that the suppliers of money capital require. Those suppliers may currently own the shares of stock in the firm and thereby automatically have a claim to the reinvested profits of the firm, or they may be suppliers of money capital funds in the external capital market. The final statements on economic valuation, therefore, will have to be deferred until the full treatment of uncertainty can be taken into account. In the meantime, the arguments presented in Chapter 3 will lay the groundwork and indicate some of the ways in which the relevant concepts have been exploited in the neoclassical tradition.

CHAPTER 2

Assets, capital, and capitalization

The conceptual foundations and technical apparatus of the theory of the firm require an understanding of the financial statements that describe the firm's economic position and structure. These are its periodic balance sheet and income statement. The examination of these documents establishes a linkage between the theory of the firm and an important dichotomy employed in many parts of economic analysis. This is the distinction between stock variables and stock analysis on the one hand and flow variables and flow analysis on the other.

On this important matter, the theory of the firm has been ambivalent. Following the recrudescence of interest in the firm's optimization problems in the 1930s, the distinguished economist Kenneth Boulding could still say, in the first edition of his *A Reconstruction of Economics* in 1950, that "the concept of the balance sheet, unfortunately, has not been employed to any extent in developing the static theory of the firm, so that as generally presented in the textbooks the firm is a strange bloodless creature without a balance sheet, without any visible capital structure, without debts, and engaged apparently in the simultaneous purchase of inputs and sale of outputs at constant rates" (1950, p. 34. See also Boulding, 1966, Vol. I, p. 305). Brian Loasby is probably not too wide of the mark when he comments on "the widespread contempt exhibited by economists for accounting (the more scandalous for not being recognized as a scandal)" (1971, p. 882). If the simple device of the balance sheet, or the firm's economic position statement, had been exploited at an earlier stage in the development of the theory, a clearer understanding would have been gained of the need to distinguish between such *assets* of the firm as *real* capital and such *liabilities* as *money* capital. But the distinction between real and money capital has not been consistently articulated.

A difference of treatment has been accorded the financial and the nonfinancial firm in this respect. The economic significance of the former, for example banks and other financial intermediaries, has stemmed partly from the portfolio of assets in which they have invested. The pools of savings flowing to them from the ultimate savers in the economy have been made available, along with the creation of new money in certain instances, to borrowers in the money capital market. It was natural, therefore, to emphasize the liabilities that the financial institutions registered on the receipt of savers' funds and the assets they acquired in their lending and investment activities. The theory of financial intermediation has investigated the criteria of optimum-asset portfolios, having regard to possible trade-offs between prospective rates of return on asset investments and the level of risks associated with them. The theory has examined also the sources from which such institutions acquire funds, in the light, particularly, of the disturbed financial conditions of the late 1970s and early 1980s and the deregulation legislation that occurred at that time (see Vickers, 1985a).

The nonfinancial firm, on the other hand, has not generally been accorded such a balance sheet analysis. Here Kenneth Boulding's indictment applies. The economic and the financial theories of the firm have led separate and unsymbiotic existences. The difficulty that static, timeless, equilibrium theorizing has had in finding a place for money led also, paradoxically, to a diminution of the significance of the financial sector in the analytical scheme of things. But there are reasons to believe that progress toward the integration of these different parts of economic analysis has lately accelerated (see Kalecki, 1937; Gabor and Pearce, 1952, 1958; Vickers, 1968; Patinkin, 1965; Davidson, 1978).

Stocks and flows in economic theory

The stock–flow dichotomy has enjoyed a lively existence in many parts of economic theory. Recall, for example, the intensive debates during the 1930s and 1940s over the correct formulation of the theory of the rate of interest. The differences of view were sharply focused in Keynes's *General Theory*, in which the rate of interest was understood as the variable that brought into equality the demand for money and the supply of money (Keynes, 1936. See also Robertson, 1940). An alternative formulation saw the rate of interest as the variable that brought into equality the supply of loanable funds and the demand for loanable funds. The first was a stock theory and the latter a flow theory. In due course, it was decided that, on a correct formulation, the two bodies of theory came to the same thing (see Harris, 1981, Chs. 15, 16; Coddington, 1983, p. 76). In its flow aspect, the interest rate was the price of loanable funds. In its stock aspect, it was the price paid for the privilege of holding money. That price was interpreted as the opportunity cost of holding money, or as the income sacrificed by not holding wealth in an alternative income-earning form, such as a short-term government security.

The stock–flow distinction was noted earlier also in connection with the interpretation of capital as a factor of production. The production function argument was not the *stock* of real capital assets held by the firm but the *flow* of services those real capital assets provided. Further, we can distinguish between the firm's stock of real capital, as that is described and valued in its balance sheet position statement at any given date, and the flow of investment expenditure, which, during any operating period, adds to that existing capital stock. Capital, that is, is a stock concept, whereas investment is a flow concept.

During each operating period, a portion of the firm's total capital stock will be worn out by virtue of its contribution to the production activity. This wear and tear, or normal wastage due to use, is referred to in the economic literature as depreciation, or as capital consumption. At the end of each accounting period, a deduction must be made from the firm's gross income stream to cover such depreciation costs. Those deductions are set aside and accumulated during the economic life of the assets so that a fund will be available to replace the assets at the end of their useful lives. Only in this way is it possible to maintain capital intact. The true residual income earned by the firm after making such depreciation deductions is available for distribution to its owners.

The stock–flow distinction has application also to the phenomenon of income itself and to the disposability of the firm's income stream. The total money capital invested in the firm by its owners, and the amount of debt or loan capital raised by the firm, stand in its position statement as stock variables, awaiting the payment of interest and dividends and, in the case of the debt, the eventual repayment on the agreed maturity date. A *stock* of money capital is entrusted to the firm in return for a *flow* of income payments, adequate in the minds of the suppliers of money capital to compensate them for the risks they bear.

Balance sheet, or economic position statement

The economic position of the firm at any date is summarized in a balance sheet statement of all of the assets owned and all of the liabilities owed by the firm. Consider the pro forma balance sheet shown in Table 2.1.

In the general case, and in an accounting sense, the balance sheet entries will be shown at what are referred to as book values. That is to say, the assets will be recorded at the values at which they were actually acquired by the firm, subject to exceptions we shall note. Similarly, the liabilities will be recorded at the value representing the actual number of dollars received by the firm from the various sources indicated. One such source of money capital is described in Table 2.1 as preferred stock. For our present purposes, this can be taken as a form of equity ownership stock, the differences between preferred and common stock being mainly twofold. First, the preferred stock is usually entitled to receive a fixed annual dividend specified in the preferred stock contract, while the common stock equity holders receive the residue of

Table 2.1 *Balance sheet*

Assets		Liabilities	
Current assets		Current liabilities	
Cash	xxx	Accounts payable	xxx
Accounts receivable	xxx	Short-term debt	xxx
Inventory	xxx	Long-term capital sources	
Fixed assets	xxx	Debt	xxx
		Preferred stock	xxx
		Owners' equity	
		Common stock	xxx
		Earned surplus	xxx
Total assets	xxx	Total liabilities	xxx

income that remains after the payment of preferred stock dividends. Second, the claim of the preferred stockholders will usually rank ahead of the claim of the common stockholders in the event of the insolvency and dissolution of the firm, though it will, of course, rank behind the claim of the debt holders. For those reasons the cost of preferred stock capital will in general be higher than that of the debt capital but lower than the cost of common stock funds. For analytical purposes, and recognizing that preferred stock financing is not used extensively in practice, we shall assume in the following chapters that the sources of money capital can be said to be simply debt on the one hand and common stock, or equity owners' funds, on the other. The debt capital funds may be obtained from either short-term or long-term sources, and in normal economic and financial market conditions the cost of the short-term will be lower than that of the long-term debt.

The owner's equity in the firm includes both the common stock account, representing the amount of funds actually received by the firm from the sale of shares of common stock, and an earned surplus account. The latter represents the accumulated value of the earnings retained in the firm during preceding operating periods. The funds corresponding to this entry will have been reinvested by the firm in assets, and they accordingly represent a genuine part of the total ownership investment. In the general case, and provided the outlook for the firm's investment and operating performance is favorable, the market value of the ownership shares of common stock will rise as the total earned surplus retained in the firm increases. The total ownership equity in the firm is sometimes referred to as the firm's net worth. In economic accounting, an entity's net worth is the difference between the total values of its assets and its nonownership liabilities.

It would be perfectly possible, of course, to construct a balance sheet or

position statement that showed the various accounts at current market values
rather than at book or historic values. If commodity prices in general had been
rising, the current market value of some of the firm's assets may be greater
than their original cost or book values. A profit would then have been made
simply by reason that the firm held the assets subject to market value appreciation. If that profit were recorded during a given time period, it would be
shown also in a capital surplus account on the liabilities side of the balance
sheet, indicating that to that extent the total value of the owners' investment
in the firm had increased. Further, the fixed assets referred to in Table 2.1
will be recorded net of the depreciation mentioned earlier. The fixed-asset
account will actually be entered at book value or acquisition cost less the total
accumulated depreciation that has been written off against the firm's income
stream each period since the assets were acquired. If the market value of fixed
assets had appreciated as a result of inflationary price changes and if it were
desired to record that fact in the firm's economic position statement, the increase in the balance sheet value of the assets would once again have to be
offset by a corresponding record of a capital surplus account on the liabilities
side. This would again indicate that the value of the owner's investment in
the firm had increased.

The information conveyed by the balance sheet can be summarized in the
following four statements. First, the total of the assets side of the balance
sheet indicates the total investment that has been made in the firm. The money
capital funds available to the firm have been invested in assets with the objective of generating an income stream and thereby economic values for the
owners of the firm. Assets are at work generating income. The economic
value of the investment, quite apart from the recorded or book value of the
assets, depends on, and is determined by, the level, time shape, and risk
characteristics of the income stream it can be expected to generate.

Second, the *structure* of the assets side of the balance sheet indicates the
structure of the investment that has been made in the firm. In any given
economic environment, there conceivably exists more than one way in which
the available money capital can be put to work in an income-earning enterprise. Each of the available investment alternatives can be looked upon as an
achievable combination of assets, and the balance sheet shows which of the
alternative combinations has been selected by the firm. This immediately raises
a twofold question. First, is it possible to establish criteria to determine whether
any particular combination of assets can be regarded as an optimum combination; and second, can it be concluded whether the firm's structural and
operating decisions, which are reflected in the combination of assets described
in the balance sheet, were in fact optimizing decisions? We shall return to this
important question.

Third, the total of the liabilities side of the balance sheet indicates the total money capital employed in the firm. It follows, of course, that as the total of the liabilities, including ownership capital, precisely equals the total of the assets, we must simply be looking at the same thing from two different points of view. In a sense this is true. But focusing attention on the description of capital employed sharpens the awareness of two significant facts. First, the availability of money capital constitutes a constraint on the investment decisions of the firm and establishes the optimization process in the firm as one of *constrained* optimization. Second, we are thereby forced to take analytical account of the distinction that this emphasizes between the money capital that is invested and the real capital assets in which the investment is made.

Fourth, it follows that in the same way as corresponding questions were raised regarding the assets side of the balance sheet, the following can now be asked with respect to the liabilities side. First, is it possible to establish criteria for determining whether a particular combination of money capital sources is in fact an optimum combination; and second, can it be concluded whether the decisions of the firm that gave rise to the particular combination of liabilities that exists were actually optimizing decisions?

Thus, the principal message of the balance sheet is a message regarding the structure of the firm. It describes the economic position of the firm at a point in time. In that sense, it is a static or stationary document. But it is a tool of dynamic analysis when it is recognized that the structure it describes, or the optimum structure to which it might be brought, is itself subject to change as the economic environment changes.

Transformation of assets and liabilities: dynamics of the balance sheet

Kenneth Boulding early perceived the necessity for an analysis of this kind as an element in the theory of the firm. He has conceived, moreover, of what he expressively referred to as the homeostasis of the balance sheet. By this he means that when, in the course of the firm's operations, it is disturbed from an existing structural state, forces will be set in motion to return it to its previously existing, and conceivably optimum, state (1950, Ch. 2). This notion of homeostasis, however, although it is useful for analytical purposes, "is clearly only a very first approximation . . . [for] it says nothing about what determines the equilibrium state itself" (p. 33), or in our terms, what determines the optimum structure of the firm at any particular time.

Boulding's perception, however, enables us to conceive of the operations of the firm as a successive transformation of assets and of liabilities. We conceive, for this purpose, of the firm's internally generated cash flow. First, money capital flows in and is reflected in an addition to the cash account on the assets side of the balance sheet and as a source of investable funds in a debt or equity account on the liabilities side of the balance sheet. As the available cash is spent on acquiring variable factors of production and materials, the cash asset is transformed into an asset called inventories, either of raw materials or work-in-progress or finished goods. At the same time, some of the cash may have been transformed into fixed assets. When in due course the firm's output is sold, the asset of finished goods is transformed into an asset called accounts receivable, and when the purchasers of goods pay their accounts, a further asset transformation occurs to reestablish the cash account. Hopefully, the final receipt of cash will exceed the cash outflow that was necessary to produce the output sold. The excess cash receipts, which will be reflected in the firm's income statement we are about to consider, will also be reflected in an increase in the owners' funds retained in the firm or in dividend payments to them.

This is Boulding's homeostasis at work. It can be linked now with the general structure of the firm's income statement.

Income statement, or economic performance statement

A logical order or priority of ideas exists at this point. Income, we can say, is prior to economic value. The economic value of any asset or investment is precisely defined as the present value, or the present discounted or capitalized value, of the income stream it can be expected to generate during its economic life. We shall return to this important matter of discounting or capitalization. For the present, we observe the general nature of the firm's income statement as shown in Table 2.2.

Consider this income statement in the light of the firm's profit function,

$$\pi_t = p_t Q_t - \sum_i b_{it} X_{it} - r_t D_t \tag{2.1}$$

where the following notation applies, with all variables being appropriately dated as indicated by the subscript t:

π = net residual income available to the owners
p = selling price per unit of output
Q = number of units of output sold
X_i = quantity of units of factor capacity employed for each factor i incorporated in the productive process
b_i = input cost per unit of factor capacity
r = average rate of interest per annum payable on funds obtained from nonowner sources of capital
D = total amount of nonowner funds employed in the firm

The equation states that the income available to the owners of the firm is the residual of the total sales revenue minus all factor costs of production and minus also the interest income paid to the providers of debt capital. The sales revenue item in Equation (2.1) is reflected in the first entry in the income

Table 2.2 *Income statement*

Total Sales		xxx
Less Variable factor costs	xxx	
Fixed factor costs	xxx	
Total operating costs		xxx
Net operating income		xxx
Less Interest on debt capital		xxx
Income before tax		xxx
Less Income tax liability		xxx
Net income		xxx
Less Preferred stock and common stock dividends		xxx
Retained earnings		xxx

statement, and the factor costs are reflected in what have been labeled total operating costs.

As in the case of the balance sheet, we are again interested principally in the *structure* of the income statement, meaning thereby (1) the proportionate division of total operating costs between the rewards to factors of production of differing kinds and durabilities and (2) the division of the net operating income between the rewards paid to the providers of debt capital and the residual earnings or rewards available to the owners of the firm. The structure of the earnings stream and of its distribution is related to two principal determining forces. First, the firm's decision regarding the optimum real capital intensity of its production process causes a division between fixed and variable factors of production or between fixed and variable costs of operation. This in turn determines the degree to which the net operating income of the firm will fluctuate when fluctuations in total sales revenue are experienced. The greater the ratio of fixed to variable costs, or the greater the degree of real capital intensity, the greater will be the magnification of fluctuation in net operating income when sales revenues fluctuate. When revenue falls, a greater proportion of it will be absorbed by fixed operating costs, causing a greater than proportionate decline in net operating income. A contrary result will occur when sales revenue increases. Second, the firm's decision regarding the optimum debt-to-equity ratio in its financing structure determines the degree of instability in the residual equity owners' income for given fluctuations in the net operating income. For a relatively large debt-to-equity ratio, a fall in net operating income will cause a greater proportion of it to be absorbed in paying the fixed contractual costs of interest on the debt capital, with, once again, a contrary result when net operating income rises.

The concept and the reporting of the firm's net income as summarized in

Table 2.2 may be subject to a number of variables and discretionary management practices that do not call for extended discussion at present. For example, the total operating costs will include, among the variable costs, the value of the materials used in production. The estimate of the value of materials used will generally be equal to the value of the materials stocks at the beginning of the production period plus the value of materials purchased during the period minus the value of inventory stocks at the end of the period. If inventory materials prices rise during the operating period, and if those higher prices are reflected in the valuation of the materials held at the end of the period, this will imply that the materials actually used in production were charged to the income statement at their earlier and lower values. Such a method of materials accounting, referred to as first-in-first-out, or FIFO, will produce a higher reported income in the presence of rising prices, resulting from a lower reported materials cost, than would occur if the opposite, last-in-first-out, or LIFO, materials accounting procedure were used. In the latter case, the final inventory stock would be valued at the earlier and lower prices, and the materials used would be included in the cost of goods sold and charged against income at the later and higher prices.

Second, a significant element of the fixed operating costs in Table 2.2 is the periodic depreciation charged against the value of the firm's assets. Various methods of depreciation may be employed. Straight-line depreciation writes off and charges against income each year an equal proportion of the asset's original cost. Alternatively, various forms of accelerated depreciation may be used. These have the effect of writing off a larger proportion of the original cost of the asset during the early years of its life. If, once again, asset prices are rising, depreciation by any of the methods suggested will gradually provide a replacement fund equal to the initial cost of the assets, but this may be lower than the actual replacement cost the higher asset prices imply. The accumulated depreciation fund will not then be sufficient to enable the firm to maintain its real capital intact by replacing its assets. In effect, some of its capital value will have been consumed during the time periods preceding the asset replacement because the lower-than-necessary periodic depreciation charges will have led to a higher-than-realistic reported income.

The depreciation charge thus affects both the balance sheet, where the asset values are shown at initial cost minus accumulated depreciation, and the income statement, where the reported income is affected in the manner indicated. But the periodic depreciation charge does not, as do other operating costs, give rise to a cash outflow from the firm. Important differences exist between the firm's overall income-generating ability and its ability to produce an internally generated cash flow. For many purposes of analysis, particularly in relation to investment expenditure decisions, it is necessary to focus attention on the *cash-flow*-generating ability, rather than the prospective *income stream,* that a project promises. All of these considerations make it necessary for extreme care to be exercised in comparing the reported incomes of different firms and in making decisions regarding portfolio investments and the choices between different firms' capital securities. This requires estimates of the expected income returns and the possible instability or riskiness of those returns that the holding of such securities provides (see Elton and Gruber, 1984; Brealey and Myers, 1984).

Operational and financial leverage

The first of two basic sources of instability in the firm's income stream is referred to as operational leverage. It results from the interposition of fixed operating costs between the sales revenue and the net operating income. It is reflected in the first half, or the so-called operating section, of the income statement. The second source of instability, which results from the interposition of fixed financial charges between the net operating income and the residual net income, is referred to as financial leverage. It is reflected in the lower half, or the financial section, of the income statement.

It will add concreteness to the analysis and will reveal the interconnections that bear on the optimization of both the operating and financial structures of the firm if we consider the information shown in Tables 2.3, 2.4, and 2.5. Here we imagine three firms of the same size, operating in the same industry

Table 2.3 *Earning ability of firm A*

Total assets	$1,000			
Debt capital	200 (interest rate 5%)			
Equity capital	800			
Financial leverage ratio	$\frac{1}{4}$			
	Internal rate of return			
	5%	10%	15%	20%
Net operating income	$50	$100	$150	$200
Interest on debt	10	10	10	10
Income before tax	40	90	140	190
Tax (50%)	20	45	70	95
Net income	20	45	70	95
Rate of return on equity, %	2.5	5.6	8.7	11.9

Table 2.4 *Earning ability of firm B*

Total assets	$1,000			
Debt capital	500 (interest rate 5%)			
Equity capital	500			
Financial leverage ratio	1			

	Internal rate of return			
	5%	10%	15%	20%
Net operating income	$50	$100	$150	$200
Interest on debt	25	25	25	25
Income before tax	25	75	125	175
Tax (50%)	12.5	37.5	62.5	87.5
Net income	12.5	37.5	62.5	87.5
Rate of return on equity, %	2.5	7.5	12.5	17.5

Table 2.5 *Earning ability of firm C*

Total assets	$1,000			
Debt capital	800 (interest rate 6%)			
Equity capital	200			
Financial leverage ratio	4			

	Internal rate of return			
	5%	10%	15%	20%
Net operating income	$50	$100	$150	$200
Interest on debt	48	48	48	48
Income before tax	2	52	102	152
Tax (50%)	1	26	51	76
Net income	1	26	51	76
Rate of return on equity, %	0.5	13	25.5	38

and the same general economic environment, having similar operating structures, and earning the same rate of return on their total investment. The latter,
or the internal rate of return, may be expressed as the percentage of net operating income to the total capital employed, or total assets at work in the

Table 2.6 *Summary of financial leverage relationships*

Degree of leverage	Rate of return on equity for indicated internal rates of return			
	5%	10%	15%	20%
Low	2.5	5.6	8.7	11.9
Medium	2.5	7.5	12.5	17.5
High	0.5	13.0	25.5	38.0
	Percentage variation in rate of return on equity for indicated changes in internal rates of return			
	Internal rate of return changing from			
	10 to 5% = −50%	10 to 15% = +50%		10 to 20% = +100%
Low	−55	55		112
Medium	−66	67		133
High	−96	96		192

firm. Imagine, however, that the structural difference between the firms is that they have adopted the differing financial structures indicated in the tables.

It is to be expected that a firm will have to pay a higher rate of interest on its debt capital as its financial leverage or debt-to-equity ratio increases, due, of course, to the increased riskiness of the debt holders' position. A nod in the direction of realism is therefore made in Table 2.5 by supposing that the rate of interest has risen from 5 to 6 percent in response to the sharply higher financial leverage ratio. In order to clarify the financial leverage effects in the briefest space, relevant data from Tables 2.3, 2.4, and 2.5 are summarized in Table 2.6. In this table, firms A, B, and C are referred to as low-, medium-, and high-leverage firms, respectively.

Several summary propositions may be adduced from the data in Table 2.6. First, in both the low-leverage and medium-leverage firms the rate of return on equity is 2.5 percent when the internal rate of return on total capital employed is 5 percent. This follows from the fact that the internal rate of return is precisely the same as the rate of interest being paid on the debt capital. No surplus earnings are therefore available to accrue to the residual owners. Only if the debt capital, when it is put to work in the firm, should earn a rate of return greater than the rate of interest being paid on the debt can the equity owners be said to receive the benefits of financial leverage.

But even in the case where no change in the owners' income occurs from a leverage effect, their overall economic position could in fact be worsened. This could occur if the potential instability introduced into their income expectations by the debt-to-equity ratio should induce an increase in the equity market's capitalization rate, or required rate of return. For this would cause a reduction in the capitalized value of their investment in ways that we shall analyze more fully. The example before us shows clearly how such effects may emerge. If the internal rate of return should be 5 percent while the rate of interest on borrowed funds should be, say, 6 percent, as in the case of the high-leverage firm, the contractual interest on the debt would absorb part of what would otherwise be the residual income of the owners, and the rate of return on the equity could fall to a very low level.

Second, in those instances in which the internal rate of return is greater than the interest rate on the debt, the rate of return on equity will be greater where the degree of financial leverage is greater, or where the debt-to-equity ratio is higher. This is shown in the last three columns of the first part of Table 2.6.

Third, for any given proportionate change in the internal rate of return, the existence of the leverage effect will give rise to a magnified change in the rate of return on the equity capital. Consider the last two columns of the lower section of Table 2.6. Increases of 50 and 100 percent in the internal rates of return caused larger rates of increase in the rate of return on equity in each of the low-, medium-, and high-leverage firms. Even more important, the degree of magnification of residual rates of return is seen to increase as the financial leverage ratio increases. But, of course, the same magnification effect can work in reverse if the underlying income-generating ability of the firm should fall. The reverse effect is depicted in the first column of the lower section of Table 2.6.

Economic decisions in the firm: production, capital, and finance

The theory of the firm has conventionally regarded the objective of the firm's management as that of maximizing the attainable profit under both short-run and long-run conditions. In the short-run analysis, the real capital stock of the firm has generally been taken as fixed. The operating decision problem was that of settling on the optimum amount of variable factors to employ in conjunction with the given plant and other elements of fixed capital. In the long run, on the other hand, all factors of production, including those that were taken as fixed in the short run, were assumed to be variable. In the long run, capital was assumed to be mobile. It could, it was imagined, migrate to other and more attractive lines of economic employment. To the extent that the theory broke out of the static mold that this summary of the short- and long-run comparison envisages, a legitimate target of management might be that of maximizing, or optimizing subject to the risks involved, the rate of growth of the firm. This is taken as the primary objective of the firm in many expressions of what we have termed the postclassical theory. In other cases, the objective might be that of maximizing the market share of the firm, subject, in some instances, to the realization of an acceptable rate of return on the capital employed.

Inadequate attention has usually been given, however, to the question of precisely what was thought to be mobile in the long run but assumed to be given and fixed in the short run. If it was real capital that was mobile, insufficient attention was given to the fact that the specificity of real capital assets diminished their economic and functional mobility. There is little reason to believe that a ready market exists for second-hand real capital assets that were initially designed for a specific economic use. If, on the other hand, it was assumed that money capital was mobile, it then became necessary to explain precisely how the money value of immobile real assets could be realized in such a way as to permit that money capital to migrate to alternative uses or other investment opportunities. The truth of the matter is that the money value of capital assets depends on the prospective income streams they are capable of generating in their existing or alternative uses. If the income-generating ability of an asset should, for any of a number of economic reasons, evaporate, the economic value of that asset will be reduced to zero, and its monetary value, if any, will be determined simply by its disposal or scrap value.

The linkage that the theory of the firm has imagined to exist between the short and the long run might not, therefore, exist. It is necessary to recognize that while money capital is homogeneous, real capital is a sum of heterogeneous units. Lachmann, in an early formulation of related theoretical problems, observed that to invest in a firm is to "de-homogenize money capital" (1956, p. 36), and he warned against the danger to analysis of what he called an "illegitimate generalization based on the homogeneity hypothesis" (p. 10).

The theory of the firm needs to distinguish between two different kinds or levels of analysis so far as the capital investment and the capital migration problems are concerned. First, we can envisage an ab initio planning problem in connection with which we can construct models of optimum enterprise structure. In that case, the theory of the firm determines the optimum relations between fixed and variable factors of production with which to produce an optimum level of output or an optimum product mix. Second, we can envisage a problem of sequential structural planning for a firm that is an established going concern. In that case, we need to understand how, at each sequential planning date in real historic time, the money capital availability that constrains the firm's structural decisions takes account of the money capital inherent in the true economic value of its assets. In some instances, claims to all or a portion of the assets may be able to be sold in the capital securities market and the funds made available for reinvestment. Or where appropriate, account may be taken of the money capital available from the liquidation value of those assets that can no longer be optimally employed in the firm. The theory of the firm has generally failed, however, to distinguish between these two very different capital investment problems, and analytical refuge has been taken in the assumption of perfect capital mobility.

More completely, realism requires us to distinguish between (i) the ab initio planning decision, (ii) the short-run operating decision, and (iii) the sequential restructuring decision of the firm. The last mentioned might lead simply to an expansion of existing facilities for the existing or closely related purposes or to a partial or total liquidation and reinvestment.

In Chapter 4 we shall establish a method of looking at the first of these decision problems. In doing so, we shall maintain the distinctions between homogeneous money capital and the heterogeneous units of real capital to which money capital is committed, at the same time as we envisage the linkage and interrelations between them. For this purpose, it is useful to conceive of a trilogy of decision problems confronting the firm. We refer to them as (i) the production decision, (ii) the investment decision, and (iii) the financing decision. The interdependence between the elements of this trilogy, the solution values of which will follow from the maximization of the value of an appropriately defined objective function, can be seen in the following way.

First, the production decision is concerned to discover (i) the optimum level of output, or the optimum level and combination of outputs in a multiproduct firm, and (ii) the optimum combination of factor inputs, both capital and variable factors, that should be employed, given the state of technological knowledge and the implied technological possibilities in the production function, to produce that optimum output. The product output decision will involve also, of course, a decision as to the market price at which the output should be sold, given the general assumption of imperfect competition or an average revenue function of the form employed in the following chapter, $p = p(Q)$. When, at a later stage of our work, fuller account is taken of uncertainty, the optimum size and structure of the firm may well be such as to afford the firm a flexible range of short-run operations. It may be desirable, in other words, to build into the firm a target level of standard excess capacity.

The decision to produce implies the presence in the firm of a production apparatus. The investment problem, therefore, is concerned to discover the optimum amount and combination of real and monetary assets in which to invest in order to establish and maintain the productive process that is necessary to produce the optimum output with the optimum combination of factor inputs.

But the decision to invest in this manner implies the need to finance the investment. It follows that the financing problem is concerned to discover the optimum combination of financing sources, or sources of money capital, that should be used to finance the optimum investment in assets necessary to maintain, at their interdependent optimum values, the size, structure, and operating processes of the firm. This financing decision may be subject, however, to whatever degree of unused borrowing capacity, or flexibility for varying possible future loan operations, it might be desired to maintain. The interdependence of the elements of the firm's structural decision trilogy will become clear. Caution must be raised against too easy an assumption of the efficiency of sequential rather than mutually determinate decision making in these important respects.

Economic decisions in the firm and economic position and performance statements

In the light of our discussion of the firm's economic balance sheet and its income or economic performance statement, we may visualize the manner in which the solutions to this trilogy of decision problems are reflected in those analytical documents. The outcomes of each of the decision problems will be reflected in two different ways in the economic statements, as reference to Tables 2.1 and 2.2 in connection with the following points will confirm. The perception of the relations between them will clarify further the interdependence between the decision problems themselves.

First, the production problem envisages a level of production and sale of output, and the sales revenue, or the level of output times the unit price at which it is sold, will appear at the head of the income statement. The production problem decision envisages also an optimum combination of factor inputs. The costs incurred by these will be reflected in the income statement as either variable or fixed operating costs. In the case of the fixed factors, it will be necessary to determine the periodic operating flow costs of real capital, including, as we have observed in a preliminary fashion already, the periodic depreciation costs. We have already noted that the structure of the operating section of the income statement will reflect the degree of operational leverage at work in the firm.

The solution to the production problem will be reflected also in the balance sheet, and here it illustrates an aspect of Boulding's homeostasis. To the extent that the production decision involves an optimum combination of variable and fixed factors of production, it will be necessary to invest in real capital assets to provide the periodic flows of fixed factor services. It is the latter, we recall, that we envisage as arguments in the firm's technological production function. That investment in real capital assets, then, will be reflected in fixed-asset accounts in the balance sheet or economic position statement.

Second, the solution to the investment problem will be reflected in both the balance sheet and the income statement. We have just seen that the decision to invest in fixed assets will be reflected on the assets side of the balance sheet. But we recall also that the investment problem is concerned with the optimum combination of real and monetary assets, and its outcome will be reflected also, therefore, in the current-assets section of the balance sheet, in the cash, accounts receivable, and inventory accounts. Additionally, the investment problem decision will be reflected in the operating section of the income statement for a reason that may escape attention because it does not give rise to immediate cash flows in the firm. We refer again to the manner in which the decision to invest in depreciable assets implies a periodic depreciation charge as an inclusion in costs against the firm's income stream.

Third, the solution to the financing problem will again be reflected in both the balance sheet and the income statement. To the extent that the financing decision determines an optimum combination of sources of money capital, envisaging a mix of debt and equity capital, the outcome will be reflected on the liabilities side of the balance sheet. Further, the need to make a fixed periodic interest payment on the debt capital will be reflected in the financial section of the income statement. The operating section of the income statement, it will be recalled, describes the income-generating ability of the total assets at work in the firm, and the financial section describes the manner in which the net operating income is distributed among the providers of the money capital funds. A portion, which constitutes a prior claim against the income stream, is paid to the debt holders, and the remainder, after the payment of taxes, becomes the residual earnings of the equity owners.

Economic valuation, or capitalization of income streams

Equation (2.1), in the context of the firm's income or economic performance statement, describes the periodic net profit that becomes the property of the residual equity owners. The theory of the firm has generally focused on this net profit as the maximand variable in the firm's optimization problem. It has, moreover, as Equation (2.1) implies, usually treated the profit problem in a static sense. It has assumed that when the firm is brought to an equilibrium posture and earnings position, the net profit will recur during each future operating period. For many reasons, however, the profit criterion is inadequate. But its deficiencies can be emphasized only when the questions of money capital and the lapse of real economic time are integrated into the firm's decision problems.

The firm must be interested not simply in the net profit that may be generated and become the property of the owners but also in what we shall call the economic value of that income. For it is this that determines the economic value of the owners' investment in the firm. In short, we replace the traditional objective of profit maximization by that of economic value maximization. That means, at one remove, the maximization of the market value of the firm's outstanding shares of common stock. To achieve this objective, it may be necessary to refrain from planning for the maximum attainable economic profit. For it is necessary to take into account also the risks being borne in the pursuit of that profit. The suppliers of money capital, given the assumption of risk aversion on the supply side of the money capital market, will in general require a higher rate of return to compensate them for undertaking higher degrees of risk. The objective of the firm, then, is to generate that income stream for the owners that, when it is valued at a capitalization rate equal to the owner's required rate of return, will attain a maximum possible value. Clearly, some difficult problems associated with the specification of that appropriate capitalization rate will need to be addressed.

It will give concreteness to the transition from profit maximization to economic value maximization if the following summary relationship is observed. Consider the profit variable defined in Equation (2.1), π_t, describing the firm's periodic net income accruing to the owners. The economic value of such an income stream over time, or, that is, the economic value of the ownership, V, will be the present discounted value, or the present capitalized value, of the income stream when that income stream is discounted at a capitalization rate equal to the owners' required rate of return. We may assume at this stage that this capitalization rate, ρ, is determined by money capital market conditions and will in general be higher or lower depending on whether the degree of risk to which the equity owners are exposed is higher or lower. We write $\rho = \rho$ (risk) to indicate the dependence of the required rate of return on the risk being borne, and we shall in due course observe the possible functional forms of that dependence.

We can therefore write

$$V = \sum_{t=1}^{\infty} \frac{\pi_t}{(1+\rho)^t} \tag{2.2}$$

or

$$V = \int_0^{\infty} \pi_t e^{-\rho t} \, dt \tag{2.3}$$

Equation (2.2) involves the familiar assumption of discontinuous discounting, whereas Equation (2.3) implies continuous discounting. In the simple case where the profit is assumed to remain constant through all future operating periods, and noting that the residual equity shares whose value we are here specifying have no maturity date and that they therefore earn in effect a perpetual or infinitely long income stream, Equations (2.2) and (2.3) both reduce to the straightforward expression

$$V = \pi/\rho \tag{2.4}$$

In these expressions, the symbol V refers to economic value. In the more complex cases that will engage us, the economic value will need to be interpreted as containing within it a greater or lesser degree of uncertainty. In the conventional theory in which uncertainty is interpreted as probabilistically reducible risk, the economic value will be interpreted as a random variable by virtue of its dependence on the time vector of periodic profit, the elements of which are also understood as random variables. The received traditions in this regard require us to bring into service the notions of the probability calculus. In the following chapter we shall examine the fundamentals of economic valuation more fully. Then in the chapters that follow, in Part II, we shall expand the neoclassical theory to specify a firm's objective function that takes full account of the money capital availability constraint. This will lead to a more complete demonstration of the mutually determinate production, pricing, investment, and financing decision solutions.

CHAPTER 3

The concept and relevance
of economic value

The concept of income is logically prior to the concept of value. The economic value of an asset depends on the future stream of benefits that the asset will, or is expected to, provide. In the case of an asset, such as we are preponderantly concerned with in the theory of the firm, which is expected to earn a specifiable amount of income or realize a definable cash flow in the future, its economic value is defined as the present value, or the present discounted or capitalized value, of that prospective income stream.

Our purpose in this chapter is to make these concepts related to economic value more precise and thereby lay the foundation for visualizing the determinants of value in more complex cases. In this chapter we shall not give an adequate account of the relevance to the valuation problem of the presence of risk or uncertainty. That important issue must await the subsequent development, in the neoclassical case, of the apparatus of probability and its application to the definition of risk and, in the later postclassical case, the development of the potential surprise analysis.

Economic valuation rests on the proposition that a dollar available today is worth more than a dollar available tomorrow or next year or at some other time in the future. This is not simply a matter of saying that a bird in the hand is worth two in the bush. For we may suppose that the expectation of receiving a dollar in the future may be held with absolute certainty. There may be no risk or uncertainty involved. In the ordinary course of affairs, a dollar received today would still be worth more than a dollar to be received in the future, for it could be invested for the period between the present and the date on which the future expected dollar will become available. The investment will then earn income in the form of a rate of interest, and when the date of expectation arrives, its accumulated value will be greater than one dollar.

We can therefore envisage what we shall call differently dated money values. We shall speak of present-dated money and future-dated money. Furthermore, we may speak of the future value of present-dated money and the present value of future-dated money. These concepts may be brought together and their relationships exhibited under the heading of what is referred to as the time value of money.

Time value of money

Consider an amount of present-dated money, referred to by the symbol P, which is invested for one year at a rate of interest of r percent per annum. The value of the investment at the end of the year, here designated as W_1, can be stated as

$$W_1 = P + rP = P(1 + r) \qquad (3.1)$$

This example assumes that the interest on the investment is added only once, at the end of the year. It thereby reflects the most extreme form of what is called discontinuous interest imputation.

If the investment were left to accumulate for another year, the value at the end of the second year could be similarly described. It would be equal to the value that the investment had attained by the end of the first year plus interest at the assumed rate of r percent per annum on that amount:

$$W_2 = W_1(1 + r) = P(1 + r)(1 + r) = P(1 + r)^2 \qquad (3.2)$$

It follows that if the investment is left to accumulate for any desired number of years, say t years, the value of the investment at the end of that time could be stated as[1]

$$W_t = P(1 + r)^t \qquad (3.3)$$

In economics, and particularly in connection with the problem of economic valuation, we are frequently interested not in the future value of a present-dated sum but in the present value of a future-dated amount of money. Present values of future-dated sums can be derived directly from the general expression contained in Equation (3.3). It follows by transposition that

$$P = \frac{W_t}{(1 + r)^t} \quad \text{or} \quad P = W_t(1 + r)^{-t} \qquad (3.4)$$

This procedure of reducing a future-dated sum to its present-value equivalent is referred to as "discounting." A more formal definition of present value is the following. The present value of a future expected sum is that amount of money that, if it were invested now at a specified compound rate of interest per annum, would amount to that future sum on the future designated date.

---

[1] The corresponding form of Equation (3.3) if continuous rather than discontinuous interest imputation and growth is assumed is $W_t = Pe^{rt}$, where the symbol e is a mathematical constant whose value approximates 2.71828. In this chapter we shall present the analysis in its discontinuous form. If the continuous forms were used, the discontinuous summations in the following section could be written as, for example, $\Sigma S_t e^{-rt}$ in place of $\Sigma S_t(1 + r)^{-t}$, or the integral $\int S(t)e^{-rt}\, dt$ could be employed. Forms of this kind will appear in Chapter 4, where more extensive use is made of the differential and integral calculus.

Present values of future expected series of money payments

Economic valuation is frequently concerned not simply with the present value of a future-dated sum but with the present value of a series of such sums. The problem can be visualized in the valuation of an income-earning asset such as a government bond. Imagine such a security with a face value of $1,000, the amount, that is to say, written on the face of the security and the amount that will be repaid to the holder when the bond matures and becomes due for repayment. Suppose that stated on the face of the bond also are words to the effect that the holder is entitled to receive an interest payment each year equal to 6 percent of the face amount of the bond. That stated rate of interest is referred to as the coupon rate. It implies that the holder will receive $60 per annum (6 percent of the $1,000 face amount) so long as he holds the bond. We can suppose, to complete the example, that the bond will mature and will be repaid (or redeemed) 10 years from the present date. The question now arises as to what value the bond would have in the capital asset market if the current rate of interest were, say, 5 percent. In that case, investors in general will be prepared to purchase and hold the bond only if they can acquire it at a price that will make it possible for them to realize a rate of return of 5 percent on their investment. Five percent is, in such a situation, the investor's opportunity cost of the investment.

By purchasing the bond, the investor would be assured of receiving in exchange for his outlay the total of (i) $60 interest payment each year for the next 10 years plus (ii) the amount of $1,000 as the redemption value of the bond when it matures 10 years from the present. We calculate the present value of these amounts, and therefore the economic value of the bond, by applying the familiar present-value rules. Using the notation V_0 to refer to the present value, we have

$$V_0 = \$60(1+0.05)^{-1} + 60(1+0.05)^{-2} + 60(1+0.05)^{-3}$$
$$+ \cdots + 60(1+0.05)^{-10} + 1,000(1+0.05)^{-10} \tag{3.5}$$

In general terms, such an expression can be written as follows, where S_t describes the annual interest cash inflow, M the maturity or redemption value, r the discount rate or the required rate of return at which the expected cash flow stream is being discounted or "valued," and n the number of years between the present and the maturity date:

$$V_0 = \sum_{t=1}^{n} S_t(1+r)^{-t} + M(1+r)^{-n} \tag{3.6}$$

The present value of the series of expected future receipts is simply the sum of the present discounted values of each of the separate elements in the expected cash flow when those cash flow elements are discounted at a discount factor equal to the investor's required rate of return.

Application to the firm's investment decisions

The logic of the firm's investment decision can be exhibited by employing the following notation and making an application of the valuation principles that have just been adduced.

S_t = expected cash inflow attributable to the proposed investment project in time period (or year) t

n = number of years in the expected economic life of the project

m = the firm's cost of money capital

k = expected true rate of profit on the project

V = economic value, or present capitalized value, of the project

C = required total money capital outlay on the project

J_n = liquidation value of the asset investment at the end of the economic life of the project

Recalling the definitions introduced in connection with the firm's balance sheet or economic position statement and its income or economic performance statement in Chapter 2, only a minimal further comment on the foregoing symbols is necessary.

First, the periodic cash inflow, S_t, is to be regarded as the enterprise net incremental cash flow properly attributable to the project being examined. It is derived by considering the total cash inflow that, it is estimated, would be generated by the firm as a whole if the project under consideration were adopted and then deducting from this the cash inflow that would be generated if the project were not undertaken. The difference will be the marginal cash flow due to the presence of the new project in the firm. The cash flow should be taken net of all operating costs but before the deduction of depreciation on the real capital assets. The reason for the latter is that in order to be economically worthwhile the cash inflow should be large enough to enable the firm to realize two objectives: (i) to set aside out of that cash flow each year an amount, by way of a contribution to a sinking fund, such that at the end of the life of the real assets employed in the project that sinking fund will be sufficiently large to provide for the replacement of the assets; and (ii) to provide, after the setting aside of that depreciation allowance, an acceptable rate of return on the money capital employed. Only if both of these objectives are realized will the capital committed to the investment be preserved intact, at the same time as the desired rate of return is realized.

Second, the firm's cost of money capital, here designated m, describes the estimated cost of capital that the firm will be required to pay in order to acquire the money capital funds necessary to finance the project. This money capital may be obtained by retaining in the firm, rather than distributing as dividends, a portion of the previously generated income. Or it may be ob-

tained by making new capital issues, by either borrowing or raising new equity, in the external money capital market. In some sense, yet to be explored
more fully, the firm's marginal cost of capital, m, will be an estimate of the
risk-adjusted rate of return that the suppliers of money capital require in order
to induce them to supply money capital to the firm and to accept the degree
of risk that that involves. We employ this discount factor in the present example even though, as we indicated at the beginning of this chapter, we are
not endeavoring to make full adjustments for risk and uncertainty at this stage.
Our concern here is simply with the logic and mechanics of economic valuation, and both the future expected cash flows and the rigorously relevant discount rate will be more fully specified in the chapters that follow.

Third, the required money capital outlay on the project, here designated C
and assumed to be made in one lump sum at the initial implementation of the
project, should take account of all necessary expenditures that have to be
made in order to bring the project to operating or cash-flow-generating condition. It is comprised of three elements: (i) the cost of acquiring the real
capital assets necessary to implement the project, (ii) the installation expenses
incurred prior to the operational date and properly attributable to the project,
and (iii) the value of the firm's incremental investment in current assets, such
as inventories and accounts receivable, which has to be made in order to
maintain the project in continuous operating and income-generating condition. The income stream generated by the project must be sufficiently large to
provide an acceptable rate of return on all capital expenditures incurred under
these three heads.

The economic value of the investment project, or what we have referred to
as the present discounted value of the future expected cash inflow stream, is
then estimated by discounting those cash flows at a discount factor equal to
the firm's cost of money capital. The expected liquidation value of the project
at its terminal date, which is referred to as J_n in Equation (3.7), will in general
include at least the nondepreciable portion of the current-asset investments
included in the total capital outlay on the project. It follows that

$$V = \sum_{t=1}^{n} S_t(1+m)^{-t} + J_n(1+m)^{-n} \tag{3.7}$$

This provides an investment decision criterion in the form of a comparison
between the economic value of the project and the money capital outlay that
is necessary to bring the project to operational condition:

$$V \gtreqless C \tag{3.8}$$

It follows that the higher the discount factor in Equation (3.7), or the higher
the cost of money capital, the lower will be the economic value of the project.

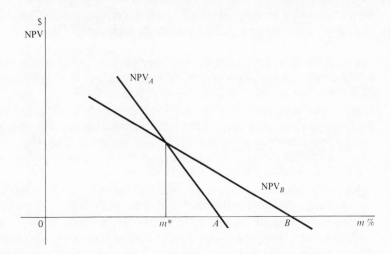

Figure 3.1

The net present value of the project, or the difference between the economic value and the money capital outlay,

$$NPV = V - C \tag{3.9}$$

similarly provides the investment decision criterion

$$NPV \gtreqless 0 \tag{3.10}$$

A net present-value function showing the dependence of the NPV on the discount factor (cost of money capital) may be described as in Figure 3.1.

This figure shows the net present-value functions for two separate investment projects, A and B. Each is negatively inclined as inferred from the preceding analysis. It could be imagined that projects A and B required the same money capital outlay and had the same economic life but that the time shape of the cash inflows was different for project A from that for project B. For higher discount factors, NPV_A falls more rapidly than does NPV_B. This would occur if project A cash inflows were expected to be higher in the later years of the life of the project. In that case, the higher discount factor would cause a larger reduction in the NPV by reason that it was applied to larger nominal magnitudes for a longer period of time.

At a cost of capital equal to $0A$ in Figure 3.1, NPV_A is equal to zero, and a comparable condition occurs at a cost of capital $0B$ in the case of NPV_B. To interpret these data, we can inspect an alternative formulation of the firm's decision problem.

Employing familiar discounting procedures, it is possible to estimate the discount factor that must be employed in order to make the present discounted value of the future expected cash inflows equal to the required capital outlay on the project. This discount factor is shown as k in

$$C = \sum_{t=1}^{n} S_t(1+k)^{-t} + J_n(1+k)^{-n} \tag{3.11}$$

The solution value of k is referred to as the project's true rate of profit or the internal rate of return. If, for simplicity, we assume that the terminal value is zero and that the periodic cash flow is constant, the solution value of k may be written as

$$k = \frac{S}{C} - \frac{S}{C}\left[\frac{1}{1+k}\right]^{n} \tag{3.12}$$

For projects of longer economic lives, or as n in Equation (3.12) increases, the true rate of profit approaches asymptotically the value S/C. This will be recognized as the reciprocal of the project's payoff period. The latter, or C/S, is the number of years it would take for the project's cumulative annual cash inflows to aggregate to the initial capital investment outlay.

Given the computation of the true rate of profit in the investment project, the investment decision criterion can be established by comparing the rate of profit with the firm's marginal cost of money capital:

$$k \gtreqless m \tag{3.13}$$

For an investment project in which a capital outlay in the present is followed by a positive return cash inflow each year during the life of the project, the criteria derived in Equations (3.8), (3.10), and (3.13) will all provide the same answer to an accept-or-reject decision.

Returning now to Figure 3.1 and recalling the definition of the true rate of profit as the discount factor that equates the economic value of the cash inflows to the money capital outlay, or the NPV to zero, the abscissa intercepts in Figure 3.1 can be understood as describing the true rates of profit in the respective investment projects.

The possibilities shown in Figure 3.1, however, illustrate the difficulties in using the investment decision criteria as ranking devices when it is desired to specify the order of ranking or desirability of different projects. If, for example, the rate-of-profit criterion were used, project B would be ranked ahead of, or would be preferred to, project A. But if the NPV criterion were used for ranking purposes, no single unambiguous answer would be provided. For at discount factors higher than m^*, project B has a higher NPV than does project A. But at discount factors below m^*, the opposite ranking occurs. We have, then, the potential problem of inverse rankings at low costs of capital.

In such an event, the economically correct order of preference will always be given by the economic value criterion, for this, as will be seen immediately, involves a more conservative reinvestment rate assumption.

The reinvestment rate assumption is understood by referring again to the solution value of the true rate of profit k in Equation (3.11). This, we recall, is derived from the periodic cash flows of S_t. The cash flow elements, in turn, can be regarded as divisible into (i) a "return-of-capital" component that is, as we have seen, placed into a sinking fund to provide for the replacement of the real assets involved in the project and (ii) a "true residual income" component. In order to conclude that the solution value of k is in fact a true rate of profit, the return-of-capital components must be able to be reinvested at the same cumulative annual rate of return as k, the rate being earned on the original project.

Consider for the moment that k is in this rigorous sense a true rate of profit. Then the residual income generated by the investment must be regarded as k percent of the original capital committed to it. Taking kC, therefore, as a measure of the true income component of the cash flow, the balance, or $S - kC$, must be regarded as the return-of-capital component available to preserve the original capital investment intact. If such an amount, $S - kC$, is reinvested at the end of the first year of the life of the project and accumulated at k percent per annum, its accumulated value at the terminal date of the project will be equal to $(S - kC) (1 + k)^{n-1}$. If all such annual reinvestment components were similarly accumulated, the condition it is desired to attain by the terminal date would be described as

$$C = \sum_{t=1}^{n} (S - kC)(1 + k)^{n-t} \tag{3.14}$$

It can be shown by algebraic manipulation that the same value of k satisfies both Equations (3.11) and (3.14). If, therefore, there is reason to believe that the periodic return-of-capital components of the cash flow cannot be reinvested at as favorable a rate as appears to be earned on the original project, then in order to maintain the capital investment intact, the annual return-of-capital components will have to be larger. In that event, the residual income components will be smaller, and the true rate of profit will accordingly be lower than was initially anticipated. The amount by which the true estimate of the rate of return must then be reduced will depend on the assumption that is made regarding the attainable reinvestment rate.

A project's NPV function will be monotonically negative as in Figure 3.1 only in connection with what we refer to as a normal investment project. This may be defined as a project for which a cash outlay in the present is followed by a positive cash inflow each period in the future. Correspondingly, a nonnormal investment project will be one in which the cash inflows are negative

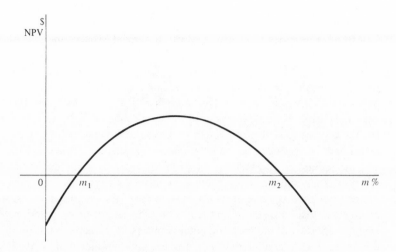

Figure 3.2

in one or more years in the future. A negative cash inflow may be caused by the need to make unusually high maintenance expenditures in a particular year. When a change of sign in the elements of the cash flow vector occurs, it can be shown that the NPV function will cross the abscissa, as in Figure 3.2, for example, as many times as the number of changes of sign in the cash flow elements.

This is because the solution value of the true rate of profit, or k in Equation (3.11), is provided by the positive roots of an nth-degree polynomial for a project whose cash flow extends for n years. For a "normal" project as defined above, the solution values of these roots converge on one positive real magnitude. Multiple solution values, or multiple roots of the relevant polynomial, occur in the "nonnormal" case. Consider a project that had a life of two years with a cash outflow to finance the project occurring at the beginning of the first year followed by a cash inflow at the end of the first and second years. This would mean that the true rate of profit would be provided by the positive root of a second-degree equation. The cash flow would contain one change of sign, negative at the beginning of the first year (the investment outflow) and positive at the end of the first and second years (the cash inflows). This one change of sign would provide one positive real root, described in Figure 3.1 by the abscissa intercept. An investment outlay today of $100, for example, may be followed by cash inflows of $10 and $110, respectively, one and two years from the present date. Equation (3.11) would then specify the rate of profit as the positive solution value of k in the equation

$100 = 10(1+k)^{-1} + 110(1+k)^{-2}$. This requires a solution of the equation $100(1+k)^2 = 10(1+k) + 110$ or the second-degree polynomial $100k^2 + 190k - 20 = 0$. This provides a positive root of 10 percent. That is the rate of profit in the project.

In the example exhibited in Figure 3.2, the project will display positive net present values for costs of capital between m_1 and m_2. But at costs of capital or discount factors outside of that range the NPV is negative. We then have what is referred to as the problem of multiple roots, or multiple solution values for k in the rate of profit equation. Given that condition, the appropriate investment decision can be made by discounting the cash flows at a specified cost of capital and formulating the problem in terms of the economic value criterion. That criterion makes the conservative assumption that the cash flows can be reinvested at a rate of return equal to the cost of capital, a less stringent assumption than is made in that respect by the rate-of-profit criterion. If, as we have envisaged, the cost of capital is interpretable as an opportunity cost, it is reasonable to assume that reinvestment opportunities will be available at that rate (see Lorie and Savage, 1955; Solomon, 1956).

Economic value and the relevance of separation theorems

The logic of the preceding analysis points to a significant proposition. Provided it is possible to specify an opportunity cost of capital or a required rate of return, or a relevant discount factor or capitalization rate at which future-dated sums may be discounted to their present values, optimization decisions should be made by maximizing present or economic values. This has become a widely accepted rule in the economics of financial optimization. It has been argued that on the assumption that borrowing and lending of money capital can take place at a designated rate of interest, intertemporal production and consumption decisions can be "separated." The so-called separation theorems that have entered the literature are highly relevant to the neoclassical (or neo-Walrasian) equilibrium theory of financial asset prices and to the significance those prices have for the firm's cost of money capital. In preparation for our encounter with that level of argument in Part II, we may look at two reasonably straightforward applications to this question of the economic valuation apparatus we have examined in this chapter. In this exposition, we shall make use of the neoclassical assumption that unlimited borrowing and lending opportunities exist in perfect capital markets and that no single borrower or lender is able, by his individual actions, to exert any impact on the assumedly equilibrium rate of interest that exists.

Consider for this purpose an individual who (1) possesses a given resource endowment at the present time, t_0, and who has the sure prospect of a future income endowment accruing at the end of one time period from the present, at t_1; (2) is confronted with definable intertemporal production opportunities

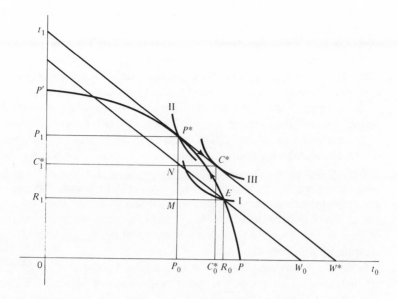

Figure 3.3

extending over the same single time period; and (3) has the opportunity of borrowing or lending over the same time period at a given and exogenously determined market rate of interest. Such a situation is described in Figure 3.3.

In Figure 3.3, the axes labeled t_0 and t_1 represent resource availabilities at each of the two time dates. The point E indicates that the individual's time vector of endowments is described by R_0 and R_1. Through the endowment point, an intertemporal production possibility or production transformation frontier, PP', is described. This indicates that by consuming less than his given endowment in the current period and devoting part of his resources to production, a larger amount of consumable resources could be made available to the individual in the following period. The extent to which this would be economically advisable would depend on his intertemporal consumption preferences, on the intertemporal production possibilities, and as we shall see, on the externally given market rate of interest.

Let us assume that a market rate of interest r is implicitly defined by the slope of the valuation line intercepting the t_0 axis at W_0. The magnitude of W_0 then describes the value of the individual's two-period endowment vector, measured in present-value magnitudes, by virtue of the fact that the valuation line passes through the endowment point E. In other words,

$$W_0 = R_0 + R_1/(1+r) \qquad (3.15)$$

and every point on the same valuation line would have the same present value.

An indifference curve through the endowment point E, labeled I, indicates that E does not lie on the highest attainable indifference curve. For by moving along the production transformation frontier from E in the direction indicated by the arrow, the individual can climb on to higher indifference curves. He would then be investing part of his currently available resources in production activities, the output of which would accrue in the following period.

The optimum extent of such an intertemporal resource reallocation will depend on the given rate of interest. The production possibility frontier is crossing a family of valuation lines that are parallel by virtue of the given rate of interest, and the optimum production point will be P^* in the diagram. At that point, the production possibility frontier is tangential to the highest attainable valuation line. Two conclusions may then be drawn. First, the marginal rate of intertemporal product transformation, or the marginal internal rate of return on resources devoted to production, is equal to the market rate of interest and, second, the individual has maximized his attainable wealth measure by W^* on the t_0 axis.

Given the endowment point E, it follows that by allocating $EM = R_0 P_0$ to production, the next period's output can be increased by $MP^* = R_1 P_1$. The total resources available for consumption in the next period would then be the sum of $0R_1$, the prospect of next period's income included in the present endowment, and $R_1 P_1$, or $0P_1 = P_0 P^*$. But even though the point P^* represents the maximum attainable wealth position, it does not represent the individual's optimum intertemporal consumption allocation.

Consider now the indifference curve labeled II, which cuts the production frontier and the valuation line at P^*. The individual can attain a higher level of utility by moving back along the highest attainable valuation line in the direction of the arrow. In Figure 3.3, he will move to the optimum-consumption point C^*, at which an indifference curve is tangential to the valuation line. At that point, the marginal rate of intertemporal resource substitution in consumption will be equal to the market rate of interest and also, therefore, to the marginal rate of intertemporal resource transformation in production.

By taking these actions, the individual has made two moves that, by virtue of the *given* market rate of interest, we can regard as *separable*, thus laying the foundation for what we anticipated as a separation theorem. This states that the optimum intertemporal consumption decision is *separable from* the corresponding production decision. The individual can thus be thought of as moving first from his endowment point E to the optimum-production point P^* and then back to the optimum-consumption point C^*. In order to make the move from P^* to C^*, the individual will *borrow* at the market rate of interest an amount of consumable resources equal to C^*N in present value terms, and he will therefore have to repay the equivalent of this amount out of the next

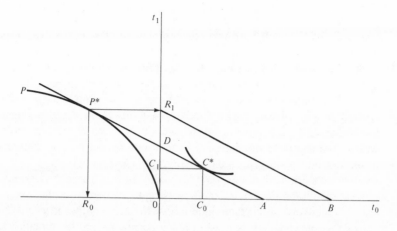

Figure 3.4

period's production, or the amount of $P*N$ in next-period values. This borrowing and subsequent repayment transmutes the optimum-production vector (P_0, P_1) into the optimum-consumption vector (C_0^*, C_1^*). It permits the individual to achieve a consumption vector that lies outside of the production possibility frontier, PP'.

Alternatively, by comparing the original endowment point E and the final-consumption point C^*, we could regard the overall operation as reducing the current consumption from the current endowment of R_0 to C_0^*, the difference between these two amounts being allocated to production. Then a further amount of $C_0^*P_0$ is borrowed and also allocated to production in order that in the next period the total amount of resources will be increased from the endowment of R_1 to P_0P^*. Out of this latter total the amount of NP^* will be used to repay borrowing, and the residue of $P_0N = 0C_1^*$ will be available for consumption.

A similar condition, focusing on the financing of resource utilization and production in the firm, can be observed from Figure 3.4. Here the firm is assumed to have no initial resource endowment, and its intertemporal production possibility frontier, described by the concave locus $0P$ in the left-hand quadrant of the figure, therefore emanates from the origin. Magnitudes to the right of the origin on the horizontal axis represent individuals' positive-resource availabilities measured in present values. Magnitudes to the left represent resource amounts borrowed by firms from individuals and employed as inputs to production.

The concavity of the production possibility frontier in the left-hand quadrant of the figure indicates that the firm experiences diminishing marginal productivity as the level of resource input is increased. In the conditions envisioned, the firm will borrow an amount equal to $0R_0$ in the present period and will use this as an input to production to realize an output of $R_0P^* = 0R_1$ in the next period. It is assumed that the firm will borrow the money capital needed to finance this production at an interest rate of r percent, given by the slope of the parallel valuation lines P^*A and R_1B. The optimality of the production point P^*, where the production possibility frontier is again tangential to a valuation line, follows from the equality between the rate of interest at which it borrows and the marginal internal rate of return in production. The amount of borrowing equals $0R_0 = R_1P^* = AB$, and the repayment out of the next period's production will equal R_1D. This implies that of the next period's production of $0R_1$, the net amount remaining to the owners of the firm will be $0D$. Alternatively, in current-value terms, the gross output from production equals $0B$, of which AB is used to repay borrowing and $0A$ remains for the owners.

The owners' intertemporal consumption opportunity set is described by the triangular space $0DA$ because the future net income of $0D$ has a present value of $0A$. The owners need not wait, however, until the acquisition of $0D$ resources in the next period before they consume. Given the market rate of interest, they may move down along the valuation line DA until they reach their optimum consumption point C^*. At that point their subjective marginal rate of substitution between present and future consumption, the slope of the indifference curve at C^*, is equal to the market rate of interest at which they have borrowed. The owners, then, will borrow $0C_0 = C_1C^*$ for present consumption, in exchange for which they will repay C_1D out of their future expected net income. The remaining part of that net income, $0C_1$, will then be available for consumption in the next period.

In this exercise, *given the market rate of interest*, the firm's investment, production, and financing decisions are *separable from* the owners' consumption decision. The form of the owners' consumption utility function, in other words, is quite irrelevant to the firm's optimum borrowing, investment, and production decisions. Given the market rate of interest and *given the ability of both the firm and its individual owners to borrow at that rate*, the only thing the firm's managers need worry about is the maximization of the present value of the future expected revenue stream of the firm. If, in the example, the firm produces at a maximum point P^*, the owners' ability to borrow at the market rate of interest, or, that is, to sell claims against their future expected income, enables them to achieve any intertemporal consumption vector they wish.

The notion of economic value that we have developed in this chapter, along with the adoption of the maximization of economic value as the firm's overriding objective, is prominently displayed in the neoclassical theory of the firm. That body of theory has not yet, however, reached a completely satisfying integration of the valuation problem with those of the simultaneous optimization of the firm's production, capital investment, pricing, and financing decisions. In the chapters of Part II that follow, we shall investigate the main lines of the integrative structures that might be forged within the neoclassical theory. We shall be able, then, to set against this body of thought the newer perspectives we shall adduce in Part III.

The neoclassical tradition

CHAPTER 4

Production, pricing, investment, and financing interdependence in the firm

The theory of the firm in a real-time, money-using economy must be grounded in the interdependent theories of production, capital investment, and finance. Traditionally, the theory of the firm has begun its analysis of production by positing a Marshallian short-run period in which, as the real capital employed in the firm was given and fixed, attention could focus on choosing the variable-factor inputs with which to produce specified levels of output. Then, at a later stage, the assumptions of the Marshallian long run took account of the possibility or desirability of varying the fixed factors also.

The problem in this scheme of things is that no significant place exists for money capital. The real capital–money capital dichotomy is not addressed. No meaningful discussion is given of the need for money capital, the sources from which it might be obtained, and the manner in which the cost and availability of it constrain the firm's structural and operating decisions. The Marshallian short-run and long-run fictions did, of course, point in the direction of an accounting for real time, as did Marshall's concern for the evolution, growth, and decay of firms. But the analogy of the "trees of the forest" (Marshall, 1920, p. 315f.), together with that of the representative firm, effectively collapsed the real-time argument to a timeless form and prepared it for Pigou's notion of the optimum size of the firm and its equilibrium condition (see Robinson, 1969, pp. v–vi). Progress in analysis requires that priority be given to what we have called the ab initio planning model of the firm, so that money capital, with all of the questions of intertemporal valuation and uncertainty that it opens up, can be integrated immediately into the theory.

We shall sketch in preliminary outline in this chapter the way in which that might most effectively be done, consistent with the thought forms of the neoclassical theory. It will not be possible to take full account initially of uncertainty or of the full significance of the passage of time. In this sense, the model is quite incomplete. We shall return to those matters. It should be emphasized, moreover, that the analysis that follows remains firmly within the neoclassical paradigm and that its principal significance lies in the manner in which it brings into focus the question of production–capital–financing interdependence. That will in due course be subject to an alternative interpretation in Part III, where the present neoclassical assumptions are amended.

We are here, moreover, envisaging a static model of long-run structural

59

optimization in the firm. The model is not at this stage dynamic, and the structural optima it brings into view are understood, as in the general neo-classical static theory, to be reproduced from period to period by the deter-minant relations in the model. The static nature of the argument implies that as the firm is not in this context growing over time, all of the net income is paid to the owners in the form of dividends. At this early stage of our work, all financing is assumed to be obtained from external sources, and the cost of money capital is correspondingly the cost of externally available funds.

Notation employed in the model

The geometry of the firm's revenue, production, cost, and profit functions will be familiar from earlier studies in the theory of the firm. Principal atten-tion will therefore be given in what follows to a straightforward algebraic statement of the theory, without the familiar geometric support. Brief com-ments will be made on some of the principal components of the model after the following list of notation employed.[1]

$\rho =$ equity owners' capitalization rate, or required rate of return, which is functionally dependent on the equity and debt cap-ital mix employed in the firm

$p =$ unit selling price of the firm's product (assuming a single-product firm), regarded as a function of the quantity of out-put produced and sold, Q, and written as $p = p(Q)$, thereby recognizing the presence of imperfect competition in the firm's output market

$X, Y =$ input factors of production (confining attention initially to a two-factor production function as a means of illustrating the principal relations involved), to be described more precisely as the number of units of the factor capacities employed

$Q =$ the level of output, shown as dependent on the level and mix of factor inputs and described in the familiar production function form as $Q = f(X, Y)$

$\gamma_1, \gamma_2 =$ unit factor costs of inputs X and Y, respectively, to be re-ferred to more precisely as the periodic operating flow costs per unit of factor capacity input

$r =$ average rate of interest on the total debt or nonownership capital employed in the firm, understood, as in the case of

---

[1] The model in this chapter is derived from that first introduced in Vickers (1968) and expanded in Vickers (1970). The argument has been reproduced in Turnovsky (1970) and has been discussed extensively in Herendeen (1975, p. 97f.).

the equity owners' required rate of return, ρ, to depend on
the debt-to-equity ratio in the firm's financing structure

K = amount of equity or ownership capital invested in the firm

D = amount of debt or nonownership capital employed in the
firm

g = net working capital requirement function, describing the
firm's net investment in working capital assets (cash, accounts receivable, and inventory, less current liabilities) as
functionally dependent on the level of output, $g = g(Q)$, or,
indirectly, $g = g[f(X, Y)]$

α, β = money capital requirement coefficients of factors X and Y,
respectively

λ = an undetermined (Lagrangian) multiplier or coefficient attached to the money capital constraint variable

Preliminary comments on elements of the model

1   Costs of debt and equity capital

Both the equity owners' capitalization rate and the average rate of interest on
the debt are dependent on the financing mix employed in the firm. They will
be determined by the supply-and-demand conditions in the equity and debt
capital sectors of the money capital market. This acknowledges the impact of
the leverage characteristics of the firm's financing structure that we noted in
Chapter 2. The higher the debt-to-equity ratio, or the higher the degree of
financial leverage at work in the firm, the greater will be the risk exposure of
both the creditors, that is the debt holders, and the residual owners. If we
assume risk aversion on the supply side of the money capital market, the
higher risks induced by higher degrees of leverage will call forth higher required rates of return on the invested money capital. This dependence will be
exhibited by the functional forms $r = r(K, D)$ and $\rho = \rho(K, D)$. Both the equity
cost and the debt cost functions will be understood to be monotonically positive. Increasing risks incur increasing money capital costs.

At several points, it will be necessary not only to speak of the overall or
average cost of money capital but also to consider the marginal cost of introducing additional capital to the firm. In the case of debt capital, for example,
the "marginal direct cost of debt" will be defined as the rate of increase in
the total interest burden of the firm that results from the employment of a
marginal unit of debt capital. The interest burden will be defined as the total
interest payments on the firm's debt capital, or rD, or, given the dependence
of the average rate of interest, r, on the debt and equity financing mix, as $r(K,$

$D)D$. The marginal direct cost of debt follows as the derivative of this interest burden with respect to debt capital.

$$\frac{\partial[r(K, D)D]}{\partial D} = r + D \frac{\partial r}{\partial D}$$ (4.1)

2   Revenue function

Observing the dependence of the unit selling price on the quantity of output sold, the firm's total revenue is described as $R = p(Q)Q$. Taking account of the dependence of output, Q, on the factors employed, the revenue function may be written as $R = p(Q)f(X, Y)$. Again it will be necessary to envisage the marginal value of this function and to consider the marginal revenue obtainable from a variation in the firm's output and sales:

$$\frac{dR}{dQ} = p + Q \frac{dp}{dQ}$$ (4.2)

Or, in instances where it is desired to envisage the dependence of revenue on, say, the incremental employment of factor X, we may write

$$\frac{\partial R}{\partial X} = \left(p + Q \frac{dp}{dQ} \right) f_x$$ (4.3)

In this last expression, the notation f_x refers to the marginal product of factor X, or the partial derivative of the production function with respect to factor $X, \partial f(X, Y)/\partial X$. Equation (4.3), therefore, describes the familiar marginal revenue product of factor X. It is equal to the marginal revenue multiplied by the marginal product of the factor.

3   Operating flow costs of factor inputs

The gamma terms in the list of notation refer to the periodic operating flow costs of the factors of production. Given that γ_1 is the flow cost of factor X, the periodic cost of employing a designated number of units of that factor will be equal to $\gamma_1 X$. If the unit flow cost should depend on the number of units of the factor being employed, the total flow cost of employing the factor during a given operating period would be $\gamma_1(X)X$. In the development of the theory, however, we shall not take a dependence of this kind explicitly into account.

In the two-factor production function that we have assumed for purposes of exposition, the periodic production cost will be

$$C = \gamma_1 X + \gamma_2 Y$$ (4.4)

Difficulty attaches to the precise specification of these flow cost elements (see Vickers, 1968, p. 127f.). If the factor in view is a completely variable factor, for example labor, the operating flow cost may frequently be specified simply as the wage rate per unit of labor input. It is in that case precisely similar to the traditional concept of the unit factor price. It may be necessary, however, for the firm to invest in certain fixed assets to make the employment of labor possible, quite apart from the investment in real capital with which the labor cooperates in production. The operating flow cost of labor may therefore include certain maintenance, servicing, and depreciation costs on associated durable assets, in the same way as those charges affect the operating flow costs of the units of durable factor capacities. Let us observe initially, therefore, the manner in which, in general, the flow cost of a unit of durable factor capacity may be specified.

The problem before us arises because the relevant asset life extends over more than one operating period. In order to maintain the presence of the asset in the firm, it will be necessary to incur in each period certain maintenance and servicing costs. At the same time, it will be necessary to charge against the income stream each period a contribution to the depreciation sinking fund that is being built up over the life of the asset to replace it when its economic life comes to an end. Only if this is done will it be possible to maintain the initial capital investment intact. This depreciation charge is based on the assumption that the asset will be regularly employed and fully used at its optimum technological intensity and will therefore be subject to regular wear and tear during its life. The operating flow cost will then be the sum of both these two cost elements, the maintenance and servicing cost plus the periodic depreciation. It will not include the interest payments on the money capital that has been raised to finance the investment in the asset. Those finance costs, which must be imputed to the factors of production whose employment the money capital makes possible, will be included as separate elements in the actual total flow costs of the factors. We shall return to that in a later section of this chapter.

Let us assume that the firm contemplates investing in a physical asset capable of providing a stipulated number of Y-capacity units per operating period. With reference to this asset, we employ the following notation:

L = economic life of the asset[2]
M = initial money capital outlay cost
S = periodic maintenance and servicing cost

---

[2] The choice of the optimum economic life of the asset gives rise to a suboptimization problem that is discussed at some length in Vickers (1968, Ch. 7). In the present introduction to the theory of the firm it is assumed that the optimum economic life of the asset is given.

T = periodic amortization or depreciation sinking fund installment
r = rate of interest assumed for sinking fund computation

The interest rate r assumed for sinking fund purposes will be an approximation to the firm's lending rate if the sinking fund is invested outside of the firm. If, on the other hand, the sinking fund is invested in income-earning assets in the firm, and thereby serves as a source of money capital that substituted for new debt or equity security issues, the sinking fund rate of interest may be approximated by an estimate of the firm's cost of external money capital. Maintenance expenditures and replacement are two different ways of providing for the productive presence of the assets in the firm, and the same sinking fund r will be used in what follows in the consideration of the maintenance and servicing costs. The periodic operating flow cost of the units of Y-factor capacity will then be the sum of the per unit values of T and S, or $\gamma_2 = (T + S)/Y$.

The periodic maintenance and servicing cost can be expected to increase during the life of the asset and may be conceived, for purposes of example, to be equal to A dollars in the first period and grow at a rate of b percent per period. In any future period, the relevant cost will therefore be Ae^{bt} dollars. The total monetary outlay connected with maintaining the productive presence of the asset in the firm is then made up of two parts: (1) the succession of periodic costs equal to Ae^{bt} and (2) the provision of M dollars for replacement purposes at the end of the life of the asset. We abstract for the present from possible changes in price levels and assume that the scrap value of the asset at the end of its life is zero.

Consider first the periodic depreciation charge. It is required that the replacement sinking fund amount to M at the end of L periods, or at the end of the life of the asset. It is therefore required that

$$M = \int_0^L Te^{rt}\, dt \tag{4.5}$$

Integrating Equation (4.5) and simplifying yields the result

$$T = \frac{rM}{e^{rL} - 1} \tag{4.6}$$

thus specifying the necessary periodic sinking fund contribution.

Similarly, the periodic maintenance and servicing cost will be equal to the constant periodic S component of a stream of payments that has the same capitalized value as the actual stream of maintenance and servicing costs made necessary by the investment. The following equation may therefore be established:

$$\int_0^L Se^{-rt}\, dt = \int_0^L Ae^{bt}e^{-rt}\, dt \tag{4.7}$$

Integrating both sides of Equation (4.7) and solving for S yields

$$S = \frac{rA}{b-r} \left(\frac{e^{bL} - e^{rL}}{e^{rL} - 1} \right) \tag{4.8}$$

Taking the periodic T and S components, it follows that $\gamma_2 = (T+S)/Y$. There may not exist, of course, a single unique way of providing a stipulated number of units of factor Y capacity per period. It may be possible to provide the requisite capacity by investing in any of several different asset structures, each having its own technological characteristics. Different types of equipment may be employed having different prospective durabilities, initial capital outlay costs, maintenance and service charge characteristics, and economic lives. A schedule of economic characteristics of different alternatives may be drawn up, where L_i, M_i, A_i, b_i, T_i, S_i, and γ_i represent the relevant data for the ith such alternative. For any given or desired level of factor Y capacity, then, the optimum real capital investment would be that which promises the minimum γ_i as thus ascertained. This magnitude should be incorporated in the planning stage in the functional relation $\gamma_i(Y)$, where the dependence of the operating flow cost on the level of the factor capacity employed is explicitly recognized.

If the employment of such a variable factor as labor carried along with it the need to invest in certain durable asset facilities in order to make the employment of labor possible, such as transportation or catering equipment, it would be necessary to estimate the optimum T and S component costs of such assets in the same way as in the foregoing durable asset case. These would then be incorporated along with the wage rate, in the true operating flow cost of the labor units.

4 Money capital requirement coefficients

The α and β terms in the list of notation describe the money capital requirement coefficients of the respective factors X and Y. They indicate, for example, that for every unit of factor Y capacity employed in the firm it will be necessary to invest β dollars of money capital in fixed assets. The specification of these coefficients follows from the preceding discussion of the operating flow cost parameters. If, for example, it was found that the optimum method of providing for the presence in the firm of Y units of factor capacity was to acquire an asset with an initial money capital outlay value of M dollars, the asset investment per unit of Y capacity would be given as

$$\beta = M/Y \tag{4.9}$$

Given the dependence of M, the money capital outlay, on the level of factor usage required, the general specification follows:

$$\beta = \beta(Y) \tag{4.10}$$

The factor's money capital requirement coefficient is again functionally dependent on the level of factor usage envisaged. The total money capital requirements for investment in fixed assets generated by the decision to employ specifiable quantities of factors X and Y can be defined as the sum of $\alpha(X)X$ and $\beta(Y)Y$.

5   *Net working capital asset requirements*

The balance sheet described in Chapter 2 indicates that in order to maintain the firm in continuous operation it will be necessary to invest part of the available money capital in cash balances, accounts receivable, and inventories of various kinds. Part of the financing sources, or part of the money capital required for this purpose, will be obtained from the current liabilities, which are also described on the balance sheet. Apart from the short-term loans from financial institutions such as the banks, funds may be made available by deferring payment of the firm's liabilities for inventory purchases, giving rise to a current liability for the corresponding amount. Taking the balance sheet total of such current liabilities from the total of current assets provides an indication of the net working capital requirements of the firm. Alternatively, the working capital requirements of the firm can be described as that portion of the current assets that is financed from long-term money capital sources. For to the extent that, as is generally the case, the current assets exceed in total the current liabilities, the latter are covering only a portion of the current-asset requirements. The remainder, therefore, must be financed from the long-term sources, long-term debt or equity capital. The reason why working capital is obtained from long-term financing sources, or why, in other words current assets normally exceed current liabilities, is that the firm thereby maintains a liquidity cushion that is deemed to be necessary to support its ongoing operations. In general, current assets are liquid in the sense that they can be turned into cash either immediately or during the firm's normal operating cycle. The current liabilities are liquid in the sense that they become due for payment at more or less frequent intervals throughout the same operating cycle.

We therefore describe a net working capital requirement function, dependent on the level of the firm's production and sales, as $g(Q)$. It will be useful in what follows to envisage such a working capital requirement function as

$$W = g[f(X, Y)] \tag{4.11}$$

showing the dependence of such money capital requirements on the firm's basic factor employment decisions.

6 *Money capital requirement function*

Making use of the variables and parameters described in the foregoing, it is possible to bring the several strands of analysis together and describe the firm's money capital requirement function. Using the symbol MCR to refer to the total money capital requirements, it follows that

$$\text{MCR} = g[f(X, Y)] + \alpha(X)X + \beta(Y)Y \tag{4.12}$$

7 *Money capital availability constraint*

At the outset of the firm's ab initio planning, it is not known what levels of factor X and Y employment will be optimal. But whatever level of production and factor use is decided upon, a total money capital requirement as defined in Equation (4.12) will be generated. Whatever level of production is chosen, it must be one that does not generate a money capital requirement greater than the money capital actually available to the firm. Defining the equity and debt capital available to the firm as K and D, respectively, the following relation must be satisfied:

$$g[f(X, Y)] + \alpha X + \beta Y \leq K + D \tag{4.13}$$

Here the fixed-asset requirements are written in the simple form, αX and βY, which, for ease of exposition, will be used in the following analysis.

When the total money capital available to the firm is being employed, or when the money capital availability constraint is operative, the inequality sign in Equation (4.13) will be replaced by the equality sign. If the level of the firm's production and factor employment were such that the inequality sign held, not all of the firm's money capital would be effectively used. In the expressive language that Lange introduced in his seminal paper in 1936, the firm would then enjoy conditions of money capital saturation. Under such conditions, in the absence of an operative money capital availability constraint, the firm has access to sufficient money capital to permit it to operate at any desired level of output with any desired combination of factor inputs. But that will not usually occur, and money capital will be for most firms in most situations a scarce resource. Moreover, the marginal cost of relaxing the money capital availability constraint, or of going to the money capital market in search of incremental funds, provides one of the important theoretical linkages we now require.

In the following analysis, the money capital availability constraint condition will be introduced, under the assumption that the constraint is operative, in the form

$$K + D - g[f(X, Y)] - \alpha X - \beta Y = 0 \tag{4.14}$$

Initial approximation to the constrained optimization model

The analysis of constrained optimization can be introduced by considering a simple problem. Let us imagine that the firm wishes to determine the combination of factors X and Y that will provide the maximum attainable profit at the same time as it satisfies a money capital availability constraint. Initially, we shall work with the firm's profit function on the assumption that no debt capital is being employed. The total money capital available is therefore simply a specified amount of equity capital. In that case, the profit function appears as

$$\pi = p(Q)f(X, Y) - \gamma_1 X - \gamma_2 Y \tag{4.15}$$

We observe again that the specification of the maximand function in this form, and in the related forms of value maximization later in this chapter, is necessary in order to ensure that the profit, or the implicit rate of return on capital, is a true reflection of the residual income available after setting aside the depreciation necessary to maintain the capital investment intact. This is because the depreciation charges, as noted previously, are included in the gamma terms describing the operating flow costs of the factors.

We now form an amended maximand function by appending to this profit function the money capital availability constraint in the form in which it will appear when it is operative. This appears in the final parentheses on the right-hand side of Equation (4.16). We have attached to this constraint condition an undetermined coefficient, λ, which will in due course be interpreted as the marginal productivity of money capital. On each occasion on which a maximand function of this amended form is written in the following analysis, we shall designate it by the symbol ϕ and refer to it as a "Lagrange function" or a "constrained objective function." In the present instance, we are concerned with the expression

$$\phi = p(Q)f(X, Y) - \gamma_1 X - \gamma_2 Y + \lambda(\bar{K} - \alpha X - \beta Y) \tag{4.16}$$

In Equation (4.16), again for ease of manipulation, we have omitted the working capital requirements from the money capital availability constraint and have focused on the fixed-asset requirements. The retention of the working capital term, as in Equation (4.14), would complicate the mathematical development further without adding significantly to the logic of the results.

The solution values of X and Y that maximize the ϕ function of Equation (4.16) will also maximize the profit function of Equation (4.15) under the conditions specified. This is true because at those solution values of X and Y the value of the expression in the final parentheses of Equation (4.16) becomes equal to zero, and the expression for ϕ is then identical with the earlier expression for the profit, π.

The firm's optimization decisions are here crystallized into the task of selecting the optimum solution values of the factor inputs X and Y. These are accordingly referred to as the firm's decision variables. The optimization task is actually performed subject to a number of what we might term constraints or limitations on the firm's actions. These include (i) the form of the revenue function, (ii) the form of the production function, (iii) the factor input operating flow costs as previously specified, and (iv) the money capital requirement coefficients. Analytically, we have substituted the revenue and production functions into the profit function. Taking the factor cost variables and the money capital requirement coefficients as specified (or calculable as previously discussed), we have in Equation (4.16) a constrained maximand function in the three unknowns X, Y, and λ. These are the two decision variables and the coefficient on the money capital constraint condition.

To discover the solution values of these variables that will provide the maximum attainable profit, we take the partial derivatives of the function in Equation (4.16) with respect to X and Y, set the resulting expressions equal to zero to satisfy the first-order optimization conditions, and combine these results with the money capital availability constraint:

$$\frac{\partial \phi}{\partial X} = \left(p + Q\frac{dp}{dQ}\right)f_x - \gamma_1 - \lambda\alpha = 0 \tag{4.17}$$

$$\frac{\partial \phi}{\partial Y} = \left(p + Q\frac{dp}{dQ}\right)f_y - \gamma_2 - \lambda\beta = 0 \tag{4.18}$$

$$\overline{K} - \alpha X - \beta Y = 0 \tag{4.19}$$

From these three equations in the three unknowns, X, Y, and λ, the solution values of the decision variables and the constraint coefficient may be determined.

If Equations (4.17) and (4.18) are rearranged by transferring the negative terms to the right-hand side of the final equality signs, and Equation (4.17) is divided by Equation (4.18), the following relation is obtained:

$$\frac{f_x}{f_y} = \frac{\gamma_1 + \lambda\alpha}{\gamma_2 + \lambda\beta} \tag{4.20}$$

This states that when the optimum combination of factors of production is employed, the ratio of the marginal products of the factors will be equal to the ratio of what we shall call their effective marginal costs. Equations (4.17) and (4.18) imply also that in such a situation the marginal revenue product of each factor will be equal to its effective marginal cost. This effective marginal cost is made up of two components. These represent, in the case of factor X, for example, the direct unit cost γ_1, or what we have termed the operating flow cost of the factor, and an additional term $\lambda\alpha$. This latter term defines the marginal imputed money capital cost that the factor is called upon to bear. This is itself made up of two terms. It is equal to the factor's money capital requirement coefficient, α, multiplied by the coefficient of the constraint variable, λ. The last term, λ, will be interpreted as the marginal productivity of money capital, the variable that is here constraining the firm's choice of its decision variables. The imputed money capital cost of factor X is therefore defined as the number of dollars of money capital investment in assets that is required for each unit of factor X employed multiplied by an imputation rate defined as equal to the marginal productivity of money capital.

If the money capital availability constraint were not operative, or if the firm enjoyed what we have referred to as money capital saturation, the solution value of λ would be zero, and the marginal productivity of money capital would be zero. Money capital would be in surplus supply. The effective marginal cost of the factor would then be defined as its direct marginal cost, or its operating flow cost, γ_1 in the case of factor X. In that case also, the ratio of the factors' marginal products, as shown in Equation (4.20), would be equal to the ratio of their direct operating flow costs.

Marginal productivity of money capital

The solution value of the coefficient on the money capital constraint condition, λ, may be interpreted as follows. At the constrained solution point, the money capital availability constraint assumes the form

$$\overline{K} = \alpha X + \beta Y \tag{4.21}$$

If, at that point, a marginal dollar of equity capital, K, is introduced to the firm, it will be possible to acquire a larger amount of the fixed assets necessary to provide for an incremental employment of factors X and Y. Given that the money capital requirement coefficients of factors X and Y are α and β, respectively, and writing the incremental employment of the factors that is now made possible as dX and dY, the marginal dollar of equity capital may be understood as applied to the acquisition of additional fixed assets, resulting from the marginal factor employments, in the proportions $\alpha\ dX$ and $\beta\ dY$. This can be expressed in other terms by taking the derivative of Equation (4.21) with respect to K. It follows that

$$1 = \alpha\ \frac{dX}{dK} + \beta\ \frac{dY}{dK} \tag{4.22}$$

The increased employment of factors X and Y that the marginal dollar of equity capital has made possible will increase the firm's attainable profit. The extent of this increase in profit can be envisaged by taking the derivative of the firm's profit function with respect to K. For this purpose, we observe that the firm's unconstrained profit function is shown in the first three terms on the right-hand side of Equation (4.16). Taking the derivative of this function with respect to K provides

$$\frac{d\pi}{dK} = \left[\left(p+Q\,\frac{dp}{dQ}\right)f_x - \gamma_1\right]\frac{dX}{dK} + \left[\left(p+Q\,\frac{dp}{dQ}\right)f_y - \gamma_2\right]\frac{dY}{dK} \qquad (4.23)$$

The first bracketed term in Equation (4.23), or $\partial\pi/\partial X$, appears in the solution condition shown in Equation (4.17), and in the equilibrium situation it takes on a value equal to $\lambda\alpha$. Similarly, the second bracketed term in Equation (4.23), or $\partial\pi/\partial Y$, takes on the value $\lambda\beta$ as shown in Equation (4.18). Substituting Equations (4.17) and (4.18) into Equation (4.23) provides, at the optimization solution values of the model,

$$\frac{d\pi}{dK} = \lambda\left(\alpha\,\frac{dX}{dK} + \beta\,\frac{dY}{dK}\right) \qquad (4.24)$$

Finally, by substituting Equation (4.22) in Equation (4.24),

$$d\pi/dK = \lambda \qquad (4.25)$$

This is the definition of λ we have been seeking. It is equal to the derivative of the firm's profit function with respect to money capital. In economic terms, it is measuring the amount by which the firm's profit could be increased by an increase of a unit of money capital. It measures, therefore, the marginal efficiency, or marginal productivity, of money capital. Money capital costs, therefore, are imputed to productive factors at a rate equal to the marginal productivity of money capital.

Effective cost and product contours and factor substitution

The optimization factor employment condition in Equation (4.20) describes, on the left-hand side, the slope of the isoproduct contour, or isoquant, determined by the form of the firm's production function. The right-hand side of the equation, the ratio of effective marginal costs, is the slope of an effective outlay contour. At the firm's optimized equilibrium, therefore, the outlay contour will be tangential to the product contour, a condition that is familiar from the textbook treatment of the theory of the firm. But the presence of a money capital availability constraint implies that the optimum-factor combination will differ from that of the money capital saturation case. Of course, under special conditions, the factor combination could be the same in both cases, but this would be so only if the ratio of the factors' money capital requirement coefficients α/β equaled the ratio of direct factor costs γ_1/γ_2. There is no reason why this particular condition should be encountered.

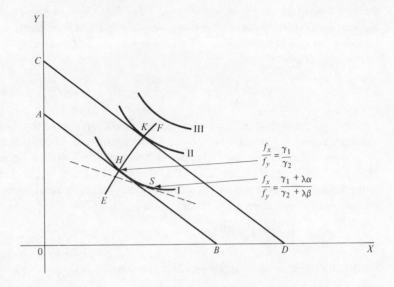

Figure 4.1

Consider now the isoproduct and isooutlay contours shown in the factor input plane in Figure 4.1.

The relative marginal factor cost line, analogous to the lines AB and CD in Figure 4.1, will in general take on a different slope in the money capital constraint case from what they will under conditions of money capital saturation. This means, as already noted, that the capital constraint induces a change in the optimum-factor combination. The direction in which the substitution of one factor for another can be expected to occur will depend on the relative money capital intensities of the factors and on the nature of the imputed capital costs that, as a consequence, the factors are required to bear.

Consider the ratio of the factors' marginal productivities, f_x/f_y, in Equation (4.20). That ratio will be lower in the capital constraint case than it will be under conditions of capital saturation if the following expression holds:

$$\frac{\gamma_1 + \lambda\alpha}{\gamma_2 + \lambda\beta} < \frac{\gamma_1}{\gamma_2} \tag{4.26}$$

Inequality (4.26) will be satisfied so long as

$$\beta/\gamma_2 > \alpha/\gamma_1 \tag{4.27}$$

The ratio f_x/f_y is the measure of the marginal rate of technical substitution between the factors at the point of optimized factor combination. But if this marginal rate of substitution is lower, then at the optimization factor combination the slope of the isoproduct curve is lower, and either of the following statements can be made. First, at the solution point, a lesser sacrifice of factor Y than would otherwise be possible can now be made for an incremental increase in factor X if it desired to remain on a given isoproduct curve; or second, a larger increment in factor X would be required to compensate for a unit loss of factor Y if it is desired to remain on a given isoproduct curve or at a given output level.

Given an operative money capital availability constraint, or given, that is, a positive marginal productivity of money capital as measured by the variable λ, the slope of the isoproduct curve at the optimum-factor combination point will be lower than it would otherwise be. Further, the greater the severity of the money capital constraint, or the larger the marginal productivity of money capital or the solution value of λ, the lower will be the slope of the isoproduct curve, or the marginal rate of substitution of factor X for factor Y. These conditions are shown by inequality (4.27) to hold so long as β/γ_2 is greater than α/γ_1. These last two ratios measure the relationship between a factor's money capital requirement coefficient and its direct unit operating flow cost, and they may be taken as measures of the money capital intensities of the factors. The entire foregoing argument can then be summed up as follows. The existence of an operative money capital availability constraint leads to a *relative* economizing on the more capital-intensive factor of production. In the case of Figure 4.1, this means that the lines describing the ratios of effective marginal costs are shallower to the X axis than would otherwise be the case.

The foregoing conclusion regarding the relative economizing on more capital-intensive factors is all that can be said at this stage. The conclusion does not permit a statement to be made about the precise change in the actual combination of factors as the availability of capital changes. For a change in the severity of the money capital constraint will cause the actual attainable level of output to change also, and the optimization solution will then be on a different isoproduct curve. In that case, the expansion path will be different from that, such as *EF* in Figure 4.1, for the firm that does not confront the money capital availability constraint. In the presence of a changing capital availability constraint, the expansion path will pass through such a point as S in Figure 4.1 and will be pulled away from the axis describing the more capital-intensive factor.

Constrained objective function and economic valuation of the ownership of the firm

We examine now the constrained maximization of the economic value of the ownership investment in the firm. Consider the objective function in Equation (4.28). The terms will be clear from previous exposition:

$$\phi = \frac{1}{\rho(K, D)} [p(Q)f(X, Y) - \gamma_1 X - \gamma_2 Y - r(K, D)D]$$
$$+ \lambda[\overline{K} + D - g(Q) - \alpha X - \beta Y] \tag{4.28}$$

The first term on the right-hand side of Equation (4.28) will be recognized as the steady-state value-of-ownership function, or $V = \pi/\rho$. In this equation, V refers to the economic value of the ownership or equity investment in the firm, and π is the profit being earned for the residual owners after the payment of all operating costs, including, by virtue of its inclusion in the gamma terms, the periodic depreciation on the firm's fixed assets, and the contractual interest on debt capital. The remaining term on the right-hand side of Equation (4.28) is the familiar money capital availability constraint, now written in expanded form to take account of the working capital requirements.

The optimization task is now that of maximizing this constrained objective function over the four decision variables X, Y, K, and D and the coefficient on the constraint condition, λ. In the first instance, it may be assumed that the amount of equity capital in the firm is given and that the objective is to decide on the optimum amount of debt capital to employ in conjunction with it. Holding the value of K as given, then, we take the partial derivatives of Equation (4.28) with respect to X, Y, and D and combine these with the constraint to provide

$$\frac{\partial \phi}{\partial X} = \frac{1}{\rho}\left[\left(p + Q\frac{dp}{dQ}\right)f_x - \gamma_1\right] - \lambda[g'(Q)f_x + \alpha] = 0 \tag{4.29}$$

$$\frac{\partial \phi}{\partial Y} = \frac{1}{\rho}\left[\left(p + Q\frac{dp}{dQ}\right)f_y - \gamma_2\right] - \lambda[g'(Q)f_y + \beta] = 0 \tag{4.30}$$

$$\frac{\partial \phi}{\partial D} = -\frac{1}{\rho}\left(r + D\frac{\partial r}{\partial D} + V\frac{\partial \rho}{\partial D}\right) + \lambda = 0 \tag{4.31}$$

$$\overline{K} + D - g(Q) - \alpha X - \beta Y = 0 \tag{4.32}$$

These conditions make it possible to specify the structural characteristics of the firm. The solution of the equation set (4.29) through (4.32), or the optimum values of X, Y, and D, provide the simultaneous solutions of the firm's production, investment, and financing problems. The optimum-production structure follows from the firm's factor usage X and Y; the optimum-asset structure is determined by the factors' money capital requirement coefficients α and β and the net working capital requirement function $g(Q)$; and the optimum amount of money capital to employ, $K + D$, and thereby the optimum debt-to-equity ratio for the given equity investment, is simultaneously determined.

On the latter question, we can examine further the condition implicit in

Equation (4.31). Here it is being said that the employment of debt capital is at its optimum level, given the equity investment, when an equality has been established between the marginal value productivity of money capital, λ, and the capitalized value of the "full marginal cost of borrowing," the negative of the first term on the left-hand side of the equation. This full marginal cost of borrowing will be further interpreted in a later chapter, where the cost of money capital is examined from a money capital market perspective. But it will be useful, in considering the following argument, to bear in mind the essential meaning of the concept.

At the beginning of this chapter we envisaged the marginal direct cost of debt as defined in Equation (4.1). That marginal direct cost exceeded the interest rate on the marginal debt, r, by reason that the increase in the amount of debt outstanding increased the overall risk exposure of the debt holders and therefore increased the average rate of interest on the debt. This was indicated by the term $\partial r/\partial D$ in Equation (4.1). This implies that when the previously existing debt matures and has to be refinanced, the new higher rate of interest will have to be paid on that refinancing debt issue also, as well as on the new debt now being issued. When new debt capital is raised and put to work in the firm, therefore, it will be necessary for it to earn a rate of return higher than simply the interest on the new debt issue. The latter magnitude, which can be referred to as the direct interest cost of the marginal debt, is described by r, the first term in the expression for the full marginal cost of debt. The additional earnings required, the $D\ \partial r/\partial D$ term in the full marginal cost of debt, describes the additional interest cost, or the additional interest burden imposed on the firm when previously existing debt is refinanced. It is shown as the amount of previously existing debt, D, multiplied by the marginal increase in the interest rate, $\partial r/\partial D$.

In isolating the full marginal cost of debt, however, as contained in Equations (4.31) and (4.42), a further term has been incorporated, namely $\partial\rho/\partial D$. This indicates that the issuance of debt capital, by reason that it increases the degree of financial leverage in the firm and thereby the risk exposure of the residual owners, can be expected to cause an increase in the owners' capitalization rate or required rate of return. The assumption of risk aversion on the supply side of the money capital market implies that both the partial derivatives in the expression for the full marginal cost of debt can be expected to be positive.

In order for the employment of marginal debt capital to be economically worthwhile, that capital, when it is put to work in the firm, must generate, over and above the return streams we have already specified, a still further increment in earnings that will have the following effect. If the new debt issue causes, via the higher financial leverage effect, an increase in the equity owners' capitalization rate or required rate of return, this will tend to cause a reduction in the market or economic value of the equity for any given level of income. It will be necessary, then, for the equity owners' net income to be increased by an amount sufficient to offset this increase in the capitalization rate. In such an event, as $V = \pi/\rho$ and the increases in π and ρ are offsetting, V will remain unchanged; and in the language of the financial market, no dilution of the equity value will have occurred. The magnitude of this necessary increase in earnings is described in the final term in the expression for the full marginal cost of debt, or $V \, \partial\rho/\partial D$. The full marginal cost of debt therefore follows, as specified, as $r + D \, \partial r/\partial D + V \, \partial\rho/\partial D$.

On the other hand, when the equity capital in the firm is increased, the degree of financial leverage will be diminished, and the risk exposure of both the debt holders and the residual owners will be reduced. We should expect, therefore, marginal impacts on the costs of debt and equity of the opposite sign from those we have just examined.

Consider now the following rearrangement of Equations (4.29) and (4.30):

$$\frac{1}{\rho}\left[\left(p + Q\frac{dp}{dQ}\right)f_x - \gamma_1\right] = \lambda[\,g'(Q)f_x + \alpha] \tag{4.33}$$

$$\frac{1}{\rho}\left[\left(p + Q\frac{dp}{dQ}\right)f_y - \gamma_2\right] = \lambda[\,g'(Q)f_y + \beta] \tag{4.34}$$

Equation (4.33) may be further interpreted as follows. The first term in the bracketed expression on the left-hand side of the equation is the marginal revenue product of factor X, and the remaining term is the direct unit flow cost of factor X. Thus the bracketed term as a whole can be understood as the surplus marginal revenue product of factor X. In the bracketed expression on the right-hand side of Equation (4.33), the first term is the incremental net working capital requirement induced by the marginal employment of factor X, and the second term is the familiar money capital requirement coefficient of the factor. The bracketed expression as a whole can therefore be regarded as a measure of the marginal money capital requirements of factor X.

With this interpretation in hand, we may write

$$\lambda = \frac{M_x/\rho}{C_x} \tag{4.35}$$

where M_x and C_x are, respectively, the surplus marginal revenue product and the marginal money capital requirement of factor X. It follows similarly from Equation (4.34) that

$$\lambda = \frac{M_y/\rho}{C_y} \tag{4.36}$$

where M_y and C_y have analogous interpretations. In Equations (4.35) and (4.36), the numerators are the capitalized values of the surplus marginal revenue products and may be referred to as the marginal value contributions of the factors. Taking these two equations together, at the optimized structure of the firm the ratios of the marginal value contribution to the marginal money capital requirement for the respective factors are equal. The marginal value contribution per dollar of money capital investment is equal for all factors employed. The marginal value productivity of money capital is equal in all lines of expenditure.

Expansion of equity investment

The analysis to this point has enabled us to specify the conditions for the maximum-value position of the owners *on the basis of a given equity investment.* We are interested also, however, in the determination of the *optimum* amount of equity investment in the firm. We need to discover the optimum structural characteristics of the firm when the optimum amount of debt capital is employed with the optimum amount of equity.

To unravel the relevant optimization conditions, reliance can be placed, as an initial approximation, on the solution value of λ, the marginal value productivity of money capital. We conceive, then, of the marginal value product of equity capital, $\partial V/\partial K$, or the partial derivative of the value function with respect to equity capital, ignoring, for the moment, the marginal impact that an increase in equity capital may have on the debt and equity capital costs. Referring to Equation (4.28) and recognizing that it incorporates on the right-hand side the ownership valuation function, $V = \pi/\rho$, we may write

$$\frac{\partial V}{\partial K} = \frac{\partial V}{\partial X}\frac{dX}{dK} + \frac{\partial V}{\partial Y}\frac{dY}{dK} \tag{4.37}$$

By substituting for the partial derivatives in Equation (4.37) the solution values shown in Equations (4.29) and (4.30) and using Equations (4.33) and (4.34), it follows that

$$\frac{\partial V}{\partial K} = \lambda[g'(Q)f_x + \alpha]\frac{dX}{dK} + \lambda[g'(Q)f_y + \beta]\frac{dY}{dK} \tag{4.38}$$

Leaving Equation (4.38) in the form indicated for the present, consider the properties of the money capital availability constraint. It follows that when the optimization conditions are satisfied and the money capital availability constraint is operative,

$$\overline{K} = g(Q) + \alpha X + \beta Y - D \tag{4.39}$$

Differentiating this equation throughout with respect to K yields

$$[g'(Q)f_x + \alpha]\frac{dX}{dK} + [g'(Q)f_y + \beta]\frac{dY}{dK} = 1 \tag{4.40}$$

From Equation (4.38) and the substitution of Equation (4.40),

$$\partial V/\partial K = \lambda \tag{4.41}$$

If λ may thus be treated as an approximation to the marginal value productivity of equity capital, reliance may be placed on the solution value of λ as an indication that the optimum amount of equity capital, and thus the overall optimum structure of the firm, is being approached. If, for example, the optimum structure of the firm is determined, subject to the constraint of a given amount of equity capital K and the solution value of λ is greater than unity, the signal is thereby being given that the economic value of the owners' investment, V, could be increased by more than one dollar by the introduction of another dollar of equity, K. When the equity investment, along with the increase in debt capital optimally associated with it, has been increased so far that the solution value of λ is unity, no further marginal investment of equity is desirable (apart from the modification introduced by the indirect effects we shall consider in the following section).

In this way, and on the level of approximation we are at present examining, reliance may be placed on the solution value of λ as the optimization signal when, as before, structural optima are determined in the manner specified in Equation (4.28). It follows from Equation (4.31) that when the solution value of λ has been depressed to unity,

$$\rho = r + D\,\frac{\partial r}{\partial D} + V\,\frac{\partial \rho}{\partial D} \tag{4.42}$$

Thus, when the introduction of debt capital, together with successively larger commitments of equity capital, has been carried far enough to depress the solution value of λ to unity, the full marginal cost of borrowing, shown on the right-hand side of Equation (4.42), will have been brought into equality with the solution value of ρ, the owners' capitalization rate or required rate of return, or the cost of equity capital.

Further comment can be made on the relation between these money capital costs at infra-optimum stages or levels of planning. We write Equation (4.31) in the form

$$\lambda = \frac{1}{\rho}\left(r + D\,\frac{\partial r}{\partial D} + V\,\frac{\partial \rho}{\partial D}\right) \tag{4.43}$$

At infra-optimum levels, when the solution value of λ is greater than unity, debt capital may be introduced even though the full marginal cost of borrowing, described in the parentheses on the right-hand side of Equation (4.43), is greater than the cost of equity capital, ρ. The explanation of this paradoxical statement resides, of course, in the fact that in the conditions envisaged, the size and structure of the firm is such that the marginal productivity of money capital is still relatively high. This is indicated by the relatively high solution value of λ. Thus a high marginal cost can be paid for debt capital so long as the marginal productivity of money capital in the firm is high enough to afford some benefit to the owners, or at least high enough to cover the full marginal cost of borrowing. For the latter takes account of the tendency for the increase in debt to raise the cost of equity [note the term $\partial\rho/\partial D$ in Equation (4.43)].

Further interpretation may be assisted by reference to Equations (4.35) and (4.36). The former may be reinterpreted as

$$C_x = M_x/\rho\lambda \tag{4.44}$$

Equation (4.44) indicates that at infra-optimum levels of planning, the surplus marginal revenue product of additional factor employments, discounted at a discount factor equal to $\rho\lambda$, should equal the marginal money capital outlay required by that factor employment. But at such infra-optimum stages, the implicit discount factor indicated is greater than the cost of equity capital, the amount of the difference being dependent on the value of λ. When the solution value of λ is unity, the discount factor, $\rho\lambda$, will be reduced to ρ.

A further approximation to money capital optimization

To this point, however, the analysis has not taken full account of the beneficial effects that can be expected to follow, on both the debt and the equity costs, from the introduction of marginal equity capital. Additional equity capital will reduce the degree of financial leverage in the firm and therefore the risk exposure of the debt and the equity holders. The necessary further interpretation can now be made most effectively by returning to Equation (4.28) and differentiating partially with respect to K, setting the partial derivative equal to 1. This is done because at the optimization margin an extra dollar of equity capital must generate at least one additional dollar of gross economic value for the owners:

$$\frac{\partial\phi}{\partial K} = -\frac{1}{\rho}\left(V\frac{\partial\rho}{\partial K} + D\frac{\partial r}{\partial K}\right) + \lambda = 1 \tag{4.45}$$

It follows from a rearrangement of Equation (4.45) that under full optimization conditions,

$$\lambda = \frac{1}{\rho}\left(\rho + D\frac{\partial r}{\partial K} + V\frac{\partial\rho}{\partial K}\right) \tag{4.46}$$

If, now, Equations (4.43) and (4.46) are compared and rearranged, it follows that under full optimization conditions

$$r + D\frac{\partial r}{\partial D} + V\frac{\partial\rho}{\partial D} = \rho + D\frac{\partial r}{\partial K} + V\frac{\partial\rho}{\partial K} = \rho\lambda \tag{4.47}$$

Thus the discount factor at which the marginal income streams should be discounted for planning purposes, $\rho\lambda$, is equal, at the overall optimum structure, to what can be referred to as the full marginal cost of debt and the full marginal cost of equity.

Equation (4.47) implies that this discount factor, $\rho\lambda$, will, in the general case of risk aversion on the part of the suppliers of money capital, be less than ρ and greater than r. That is,

$$r < \rho\lambda < \rho \qquad (4.48)$$

This is because in the general case $\partial r/\partial D$ and $\partial\rho/\partial D$ in Equation (4.47) can be expected to be positive, and $\partial r/\partial K$ and $\partial\rho/\partial K$ will be negative. Increases in debt will increase financial leverage and, by causing an increase in the debt holders' and the equity holders' risk, will lead to increases in r and ρ. The opposite effects will follow from an increase in equity capital. Moreover, it follows that *when full account is taken of these indirect marginal effects*, $\rho\lambda < \rho$ implies $\lambda < 1$.

While this is so, it will nevertheless remain true that the total derivative of V with respect to K will be equal to unity at the overall optimum structure point. This can be seen by considering the derivation of dV/dK from the basic constrained objective function in Equation (4.28):

$$\frac{dV}{dK} = \frac{\partial V}{\partial X}\frac{dX}{dK} + \frac{\partial V}{\partial Y}\frac{dY}{dK} + \frac{\partial V}{\partial r}\frac{dr}{dK} + \frac{\partial V}{\partial \rho}\frac{d\rho}{dK} \qquad (4.49)$$

Performing the differentiations and substituting equivalent values from the solution conditions in Equations (4.29) and (4.30) and Equation (4.45), it follows that

$$\frac{dV}{dK} = \lambda[g'(Q)f_x + \alpha]\frac{dX}{dK} + \lambda[g'(Q)f_y + \beta]\frac{dY}{dK} + (1 - \lambda) \qquad (4.50)$$

This somewhat complex result follows directly from the preceding argument. Note that the last two terms on the right-hand side of Equation (4.49) together describe the effect on the economic value of the equity, V, that results from the changes in r and ρ, in both cases reductions, as K is increased. Taken together, they represent $\partial V/\partial K$. First, as the interest rate on the debt, r, is reduced, this will reduce the firm's debt interest burden by $D\,\partial r/\partial K$, and a correspondingly larger residual net income will become available to the equity owners and increase the value of the equity. Second, the reduction in the equity capitalization rate, ρ, will introduce the equivalent of an increase in the equity earnings stream equal to $V\,\partial\rho/\partial K$. Both of these beneficial effects on the value of the equity are shown in the first term on the left-hand side of the final equals sign in Equation (4.45). In that equation they are capitalized at the equity capitalization rate, thereby defining, after taking account of the signs in the equation, the overall effect on the value of the equity resulting from the reduction of r and ρ. This resulting overall increase in equity value is seen, by transposition of Equation (4.45), to equal $1 - \lambda$. This result, we observe, is also described in the sum of the last two terms on the right-hand side of Equation (4.49), thus making possible the substitution of $1 - \lambda$ in Equation (4.50).

Substituting Equation (4.40) in Equation (4.50) results in

$$\frac{dV}{dK} = \lambda + (1 - \lambda) = 1 \tag{4.51}$$

The analysis in this chapter of structural planning and money capital utilization in the firm suffices for our present restricted purposes. We have looked at the decision problems of the firm as it stands at a point in time and at the determinants of its equilibrium structures. In doing so, we have highlighted, from the paradigmatic perspectives within which the analysis moves, the strands of causation the firm must take into account in deciding its best next move at its structural planning date. But we have not as yet taken significant account of the problem of uncertainty, nor would we wish to be understood to say that the firm is necessarily confronted with stable and well-defined functional relations of the kinds we have examined. We have intended, rather, to bring into focus the lines of causation and general relationships involved, leaving open for the present the possibility that greater or lesser degrees of instability may be assumed to surround those functional relations. We shall return to those highly important questions.

CHAPTER 5

Probability, risk,
and economic decisions

The question of risk or uncertainty has not yet been brought explicitly into our analysis. It has so far been incorporated only indirectly or in a proxy fashion. In our discussion of the risk exposure of the debt and equity holders in the firm, for example, we examined the impact on their positions of the degree of financial leverage in the firm's financing structure. But recent advances in the theory of the firm have attempted to handle the question of uncertainty in a more direct fashion. It has generally been assumed that the economic variables entering into the analysis could be interpreted as random variables that are describable by subjectively assigned probability distributions. It is risk in that sense that we shall discuss in this chapter.[1] We shall be concerned with what has been called variability risk, or risk described by the degree of random disturbance in the economic variables that affect the operating results of the firm. An even more fundamental risk, that of the default, bankruptcy, and possible liquidation of the firm, has not been accorded as extensive a treatment.

In focusing on the variability risk, the decision maker has frequently been assumed to choose alternatives on the basis of a utility function defined over the possible profit, economic value, or rate of return that could be generated and the degree of risk involved. The risk, in turn, has been measured by the dispersion parameter of an appropriately defined probability distribution of outcomes. The introduction of a utility function defined over random possible outcomes shifts the theory to what we shall designate as stochastic utility. In the notion of stochastic utility, the probability analysis makes, from the point of view of the received traditions, its ultimate impact on the theory of economic behavior.

Probability and probability distributions

Consider the information on two investment alternatives contained in Table 5.1. We wish to examine the criteria on which their relative attractiveness to the firm may be assessed.

[1] Our present objectives make it neither possible nor necessary to discuss the extensive literature on the application of probability analysis to the decisions of the firm. For a survey of the subject, see Hey (1979), Ford (1983), Weiss (1984), and the extensive references cited there, and for an earlier and important study, see Ozga (1965).

Table 5.1

Proposal A		Proposal B	
Probability	Cash flow ($000)	Probability	Cash flow ($000)
0.10	20	0.10	25
0.20	30	0.20	30
0.40	40	0.40	35
0.20	50	0.20	40
0.10	60	0.10	45

The data indicate that the firm has reason to believe that the periodic cash flows would range between $20,000 and $60,000 in the case of proposal A and between $25,000 and $45,000 for proposal B. These beliefs, presumably, would be based on an understanding of the firm's past performance in connection with similar investments, the general nature of the economic environment in which the investments would be undertaken, and estimates of the likely trends and instabilities in external economic forces bearing on the firm. The probability data should be read to mean that for proposal A, for example, the investment decision maker believes there is a 10 percent chance that the cash flow will fall as low as $20,000 and a similar 10 percent chance that it will be as high as $60,000. Taking each of the possible cash flow levels, and assigning to each of them in this way a probability of occurrence, the first two columns in Table 5.1 can be read as a probability distribution of the cash flow on Proposal A. In all such probability assignments, the decision maker will allocate a probability magnitude to all the elements of the range of possible outcomes he is prepared to contemplate, and the sum of the assigned probabilities must accordingly be equal to unity. A similar procedure establishes the probability distribution of the cash flow on proposal B, shown in the last two columns of Table 5.1.

The cash flows on the projects, it will be noted, are symmetrical around an average level of $40,000 for project A and $35,000 for proposal B. Which, then, is the more attractive investment opportunity? We may suppose that both proposals would involve the same initial capital investment, so that we can concentrate analysis on the shape of the cash inflow prospects in each case. We observe that while proposal A offers the prospect of a higher average cash flow, it also contemplates a wider range within which the actual realized cash flow may fall. It might seem, therefore, that it has associated with it a higher degree of risk. The question arises whether the higher possible cash flow from proposal A would be large enough to offset, in the mind of the decision maker, the higher degree of risk that it involves.

Table 5.2 *Computation of expected value and variance of cash flows on proposal A*

Prob-ability p_i	Cash flow x_i ($000)	p_ix_i	$x_i - E(x)$ $= d_i$	$(d_i)^2$	$p_i(d_i)^2$
0.10	20	2	−20	400	40
0.20	30	6	−10	100	20
0.40	40	16	0	0	0
0.20	50	10	10	100	20
0.10	60	6	20	400	40
		$\sum p_ix_i = \overline{40}$			$\sum = \overline{120}$

In Table 5.2, we have set out a computation of the two most important pieces of information contained in the basic data for proposal A. We are interested, first, in what is termed the *expected value* of the cash flow, or the expected value, sometimes referred to as the mathematical expectation, of the probability distribution of the cash flow and, second, in a measure of the dispersion of the probability distribution. We take as a measure of the latter the so-called *variance* (or its positive square root, the *standard deviation*) of the distribution.

On the basis of Table 5.2, we can set out the initial definitions relating to the probability analysis.

Definition 1

The *expected value* of a random variable, sometimes referred to as the expected value of the probability distribution of the random variable, is equal to the weighted average value of the possible outcomes, where each such possible outcome is weighted by the probability of its occurrence. Notationally, the expected value is written as follows:

$$E(x) = \sum_i p_i x_i \qquad (5.1)$$

In the examples contained in Tables 5.1 and 5.2, the random variable x describes the possible cash flows, and x_i refers to the ith possible value of that variable.

As the sum of the weights in this case, using the probabilities as the weights, is unity, the expected value is simply the sum of the possible outcomes times their probabilities. This is shown at the bottom of the third column of Table 5.2. The expected value may also be written as μ.

We may estimate also the extent to which, on the average, the possible outcomes of the random variable are distributed around, or dispersed away from, their average or expected value. We are interested for this purpose in the deviation, or difference, of each possible outcome from that expected value. These are shown in the fourth column of Table 5.2. But if we were to take the simple differences as indicated there, the sum of those differences would equal zero, thus diminishing their manipulability. We therefore take the square of the differences, as shown in the fifth column of Table 5.2, and then, as indicated in the final column, we reach the following definitions.

Definition 2

The *variance* of the probability distribution is equal to the weighted average value of the squares of the deviations of the possible outcomes from their expected value, where each such squared deviation is weighted by the probability of its occurrence. That probability is the same as the probability attaching to the outcome whose squared deviation is being considered.

Definition 3

The *standard deviation* of the probability distribution is the positive square root of the variance.

The variance and standard deviation are written as

$$\text{Var}(x) = \sigma_x^2 = \sum_i p_i [x_i - E(x)]^2 \tag{5.2}$$

$$\sigma_x = \sqrt{\sum_i p_i [x_i - E(x)]^2} \tag{5.3}$$

Proposal A in Table 5.1 therefore has the following characteristics. Its expected cash flow is $40,000; the variance of the cash flow is $120 (thousands squared); and the standard deviation is $10,950.

A further measure of risk that enables comparisons to be made between distributions that are described over different levels and ranges of possible outcomes may be defined.

Definition 4

The *coefficient of variation*, sometimes referred to as the relative standard deviation, is equal to the standard deviation divided by the expected value.

The coefficient of variation of proposal A, therefore, is $10.95/40 = 0.27. The coefficient of variation, being a measure of relative risk, is a pure number.

Proposal B in Table 5.1 may be analyzed in a manner similar to that adopted in Table 5.2 with respect to proposal A. The comparisons in Table 5.3 between proposals A and B may then be derived.

We conclude that proposal A, while it offers a higher expected cash flow, does have associated with it a higher degree of variability risk, as defined by

Table 5.3 *Comparative probability data for proposals A and B*

Statistical characteristic	Proposal A	Proposal B
Expected value	$40,000	$35,000
Standard deviation	10,950	5,480
Coefficient of variation	0.27	0.16

either the standard deviation of outcomes or the coefficient of variation. The firm could conceivably opt for the relatively safer proposal B, even though by doing so, it would be sacrificing the prospect of a somewhat higher possible cash flow. It is not possible to say immediately which would be the "proper" or the optimal decision. That must depend on the degree of risk aversion with which the firm's decision makers, acting on behalf of the owners of the firm, face their management tasks.

The probability distributions we have envisaged so far describe the probabilities attached to certain discrete or uniquely specified possible outcomes, and they are referred to as discrete distributions. In actual fact, the variable *x*, here representing dollar values of cash flows, may range over a continuous scale of possible values. In that case, the probability distributions will be representable as continuous functions such as depicted in Figure 5.1. In this figure, two continuous probability distributions are shown, approximating the general expected value and variance characteristics of the discrete distributions describing proposals A and B.

In the case of a continuous probability distribution, the total area under the curve describing the "probability density function" must equal, or integrate to, unity. We can focus on the area under the continuous probability distribution between any pair of values of the variable described on the horizontal axis and express this as a proportion of the total area under the curve. That proportion or ratio will then describe the probability that the value of the variable will fall within the range between the pair of values indicated. The expected value and variance for the continuous distributions are computed as follows, where *x* is again a suitably defined random variable:

$$E(x) = \int_a^b xp(x)\, dx \tag{5.4}$$

and

$$\text{Var}(x) = \sigma_x^2 = \int_a^b [x_i - E(x)]^2 p(x)\, dx \tag{5.5}$$

In Equations (5.4) and (5.5), $p(x)$ represents the form of the continuous probability density function, and a and b represent the lower and upper limits of the range of the random variable.

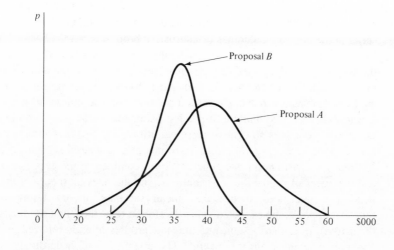

Figure 5.1

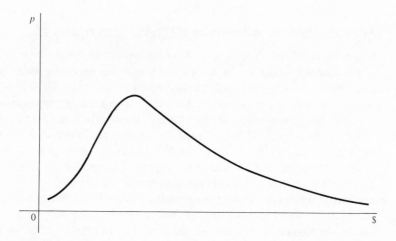

Figure 5.2

The probability distributions of the outcomes may not be of the symmetrical form that has so far been assumed. In Figure 5.2, a "positively skewed" distribution is shown. The cash flow described by such a distribution would hold out the prospect of only a moderate average or expected value, but also the possibility, however small, of very high values.

The firm's decision makers could very well be attracted to such a prospect. In that connection, we may anticipate our discussion of the utility functions of investors that exhibit varying degrees of risk aversion. The firm may choose between alternative proposals, or between the probability distributions describing the possible outcomes of alternative proposals, on the basis of a utility function defined over the expected values and variances, and possibly also the skewness, of the probability distributions. The form of the utility function may be such that (i) the firm is attracted to higher expected returns, so that the expected-value variable generates a positive marginal utility; (ii) it is averse to variability risk, so that the dispersion parameter, or the standard deviation of returns, generates a negative marginal utility; and (iii) it is attracted to, or derives a positive marginal utility from, positive skewness, such as described in Figure 5.2. Attention has generally been confined to the expected values and variances of probability distributions, and the relevant theory of decision making is widely described as the "mean–variance" theory. Using alternative terminology, the expected value is referred to as the "first moment about the origin" of a distribution, and the standard deviation is referred to as the "second moment about the mean." These statistics are accordingly said to describe the first and second moments of the probability distribution. The measure of skewness is similarly referred to as the third moment.

Asset combinations and covariance between asset returns

In making asset investments or in choosing a portfolio combination of securities, a decision maker will not generally base his decisions solely on the risk–return characteristics of individual assets or securities. He will be concerned also with the relationships that exist between the return streams generated by the various assets. If, for example, the rates of return on two assets, A and B, were observed to be "positively correlated," then when the return on A increased, the return on B would do likewise. Asset returns that are "negatively correlated" would move over time in opposite directions. This possibility gives rise to the concept of economic diversification. Diversification exists when investable money capital is distributed over assets whose prospective income streams are less than perfectly correlated. In that case, not all the income streams on all the assets rise and fall together, or to the same relative degree, over time. Indeed, if some asset income streams are negatively correlated with others, and they therefore rise when the others fall, the benefits of overall risk reduction are being achieved to a higher degree. For then "what is lost on the swings is being made up on the roundabouts." We approach this important question by examining the concept of the "covariance" between asset returns.

Consider the probability distributions of rates of return on two securities, A and B, described in Table 5.4. In this example, the rates of return on the securities, R_A and R_B, are interpreted as random variables, analogous to the

Table 5.4 *Probability distributions of rates of return*

Probability	Rate of return on security A (%)	Probability	Rate of return on security B (%)
0.10	5	0.10	3
0.20	6	0.20	4
0.40	10	0.30	5
0.20	12	0.30	6
0.10	15	0.10	8

Table 5.5 *Comparative probability data for securities A and B*

Statistical characteristic	Security A	Security B
Expected value, %	9.6	5.2
Standard deviation, %	2.97	1.33
Coefficient of variation	0.31	0.26

random variable x in the preceding definitions. An analysis of the mean return and variance characteristics of these two probability distributions reveals the summary data shown in Table 5.5.

Here again we have an example of two investment opportunities in which the one promising the higher rate of return, based on the investor's subjective probability distributions, also confronts the investor with the higher degree of risk. Based on both the absolute standard deviation and the coefficient of variation, security A is the more risky opportunity. But it is necessary to take account also of the degree to which covariation occurs, or is likely to occur, over time, between the two rates of return. We therefore examine in more detail the measures of covariation referred to as covariance and correlation.

For this purpose, we may imagine that simultaneous observations of the rates of return generated by the two securities are made and recorded in Table 5.6. To determine the degree of the covariation in these rates of return, we set out in Table 5.7 the details of the covariance computation.

As Table 5.7 indicates, we are interested now in the simultaneous deviation of the rates of return on securities A and B from their expected values. The data in columns 2 and 4 of the table, given the fact that the expected values of the rates of return have been calculated to be 9.6 and 5.2 percent, respectively, provide the simultaneous deviations in columns 3 and 5. In the final

Table 5.6 *Simultaneously observed rates of return on securities A and B*

Observation number	Security A (%)	Security B (%)
1	12	5
2	6	4
3	6	3
4	12	4
5	10	6
6	15	6
7	10	8
8	10	5
9	5	6
10	10	5

Table 5.7 *Computation of covariance between rates of return on securities A and B*

Simultaneous observation number	Rate of return on A, R_A (%)	$R_A - E(R_A)$ $= d_a$	Rate of return on B, R_B (%)	$R_B - E(R_B)$ $= d_b$	$d_a d_b$
1	12	2.4	5	−0.2	−0.48
2	6	−3.6	4	−1.2	4.32
3	6	−3.6	3	−2.2	7.92
4	12	2.4	4	−1.2	−2.88
5	10	0.4	6	0.8	0.32
6	15	5.4	6	0.8	4.32
7	10	0.4	8	2.8	1.12
8	10	0.4	5	−0.2	−0.08
9	5	−4.6	6	0.8	−3.68
10	10	0.4	5	−0.2	−0.08
					$\sum = 10.80$

column of the table, we record the product of those simultaneous deviations. We are now interested in the weighted average value of those products, or the "expected value" of the product of the simultaneous deviations. We therefore take the weighted average value of the product terms, where each such product term is weighted by the probability of its occurrence. That statistic defines the extent to which the rates of return are fluctuating together.

In the present case, each recorded product term has a 10 percent probability of occurring, so that if each product were multiplied by that probability and the results then added to provide a probability weighted sum, the result would be equal to 1.08. This figure of 1.08 is then the measure of covariance for which we have been seeking. We therefore state:

Definition 5

The *covariance* between two random variables is defined as the weighted average of the products of the simultaneous deviations of each of the random variables from its expected value, where each such product of deviations is weighted by the probability of its occurrence.

Notationally, the covariance, in this case the covariance between the rates of return on securities A and B, is written as

$$\text{Cov}(R_A, R_B) = \sigma_{AB} = \sum_A \sum_B p(R_A, R_B)[R_A - E(R_A)][R_B - E(R_B)] \quad (5.6)$$

In this expression, $p(R_A, R_B)$ represents the joint probability, or the probability of the occurrence together of the R_A and R_B values that give rise to the deviations contained in the product terms. The expression for the covariance can be written alternatively as

$$\sigma_{AB} = E\{[R_A - E(R_A)] [R_B - E(R_B)]\} \quad (5.7)$$

The definition and computation of the covariance parallels that of the variance of a random variable. In fact, the variance is a special case of the covariance and can be understood as the covariance of a random variable with itself. In other words, the formula for the covariance given in Equation (5.7) reduces to that for the variance when the variables R_A and R_B are identical. A further economy of notation describing the variance of the ith random variable in a set of N variables and the covariance between the ith and the jth random variable is the following:

$$\text{Var}(R_i) = \sigma_{ii} \qquad i = 1, \dots, N \quad (5.8)$$

$$\text{Cov}(R_i, R_j) = \sigma_{ij} \qquad i \neq j, \, i, j, = 1, \dots, N \quad (5.9)$$

Correlation between random variables

The descriptive statistics we have so far derived from the probability distributions depend on the units in which the original data are measured. If, for example, variables denominated X and Y were, in an appropriate context, measured in feet rather than in inches, the deviations from the expected values, of the kind shown in Table 5.7, would change by a factor of 12, and hence the covariance, σ_{XY}, would also change to a corresponding degree. In order to obtain a measure of the covariation between two random variables that is unaffected by the units of measurement, we can normalize the deviations by dividing them by the standard deviation of the distribution.

The resulting measure, a pure number, is referred to as the correlation coefficient, and the correlation between the ith and the jth random variables in a set of variables is written as

$$\rho_{ij} = \frac{\sigma_{ij}}{\sigma_i \sigma_j} \qquad i \neq j, \ i, j = 1, \ldots, N \qquad (5.10)$$

If $i = j$, $\rho_{ij} = 1$.

We accordingly have:

Definition 6

The *correlation* between two random variables is defined as the covariance between them divided by the product of their standard deviations.

Using the expected-value notation of Equation (5.7), the correlation coefficient for the rate-of-return example in Table 5.7 can be written as

$$\rho_{AB} = E\left[\left(\frac{R_A - E(R_A)}{\sigma_A} \right) \left(\frac{R_B - E(R_B)}{\sigma_B} \right) \right] \qquad (5.11)$$

It follows that on the basis of the data in Table 5.7 the correlation between the random variables is

$$\rho_{AB} = \frac{\sigma_{AB}}{\sigma_A \sigma_B} = \frac{1.08}{(2.97)(1.33)} = 0.27 \qquad (5.12)$$

The correlation coefficient will always lie between -1 and 1. In the present case of securities A and B, a moderate, not a high, degree of correlation exists. In our subsequent discussion of security portfolio composition and financial asset market theory, we shall make use of Equation (5.10) to write

$$\sigma_{ij} = \rho_{ij} \sigma_i \sigma_j \qquad i \neq j, \ i, j = 1, \ldots, N \qquad (5.13)$$

Much depends, for the possibility of reducing portfolio risk by engaging in asset diversification, on the magnitude of the correlation coefficient between all possible pairs of rates of return on assets, as well as the variances, or the standard deviations, on the individual assets' own rates of return. Because the signs on the standard deviations are positive, the sign of the correlation coefficient follows the sign of the covariance. The lower the correlation, including the possibility of negative value as low as -1, the greater the risk reduction that can be achieved by asset diversification.

Linear combinations of random variables: expected values, variances, and covariances

In this and the following sections we shall consider the significance of the expected values and variances of combinations of random variables. By doing so, we shall lay the foundation for the traditional theory of the selection of asset portfolios.

Imagine that a random observation X_i is made from a set of values of a variable X whose distribution is described by a probability density function having an expected value $E(X)$ and a standard deviation σ_X. Similarly, we visualize a random observation Y_i drawn from a distribution of a variable Y having an expected value and a standard deviation of $E(Y)$ and σ_Y. Imagine now that a new variable S is defined as the sum of the simultaneous observations of these X and Y variables. We must interpret S as a random variable because any variable that is a function of one or more random variables is itself a random variable. We now write

$$S = X + Y \tag{5.14}$$

It can be shown that

$$E(S) = E(X) + E(Y) \tag{5.15}$$

leading to:

Proposition 1

The expected value of a sum of random variables is equal to the sum of the expected values of the random variables.

Interest frequently attaches to the weighted sum of random variables, where, for example, denoting the weighted sum as S,

$$S = w_1 X + w_2 Y \tag{5.16}$$

where w_1 and w_2 are the weights attached to the random variables. It then follows that

$$E(S) = w_1 E(X) + w_2 E(Y) \tag{5.17}$$

leading to:

Proposition 2

The expected value of a weighted sum of random variables is equal to the weighted sum of the expected values of the random variables.

The computation of the variance of a sum of random variables is a little more complicated. Using the expected-value notation, and writing the variance of a random variable as

$$\text{Var}(X) = E\left[[X - E(X)]^2\right] \tag{5.18}$$

the variance of the sum of the random variables X and Y, Var (S), can be written as

$$\text{Var}(S) = E\left[[S - E(S)]^2\right] \tag{5.19}$$

or

$$\begin{aligned} \text{Var}(S) &= E\left[\left\{(X + Y) - [E(X) + E(Y)]\right\}^2\right] \\ &= E\left[\left\{[X - E(X)] + [Y - E(Y)]\right\}^2\right] \end{aligned} \tag{5.20}$$

We now let $[X - E(X)] = d_x$, or the deviation of the X magnitudes from their expected values, and similarly let $[Y - E(Y)] = d_y$. Equation (5.20) can then be written as

$$\text{Var}(S) = E\left[[d_x + d_y]^2\right] \tag{5.21}$$

Recalling the elementary proposition that

$$(a + b)^2 = a^2 + b^2 + 2ab$$

we can apply this formula on the right-hand side of Equation (5.21) and write the resulting expression for Var(S) as

$$\text{Var}(S) = E[d_x^2 + d_y^2 + 2d_x d_y] \tag{5.22}$$

Placing the expectation operator inside the brackets in Equation (5.22) in accordance with Proposition 1, the expression for the variance becomes

$$\text{Var}(S) = E(d_x^2) + E(d_y^2) + 2E(d_x d_y) \tag{5.23}$$

We recognize that the expectation terms on the right-hand side of Equation (5.23) describe, respectively, the variance of X, the variance of Y, and the covariance between X and Y. The final expression for the variance of the sum of the random variables is therefore

$$\text{Var}(S) = \text{Var}(X) + \text{Var}(Y) + 2\,\text{Cov}(X, Y) \tag{5.24}$$

We can therefore state:

Proposition 3

The variance of the sum of a pair of random variables is equal to the sum of the variances of the variables plus twice the covariance between them.

The expected value of the sum of the random variables, as defined, for example, in Equation (5.15), takes no account at all, and is in fact quite independent of, whatever covariation might exist between the random variables. But the covariance between the variables, as in Equation (5.24), enters in an important way into the determination of the variance of the sum. Much depends, therefore, on the magnitude of the covariance and, in particular, on the sign of the covariance term.

We can see the impact of this in another way. Making use of Equation (5.13), we write

$$\text{Var}(S) = \text{Var}(X) + \text{Var}(Y) + 2\,\rho_{XY}\sigma_X\sigma_Y \qquad (5.25)$$

Thus the variance of the sum depends crucially on the sign, as well as the magnitude, of the correlation between the variables. If the correlation between the random variables is negative, or if, that is, $\rho_{XY} < 0$, the variance of the sum will be less than the sum of the variances of the underlying random variables. If the random variables in the sum were the rates of return on assets, the combination of assets whose income streams were negatively correlated would lead to a minimization of the asset portfolio risk. This again is the meaning of economic diversification. Risk reduction can be achieved by combining assets in such a way the correlation between the income streams of given pairs of assets is less than 1. No risk reduction can be accomplished, however, and therefore no economic diversification exists, if investments are made in assets whose income streams are perfectly correlated.

The example of asset portfolios motivates our interest in the weighted sums of random variables, where, for example, the weights attached to the variables describe their relative importance in the portfolio. The variance of a weighted sum such as S in Equation (5.16) can be written as

$$\begin{aligned}
\text{Var}(S) &= E\Big[[S - E(S)]^2\Big] \\
&= E\Big[\big\{(w_1 X + w_2 Y) - [w_1 E(X) + w_2 E(Y)]\big\}^2\Big] \\
&= E\Big[\big\{w_1[X - E(X)] + w_2[Y - E(Y)]\big\}^2\Big] \\
&= E\Big[[w_1 d_x + w_2 d_y]^2\Big] \\
&= E[w_1^2 d_x^2 + w_2^2 d_y^2 + 2w_1 w_2 d_x d_y] \\
&= w_1^2 E(d_x^2) + w_2^2 E(d_y^2) + 2w_1 w_2 E(d_x d_y) \qquad (5.26)
\end{aligned}$$

This expression reduces to the following definition of the variance of the weighted sum of random variables:

$$\text{Var}(S) = w_1^2 \text{Var}(X) + w_2^2 \text{Var}(Y) + 2w_1 w_2 \text{Cov}(X,\,Y) \qquad (5.27)$$

leading to:

Proposition 4

The variance of the weighted sum of a pair of random variables is equal to the weighted sum of the variances of the variables (where the weights are the squares of the weights attached to the underlying random variables) plus twice the product of the weights times the covariance between the random variables.

The random variables included in the sum or weighted sum may, of course, be extended to any desired number. Let us suppose that a sum of three variables is defined as

$$S = X + Y + Z \tag{5.28}$$

It follows from the foregoing that

$$E(S) = E(X) + E(Y) + E(Z) \tag{5.29}$$

and

$$\mathrm{Var}(S) = \mathrm{Var}(X) + \mathrm{Var}(Y) + \mathrm{Var}(Z) + 2\,\mathrm{Cov}(XY) \\ + 2\,\mathrm{Cov}(XZ) + 2\,\mathrm{Cov}(YZ) \tag{5.30}$$

We must therefore be interested in the covariances between all possible pairs of random variables included in the sum. In the case of a large number of variables, the number of covariance terms that have to be considered mounts rapidly. It is equal to the number of pairs of items that can be defined from the set of, say, n variables included in the sum. Using factorial notation, this is defined as $n!/2!(n-2)!$. A more compact way of handling this notational problem, and of visualizing the variances of sums and weighted sums of random variables, is available. It takes up the concept of the variance–covariance matrix, frequently referred to simply as the covariance matrix.

Covariance matrix

A matrix is a rectangular array of numbers or variables (which may be, and in the present instance will be, a square array) each element of which represents a magnitude or value in which we are for some reason interested. The array of numbers is usually enclosed in square brackets. If we write the variance and the covariance terms in the forms shown in Equations (5.8) and (5.9), Equation (5.30) may be written as

$$\sigma_S^2 = \sigma_{XX} + \sigma_{YY} + \sigma_{ZZ} + 2\,\sigma_{XY} + 2\,\sigma_{XZ} + 2\,\sigma_{YZ} \tag{5.31}$$

For convenience of notation, we shall now refer to the variables X, Y, and Z as variables 1, 2, and 3, respectively. We can then set out the variance and covariance terms included in the summation in Equation (5.31) in the form

$$\begin{bmatrix} \sigma_{11} & \sigma_{12} & \sigma_{13} \\ \sigma_{21} & \sigma_{22} & \sigma_{23} \\ \sigma_{31} & \sigma_{32} & \sigma_{33} \end{bmatrix} \tag{5.32}$$

The variance of the sum of random variables, comparing (5.31) and (5.32), will be the summation of all of the terms included in the matrix, the so-called covariance matrix, in (5.32). The covariance matrix has a number of highly important properties. First, it is, of course, square and is in this case said to be of dimension 3×3, or three by three. It has three rows and three columns. This is because we must take into account the covariance of each of the variables with each of the other variables.

Second, the elements on the principal diagonal of the matrix, here shown as σ_{11}, σ_{22}, and σ_{33}, define the variances of the random variables. Including these in the sum therefore takes account of the first three terms in the summations on the right-hand sides of Equations (5.30) and (5.31).

Third, the symmetry of the matrix, meaning that for each term on the northeast of the principal diagonal there is a corresponding, and equal, term on the southwest of the diagonal, follows from the fact that the covariance between, say, the second and the third random variables is, of course, the same as the covariance between the third and the second.

Fourth, the dimension of the covariance matrix will be equal to the number of random variables in the summation, for example the number of assets included in an investment portfolio.

Finally, it follows that an extremely straightforward way exists of visualizing the effect on the variance of a sum of random variables if an additional variable is added to the sum. In the covariance matrix for the simple unweighted sum shown in (5.32), the addition of a fourth variable would expand the variance of the sum by (i) adding a new term, σ_{44}, to the principal diagonal; (ii) adding a row of covariance terms along the bottom of the matrix, $(\sigma_{41}, \sigma_{42}, \sigma_{43})$; and (iii) adding a corresponding column of covariances to the right-hand side of the matrix. The matrix then assumes dimension 4×4.

Covariance matrix of a weighted sum of random variables

When the sum of random variables is a weighted sum (as occurs in connection with an asset investment portfolio), the specification of the variance in matrix notation is somewhat more complicated. It becomes even more important, however, for economy of notation and for the visualization of the results.

We must now specify, first, what is referred to as the vector of weights attached to the underlying random variables. A vector is a column of elements or numbers enclosed in square brackets, and in the present example the elements would be the weights assigned to each of the variables in the sum.

Employing, as before, the lowercase w_i to refer to the weights, we shall denote the vector by the uppercase W. In the sum of three variables, the vector of weights is written as

$$W = \begin{bmatrix} w_1 \\ w_2 \\ w_3 \end{bmatrix} \tag{5.33}$$

It is frequently necessary to envisage a so-called row vector of elements, which is understood as the transpose of a column vector. The transpose of the vector in (5.33), notationally referred to as W', appears as

$$W' = [w_1, w_2, w_3] \tag{5.34}$$

Conceptually, the matrix shown in (5.32) can be visualized as a set of column vectors. It can also be visualized as a set of row vectors. In general, an $m \times n$ matrix is one that has m rows and n columns. Alternatively, we can say that a column vector containing m elements is a matrix of dimension $m \times 1$. The transpose, or the corresponding row vector, would be a matrix of dimension $1 \times m$. The vector in (5.33), for example, can be interpreted as a matrix of dimension 3×1.

There exists an extensive and powerful algebra of vectors and matrices, but the main aspect of this that we need to investigate for our present purposes is the operation of multiplication. The quite simple operation of matrix multiplication may appear, at first blush, to be unusually complex. But it can be considerably simplified by examining first the multiplication of vectors. In examining this operation, we should bear in mind that vectors are, as we have seen, a special form of matrix. The steps in the multiplication process that forms the product of vectors will all be reflected in the extension of the ideas to the multiplication of matrices of larger dimension.

Let us review, as an example, the calculation of the expected value of a random variable. Equation (5.1) provided the definition of the expected value, and if we now take the probabilities shown there as the weights, the expected value is interpretable, as before, as a weighted sum of possible values or outcomes. The expression for the expected value can then be written as

$$E(x) = \sum_i w_i x_i \tag{5.35}$$

We can now reinterpret this multiplication in terms of vector algebra by visualizing both (i) a vector of possible outcomes, x_i, and (ii) a vector of weights, w_i. The expected value of the variable x is then defined as the product of the X-vector of possible values of the variable and the W-vector.

Generalizing this procedure will explain the operation in more detail. We shall now use the symbol X to denote a vector of variables (not to be confused with the previous use of x to refer to a single variable). For example, the variables X, Y, and Z in Equation (5.28) can now be understood to be represented by x_1, x_2, and x_3, as shown in

$$X = \begin{bmatrix} x_1 \\ x_2 \\ x_3 \end{bmatrix} \tag{5.36}$$

We also have a vector of weights in (5.33).

The vector multiplication now proceeds as follows. We multiply the first element of the X-vector by the first element of the W-vector to obtain $w_1 x_1$. We then multiply the second element of the X-vector by the second element of the W-vector, and so on throughout the range of elements. This provides a set of product terms of the kind indicated. If we then take the sum of those product terms, we have precisely what is described as the product of the two vectors. What we have accomplished, in performing these successive multiplications of X-vector elements by W-vector elements and adding the results, is what is known as the operation of the multiplication of vectors. It is sometimes referred to also as taking the inner product of vectors. Notationally, the operation is written in summary form as $W' \cdot X$. It is also referred to as the dot product, because the dot between the transpose of the W-vector on the left and the X-vector on the right is understood as the sign indicating multiplication.

Vectors are said to be "conformable for multiplication" only if they contain the same number of elements. Moreover, it is usual to write the vectors being multiplied together in the form

$$W' \cdot X = [w_1, \ w_2, \ w_3] \begin{bmatrix} x_1 \\ x_2 \\ x_3 \end{bmatrix} \tag{5.37}$$

That is to say, the vector on the left is written as a row vector, or as the transpose of the vector of weights, and that on the right is written as a column vector. Recalling that we have already interpreted a column vector containing m elements as a matrix of dimension $m \times 1$ and its transpose as a matrix of dimension $1 \times m$, we can now refer to this vector multiplication as the simplest form of matrix multiplication. Taking this view of things, we note that the matrix on the left [the 3-element row vector in (5.37)] contains as many *columns* as the number of *rows* contained in the matrix on the right [the 3-element column vector in (5.37)]. This fact should be recognized clearly and borne in mind in what follows. It specifies the very important rule that must be satisfied in order to enable us to say that matrices are "conformable for multiplication." When we deal with higher-order matrices, instead of the simple $1 \times m$ and $m \times 1$ matrices we have in the vector multiplication case, we shall see again that matrices can be multiplied together only if this rule is satisfied. The matrix on the left must have as many columns as the number of rows in the matrix on the right. By way of final definition, a matrix of dimension 1×1 is simply a single number. It is referred to as a scalar.

An interesting result follows from the foregoing. When we multiply a $1 \times m$ vector on the left by an $m \times 1$ vector on the right, as we have done in (5.37) in the 3-variable example, we obtain as the result a 1×1 matrix, or a scalar. The number of rows in the matrix that gives the result of the multiplication, the so-called product matrix, will be the same as the number of rows in the matrix on the left, and the number of columns in the product matrix will be the same as the number of columns in the matrix on the right. Thus, for example, the multiplication of an $m \times n$ matrix by an $n \times m$ matrix will provide a product matrix of dimension $m \times m$. We must now expand these ideas to demonstrate the multiplication of matrices of higher order.

Recall the covariance matrix shown in (5.32), which we shall refer to in what follows by the symbol V, and the vector of weights shown in (5.33). Interpreting the transpose of the vector of weights as a matrix of dimension 1×3, we observe that such a matrix and the covariance matrix are conformable for multiplication. We set them together in the following way:

$$[w_1, w_2, w_3] \begin{bmatrix} \sigma_{11} & \sigma_{12} & \sigma_{13} \\ \sigma_{21} & \sigma_{22} & \sigma_{23} \\ \sigma_{31} & \sigma_{32} & \sigma_{33} \end{bmatrix} \qquad (5.38)$$

Multiplying the row vector by the first column of the matrix on the right, we obtain, by applying now familiar procedures, a scalar equal to the sum of $w_1\sigma_{11} + w_2\sigma_{21} + w_3\sigma_{31}$. If, similarly, we multiplied the row vector on the left by the second column of the covariance matrix, we would obtain another scalar result. We could again obtain a further scalar result by multiplying the row vector by the third column of the covariance matrix. By performing the multiplication envisaged in (5.38), we would obtain a product matrix of dimension 1×3. This would be written in the form

$$W'V = \left[\sum w_i\sigma_{i1}, \sum w_i\sigma_{i2}, \sum w_i\sigma_{i3} \right] \qquad i = 1, 2, 3 \qquad (5.39)$$

In Equation (5.39), we have omitted from the left-hand side, for economy of notation, the dot that was employed in the illustrative example in Equation (5.37).

We now take this 1×3 matrix and multiply it by the vector of weights, this time placing the vector of weights on the right-hand side. This is necessary because the vector of weights, being interpretable as a 3×1 matrix, will then be conformable for multiplication with a matrix on the left of dimension 1×3. So then, having the product matrix derived from (5.38) on the left [the 1×3 matrix in (5.39)] and the vector of weights on the right (a 3×1 matrix), the resulting product matrix will be of dimension 1×1, or a scalar.

To obtain this result, we proceed substantially as before. The operation is defined in Equation (5.40). We take the first element of the row matrix on the left and multiply it by the first element of the column vector on the right. This multiplication will provide us with a scalar. We repeat the procedure and multiply the second element of the row matrix on the left by the second element of the vector on the right. This provides a second scalar. Then we obtain another scalar by multiplying the third element of the row matrix by the third element of the vector on the right. We have, then, three scalar products. Adding these products provides a scalar sum, which is the result we have been searching for. It is the product of the 3-element row vector and the 3-element column vector. It is an application of the operation of the multiplication of vectors that we illustrated initially. It provides, in fact, the variance of the weighted sum of random variables. The operation can be summarized as follows:

$$W'VW = \left[\sum w_i \sigma_{i1}, \ \sum w_i \sigma_{i2}, \ \sum w_i \sigma_{i3} \right] \begin{bmatrix} w_1 \\ w_2 \\ w_3 \end{bmatrix} \qquad i = 1, 2, 3 \qquad (5.40)$$

Let us recall what we have done. Employing the notation V to refer to the covariance matrix and W to denote the vector of weights, we have performed a two-stage matrix multiplication that can be summarized in matrix notation as

$$\text{The variance of the weighted sum} = W'VW \qquad (5.41)$$

leading to:

Proposition 5

The variance of a weighted sum of random variables is equal to the transpose of the vector of weights multiplied by the covariance matrix multiplied by the vector of weights.

We may make a final interpretation of the result achieved by effecting the multiplications in Equations (5.39) and (5.40) leading to the variance of the weighted sum as defined in Equation (5.41). Setting out the full expansion of Equation (5.40), we have

$$\begin{aligned} W'VW &= w_1 \left(\sum w_i \sigma_{i1} \right) + w_2 \left(\sum w_i \sigma_{i2} \right) + w_3 \left(\sum w_i \sigma_{i3} \right) \\ &= w_1^2 \sigma_{11} + w_1 w_2 \sigma_{21} + w_1 w_3 \sigma_{31} + w_2 w_1 \sigma_{12} \\ &\quad + w_2^2 \sigma_{22} + w_2 w_3 \sigma_{32} + w_3 w_1 \sigma_{13} + w_3 w_2 \sigma_{23} + w_3^2 \sigma_{33} \qquad (5.42) \end{aligned}$$

This sum may be restated in terms that reflect precisely the variance of the weighted sum defined in Equation (5.27), noting again the symmetry in the covariance terms included in the summation in Equation (5.42). For example, σ_{21} is the same as σ_{12}.

To reinforce the procedures of this important matrix multiplication, let us work through an analogous example. We shall define a 3-element vector and a 3×3 matrix as follows (the numbers in the example are used simply for illustrative purposes and have no actual or theoretical meaning or application):

$$W = \begin{bmatrix} 2 \\ 3 \\ 5 \end{bmatrix} \qquad V = \begin{bmatrix} 3 & 7 & 5 \\ 1 & 4 & 6 \\ 2 & 1 & 3 \end{bmatrix}$$

We wish to calculate the product of $W'VW$. It follows that

$$W'V = [2, 3, 5] \begin{bmatrix} 3 & 7 & 5 \\ 1 & 4 & 6 \\ 2 & 1 & 3 \end{bmatrix} = [19, 31, 43]$$

Referring to the result of this multiplication as matrix M of dimension 1×3, and multiplying it now by the W-vector on the right, we have

$$MW = [19, 31, 43] \begin{bmatrix} 2 \\ 3 \\ 5 \end{bmatrix} = [346]$$

Thus, the scalar 346 is the result of the multiplication $W'VW$.

Variance of a weighted sum of random variables

Given that the variance of a weighted sum of three random variables can be expressed as the matrix product $W'VW$, we can extend the argument and envisage the variance of a weighted sum of n random variables. The magnitude n may be, for example, the number of financial assets included in an investment portfolio, or the number of assets in an opportunity set from which an optimal portfolio is selected. We thus envisage a vector of weights defined as $W' = [w_1, w_2, \cdots, w_i, \cdots, W_n]$. Similarly, we envisage an $n \times n$ covariance matrix. The latter takes the general form

$$V = \begin{bmatrix} \sigma_{11} & \sigma_{12} & \cdots & \sigma_{1n} \\ \sigma_{21} & \sigma_{22} & \cdots & \sigma_{2n} \\ \vdots & \vdots & \ddots & \vdots \\ \sigma_{n1} & \sigma_{n2} & \cdots & \sigma_{nn} \end{bmatrix} \tag{5.43}$$

Such a covariance matrix may be multiplied by the transpose of the vector of weights on the left (that is, premultiplied), and by the vector of weights on the right (that is, postmultiplied) to provide the variance of the weighted sum. If we envisage the set of random variables as describing the rates of return on the securities in a portfolio, we could summarize as follows the effect on the variance of the portfolio rate of return that results from adding a new asset to the portfolio. First, the addition of the asset would introduce a new variance term to the principal diagonal of the covariance matrix, which would then be of dimension $(n+1) \times (n+1)$. Second, we should add a row of covariance terms along the bottom of the covariance matrix and a corresponding column of covariance terms on the right-hand side of that matrix. Third, we should also change the vector of weights that would become an $n+1$-element vector. If, moreover, the weights were taken to be the proportion of the total portfolio represented by the different assets (making it necessary for the weights to sum to unity), the introduction of a new asset would necessarily change the weights given to all of the previously existing assets in the portfolio.

Having calculated the variance of the weighted sum of random variables, we can summarize the results for the n-variable case as follows, where S again refers to the weighted sum:

$$\text{Var}(S) = \sum w_1^2 \text{Var}(x_i) + 2 \sum_{i=1}^{n} \sum_{j>i}^{n} w_i w_j Cov(x_i x_j) \qquad (5.44)$$

Employing alternative notation, this can also be written as

$$\text{Var}(S) = \sum_i \sum_j w_i w_j \sigma_{ij} \qquad (5.45)$$

Again, recalling the definition in Equation (5.13),

$$\sigma_{ij} = \rho_{ij} \sigma_i \sigma_j$$

the final term in Equation (5.44) can be replaced by the term

$$2 \sum_{i=1}^{n} \sum_{j>i}^{n} w_i w_j \rho_{ij} \sigma_i \sigma_j$$

This development will have application in the discussion of the theory of financial asset markets and the firm's cost of money capital. We conclude this chapter by considering in a preliminary fashion the economic opportunities provided by asset combinations in the light of the different degrees of correlation that might exist between individual asset returns.

Application of probability and risk: two-asset portfolio opportunity locus

With the foregoing definitions and computational procedures in hand, we may return to the two-security example we considered earlier in this chapter. We envisage now the possibility of investing in two assets, A and B, where the rates of return on the assets are described by probability distributions with

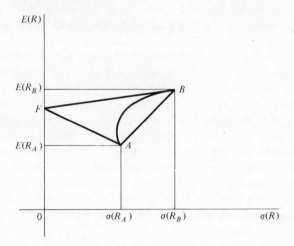

Figure 5.3

expected values and variances of $E(R_A)$, $E(R_B)$, $\text{Var}(R_A)$, and $\text{Var}(R_B)$, respectively. We shall refer to the weights assigned to each of the assets as the proportion of the portfolio accounted for by each asset, designated as w_A and w_B. Denoting the rate of return on the portfolio as R_p, where the subscript here focuses our attention on the portfolio outcome, the expected rate of return on the portfolio will be interpretable as the weighted sum of the rates of return on the individual assets comprising the portfolio. It follows that the expected value and the variance of the rate of return on the portfolio can be defined as

$$E(R_p) = w_A E(R_A) + w_B E(R_B) \tag{5.46}$$

and

$$\text{Var}(R_p) = w_A^2 \text{Var}(R_A) + w_B^2 \text{Var}(R_B) + 2w_A w_B \text{Cov}(R_A, R_B) \tag{5.47}$$

The covariance term in Equation (5.47) may be written alternatively as

$$\text{Cov}(R_A, R_B) = \rho_{AB} \sigma_A \sigma_B \tag{5.48}$$

Consider now the coordinates of the asset A and B investment opportunities in the risk–return plane in Figure 5.3. We there refer to the risk of an asset as indicated by the standard deviation of its rate of return. Let it be supposed that the asset returns are perfectly correlated, or that $\rho_{AB} = 1$. Then if Equation (5.48) is substituted into Equation (5.47), it follows that the variance of return on the portfolio can be written as

$$\text{Var}(R_p) = [w_A\sigma_A + w_B\sigma_B]^2 \tag{5.49}$$

where the standard deviations of the rates of return on the assets are now written as σ_A and σ_B. This follows from the fact that as the correlation between asset returns is assumed to be unity, the variable ρ_{AB} falls out of the expression for the portfolio variance. By expanding the right-hand side of Equation (5.49), the result in Equation (5.47) [after the substitution of Equation (5.48)] is obtained. Equation (5.49) implies that

$$\sigma(R_p) = w_A\sigma_A + w_B\sigma_B \tag{5.50}$$

In this special case of perfectly correlated asset returns, the standard deviation of the portfolio rate of return is equal to the weighted sum of the standard deviations of the rates of return on the assets contained in the portfolio. We can now trace out, in the light of these definitions, the effect on what we shall call the portfolio investment opportunity frontier, or the portfolio opportunity locus, as this is determined by different possible values of the correlation coefficient ρ_{AB}.

This portfolio opportunity locus, such as the locus AB in Figure 5.3, may or may not be linear. It describes the rate at which an investor, by varying the proportionate combination of securities A and B in the portfolio, can vary both the expected return on the portfolio and the degree of risk as measured by the standard deviation of the portfolio rate of return. If, for example, only security A were held, the portfolio risk–return characteristics, $E(R_p)$ and $\sigma(R_p)$, would be described by the risk–return characteristics of security A, or by the coordinate point A in Figure 5.3. By introducing security B to the portfolio and investing in a weighted combination of the two assets, the resulting portfolio return and risk will be described by a different point in the locus AB. The slope of this locus therefore describes the rate at which the portfolio expected rate of return can be increased in compensation for undertaking a higher degree of portfolio risk.

We note that in the two-asset case the value of w_B may be written as $1 - w_A$. A change in the proportions in which the assets are combined in the portfolio may then be reflected simply in a variation in the magnitude of w_A. We may substitute $w_B = 1 - w_A$ in Equation (5.46) and differentiate with respect to w_A, thus observing the effect on the portfolio return of increasing the relative weight of asset A:

$$\frac{dE(R_p)}{dw_A} = E(R_A) - E(R_B) \tag{5.51}$$

Similarly, differentiation of Equation (5.50) with respect to w_A implies

$$\frac{d\sigma(R_p)}{dw_A} = \sigma_A - \sigma_B \tag{5.52}$$

Dividing Equation (5.51) by Equation (5.52) provides the explicit relation between $E(R_p)$ and $\sigma(R_p)$ that we have anticipated:

$$\frac{dE(R_p)}{d\sigma(R_p)} = \frac{E(R_A) - E(R_B)}{\sigma_A - \sigma_B} \tag{5.53}$$

Equation (5.53) then describes the rate at which the portfolio rate of return can be increased by increasing the degree of risk contained within it. This rate of change describes, as we have seen, the portfolio opportunity locus. In the present case, which has been derived from the assumption that the rates of return on the underlying assets are perfectly correlated, the opportunity locus is linear. This follows from the fact that the magnitude of all of the terms on the right-hand side of Equation (5.53) are given and fixed once the forms of the probability distributions of the separate asset returns are specified.

If the value of ρ_{AB} in the preceding derivation were less than unity, or if the asset returns were less than perfectly correlated, it would follow from Equation (5.47) [after the substitution, as before, of Equation (5.48)] that the portfolio variance, and accordingly its standard deviation of rate of return, would be lower than for the case of $\rho_{AB} = 1$. We can consider the case where $\rho_{AB} = -1$. It follows from Equations (5.47) through (5.50) that

$$\sigma(R_p) = w_A \sigma_A - w_B \sigma_B \tag{5.54}$$

or, recalling that $w_A + w_B = 1$,

$$\sigma(R_p) = w_A \sigma_A - (1 - w_A)\sigma_B \tag{5.55}$$

In this case a zero-risk portfolio may be achieved, *given the assumptions regarding the risk–return characteristics of the assets and the assumed covariance between their rates of return,* if Equation (5.55) is set equal to zero and solved for w_A. The result indicates that this is achieved by setting

$$w_A = \sigma_B/(\sigma_A + \sigma_B) \tag{5.56}$$

Generating a similar result for w_B by taking $w_B = 1 - w_A$, it can be shown that the zero-risk portfolio will be achieved when the assets are combined in such proportions that $w_A/w_B = \sigma_B/\sigma_A$, or when the ratio of their weights is equal to the inverse of the ratio of the standard deviations of their rates of return.

When the correlation between the asset returns, therefore, is equal to -1, the portfolio opportunity locus in Figure 5.3 degenerates to the two-segment linear locus *AFB*, where the point *F* reflects the zero-risk combination of assets. The prospect of a zero-risk portfolio is possible because, under the assumptions stated, variation in the rate of return on one of the assets is precisely offset by (is negatively correlated with) the simultaneous variation in the rate of return on the other asset.

In actual fact, interest usually attaches to the possibility that the correlation coefficient will lie between -1 and 1, such as in the example discussed in Tables 5.4 through 5.7. The portfolio opportunity locus will be of the kind shown in Figure 5.3 as the nonlinear locus AB lying between those already derived for the extreme cases of perfectly positive and perfectly negative correlation. The correlation between the assets may in certain cases be zero. In such an event, it will be possible to determine the point on the nonlinear locus such as AB that provides the minimum-risk portfolio.

Given that the correlation coefficient is equal to zero, it follows from Equation (5.47) [after the substitution, as before, of Equation 5.48)] that the variance of the portfolio return will be equal to the weighted sum of the variances of the individual assets. Writing this variance as

$$\sigma_p^2 = w_A^2 \sigma_A^2 + (1 - w_A)^2 \sigma_B^2 \tag{5.57}$$

we may take the derivative with respect to w_A and set it equal to zero to find the minimum-risk portfolio. It can be shown that this will be achieved when the assets are combined in such a proportion that $w_A/w_B = \sigma_B^2 \sigma_A^2$. In this case, the ratio of the asset weights will equal the inverse of the ratio of the variances of their rates of return rather than the inverse of the ratio of their standard deviations that we observed in the case where $\rho_{AB} = -1$.[2]

---

[2] The extensive literature in the area discussed in this section stems from the seminal work of Markowitz (1952, 1959), Sharpe (1964, 1970), and Lintner (1965). See also Tobin (1965), Mossin (1973), Arrow (1971), Hicks (1967), Vickers (1978), and Ford (1983).

CHAPTER 6

Utility, uncertainty, and the theory
of choice

The objective of economic theory, it is frequently suggested, should be that of explaining "human behaviour as a relationship between ends and scarce means which have alternative uses" (Robbins, 1935, p. 16). In this conception of things, the problem of allocation comes sharply into prominence. It has led to the view that economic theory is concerned essentially with the logic of choice. Difficulties inhere in the constriction of economics to such a narrow focus, but it has given rise to extensive investigations into the criteria of choice or action.

Classically, the criterion on the production side of the economy has been that of profit maximization or, as we have seen, the maximization of economic value. On the consumption side, the criterion has generally been the maximization of utility or satisfaction, and a considerable body of theory has developed around the notion of the consumer's utility function. This provides a linkage with our present analysis, pointing to the possibility that decision makers' utility functions may be defined, not only over assumedly known conditions or entities, but over variables whose values can be specified only probabilistically. We raise, therefore, the possibility of what we refer to as the theory of stochastic utility, or of utility functions defined over stochastic arguments. In this chapter we shall examine a number of basic and related propositions that project analogies onto the theory of the firm.

Utility function

It is not necessary to assume that utilities, or degrees of satisfaction, are measurable in cardinal units. The theory in its developed form has become a theory of ordinal, rather than cardinal, utility (see Stigler, 1950; Shackle, 1967, Chs. 7, 8; Page, 1968; Bernoulli, 1968; Friedman and Savage, 1968; von Neumann and Morgenstern, 1953, 1968). An individual is assumed for this purpose to be able to order all possible pairs of objects of choice, say commodities X and Y, in such a way as to state that he prefers X to Y, or Y to X, or that he is indifferent between them. Only one such statement, of course, is assumed to be applicable to each given pair of objects. Moreover, the statement that the individual prefers X to Y (ranks X ahead of, or superior to, Y in his "preference ordering") and Y to Z implies that he prefers X to Z. In formal terms, the first statement will reappear as the axiom of completeness of ordering and the second as an instance of the axiom of transitivity.

These postulates, together with other assumptions we shall explore more fully, lead to the implication that the individual can describe his preference ordering by an ordinal utility function. This means that he can assign real numbers or specifications of magnitude to each of the objects of choice but that those numbers do not represent *absolute* magnitudes of the amount of satisfaction the objects of choice provide or are expected to provide. The numbers indicate merely an order of ranking. It follows that if an ordinal utility function is taken to represent a preference ordering, any monotonically increasing transformation of that function will also represent the ordering. The ordinal utility function, that is to say, is not unique. Or in other terms, it is unique only up to a monotonically increasing transformation. By this term, the following is implied.

We can suppose that $U = f(X, Y)$ describes a utility function defined over objects of choice consisting of quantities of commodities X and Y. Imagine that another utility index, or utility function, $T = g(U)$ is defined by applying a monotonically increasing transformation to the function U. The function $g(U)$ is a monotonically increasing transformation of U if $g(U_1) > g(U_0)$ whenever $U_1 > U_0$. Then the utility function T also represents the preference ordering. It follows that if, working with the original utility function, a number of 60 is assigned to one combination of X and Y and a number of 30 is assigned to a second such combination, it is not possible to say that the first combination provides twice as much utility as the second.

In order to be able to say, moreover, that a preference ordering can be represented by an ordinal utility function, or that it is, in formal terms, a representable preference ordering, a number of characteristics of the ordering must be present. First, in addition to the notions of completeness and transitivity, the set of possible objects of choice must be "connected." That is to say, if A_1 and A_2 are combinations of commodities in the opportunity set available to the individual, it must be possible to proceed from A_1 to A_2 along a continuous path of such combinations. This important assumption of continuity will reappear in a significant guise in the theory of preference orderings over stochastic outcomes. Second, we can consider all the combinations of commodities in the closed opportunity set that are at least as well liked as a given combination, say A_1, and also the set of combinations that are preferred to A_1. This means that if we envisaged an infinite sequence of commodity combinations in, say, the set of combinations preferred to A_1 and such a sequence converged to a limiting combination of A_0, that limiting combination A_0 would also be preferred to A_1.

Let us consider an ordinal utility function

$$U = f(X, Y) \tag{6.1}$$

It may appear that we could envisage the increment of utility that would result from adding a marginal increment of, say, commodity X to the consumption combination. It might be thought that in this way, assuming the utility function possesses appropriate differentiable properties, we could define the partial derivative of the utility function with respect to X as the marginal utility of X. But difficulties attach to such an interpretation of the ordinal and non-unique utility function we have just described. We shall be interested, however, in the *ratio* of the marginal utilities of the commodities, and this, which is quite properly reflected in the ratio of the partial derivatives of the utility function, has valid and significant meaning. Such a ratio remains defined over a monotonically increasing transformation of the original utility function.

We may take, for example, the function $U = aX + bY$ and a monotonic transformation of it, $T = U^2$. The function T can then be written $T = a^2X^2 + b^2Y^2 + 2abXY$. The ratio of the partial derivatives of the function U can be shown to be equal to a/b. When the similar ratio of partial derivatives is calculated from the function T, it is found to be equal once again to a/b. This ratio of partial derivatives will be referred to as the marginal rate of substitution between the commodities, or between whatever happens to be defined as the objects of choice that form the arguments of the utility function.

At this point, the sole property of the consumer utility function in which we are interested is the manner in which it gives rise to a commodity indifference map. This map is made up of a family of indifference curves in the commodity space such that each curve in the family describes a set of commodity combinations that afford the individual the same level of utility. In that sense, he is indifferent between them. They rank equally in his representable preference ordering. Members of such a family of indifference curves are shown in Figure 6.1.

The marginal rate of substitution between the arguments in the utility function, in this case commodities, can be developed in the following manner. Consider the utility function in Equation (6.1). We are interested in the change in the value of the function that would result from a simultaneous change in the magnitude of the arguments X and Y. We specify this by writing the total differential of the function:

$$dU = \frac{\partial U}{\partial X}\, dX + \frac{\partial U}{\partial Y}\, dY \tag{6.2}$$

Notationally, $\partial U/\partial X$ and $\partial U/\partial Y$ in Equation (6.2) may be referred to as f_x and f_y, respectively. The overall change in the value of the utility function is defined as the rate of change with respect to commodity X, or the partial derivative with respect to X, multiplied by the amount of the change in X, that

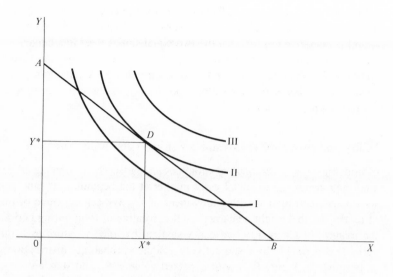

Figure 6.1

is, dX, plus the rate of change with respect to Y multiplied by the amount of the change in Y.

We consider now a simultaneous change in the arguments X and Y that leaves the individual on the same indifference curve, or at the same level of utility. In that case we can set Equation (6.2) equal to zero. It follows by transposition that

$$\frac{dY}{dX} = -\frac{f_x}{f_y} \qquad\qquad (6.3)$$

The derivative dY/dX shown in Equation (6.3) describes the slope of the indifference curve in Figure 6.1. We conclude, therefore, that the slope of the indifference curve is defined as the negative of the ratio of the partial derivatives of the utility function, or as the ratio of the marginal utilities. It defines the marginal rate of substitution between the commodities X and Y, or the rate at which, in order to remain at the same level of utility, the individual is willing to substitute commodity X for commodity Y.

The consumer's utility maximization problem may be solved against an income constraint that restricts him to an attainable commodity combination, or to an attainable commodity set such as the area $0AB$ in Figure 6.1. At the optimum-commodity combination point, or at the point of constrained utility maximization, the slope of the indifference curve will be equal to the slope of the relative commodity price line AB that forms the boundary of the attainable set in the commodity space. The location of that boundary is set by the total income or resources available for consumption. The fact that the budget constraint is operative ensures that the two equal slopes meet in a tangency. This tangency condition is shown in Figure 6.1 at point D. The individual will consume X^* of commodity X and Y^* of commodity Y. An analogous tangency condition will occur in the case of a portfolio investor's optimization over a stochastic utility function.

Utility and probability: investor's risk-aversion utility function

Consider now the investment opportunities and prospects confronting an investor who approaches the financial asset market at the beginning of time period t with a specified total wealth endowment of W_t. We can conceive of the rate of return, R_t, that might be earned on that wealth portfolio during period t. In the manner of Chapter 5, we can visualize that rate of return as a random variable describable by a subjectively assigned probability distribution, such as is shown in Figure 6.2, with expected value $E(R_t)$ and standard deviation $\sigma(R_t)$. The probability distribution of the rate of return might or might not be the approximation to the normal distribution depicted in Figure 6.2. If the distribution is assumed to be normal, the third moment, or the measure of skewness, will be equal to zero, and the investor's attention will be focused on the first two moments, the expected value and the standard deviation. This is the usual form of distribution assumed in the traditional theory, which is accordingly referred to as the mean–variance theory of investor's portfolio optimization.

Consider now the potential accumulated value of the investor's wealth at the end of time period t:

$$W_{t+1} = (1 + R_t)W_t \tag{6.4}$$

As the rate of return on the portfolio is a random variable, we must interpret the end-of-period wealth, W_{t+1}, as a random variable also. We are interested, then, in the attractiveness to the investor of, or the different possible levels of utility provided by, the possible values of W_{t+1}. It follows that we can focus on the properties of the random rate of return that generates the stochastic nature of the wealth variable. For purposes of exposition we shall assume an ordinal utility function defined over this random rate of return, and for concreteness we shall assume it to be a second-degree utility function of the form

$$U(R) = aR - bR^2 \tag{6.5}$$

This function specifies the level of utility that the individual would attach to different outcome values of the rate-of-return variable. As utility is now a function of a random variable, however, utility itself must be interpreted as a

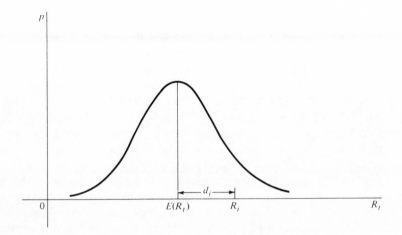

Figure 6.2

random variable. This implies that Equation (6.5) does not possess differentiable properties. No meaning attaches to the derivative of a random variable with respect to another random variable. No meaning would attach, therefore, to the notion that the marginal utility of the rate of return might be described by the derivative of the utility function with respect to the return variable. In order to address the concept of marginal utility, the utility function in Equation (6.5) must be transformed into another function that does have differentiable properties.

We accomplish this transformation by taking the expected values of both sides of Equation (6.5). The development in Chapter 5 implies that

$$E[U(R)] = aE(R) - bE(R^2) \tag{6.6}$$

The second term on the right-hand side of Equation (6.6), the expected value of the square of the underlying random variable, can be shown to be equal to the sum of (i) the square of the expected value and (ii) the variance of the probability distribution of the random variable. That is,

$$E(R^2) = [E(R)]^2 + \text{Var}(R) \tag{6.7}$$

This can be confirmed from an inspection of the probability distribution in Figure 6.2. Consider the possible outcome recorded in Figure 6.2 as R_i. This deviates from the expected value by the amount d_i. It can therefore be written as $R_i = E(R) + d_i$. Taking the square of this magnitude provides

$$R_i^2 = [E(R)]^2 + d_i^2 + 2E(R)d_i \tag{6.8}$$

Equation (6.6), however, requires us to evaluate the expected value of R^2. We therefore take the expected value of Equation (6.8). In doing so, we interpret the expected values of the terms on the right-hand side of the equation in the following manner. The expected value of the first term, the expected value of the square of the expected value of the distribution, is simply the square of the distribution's expected value. This is because that expected value is a datum, or a constant, once the form of the underlying probability distribution has been specified as in Figure 6.2. The expected value of the second term, or $E(d_i^2)$, is recognizable as the variance of the probability distribution. Finally, the expected value of the third term, or $2E(R)E(d_i)$, is equal to zero because the last element in this expression is simply the weighted sum of the deviations of the possible values of the variable from their average, or expected, value weighted by their associated probabilities. We therefore write the expected value of Equation (6.8) in the form of Equation (6.7) as required.

Taking Equation (6.7) and substituting into Equation (6.6) and writing the expected value of the probability distribution of the rate of return as μ and the variance as σ^2, the expected utility function can be written as

$$E(U) = a\mu - b\mu^2 - b\sigma^2 \qquad (6.9)$$

It is important to note what has been accomplished by this transformation. We have taken a *second*-degree utility function defined over the random variable rate of return and have transformed that into an *expected* utility function defined over the first *two* moments of the probability distribution of the underlying random variable. If there had been reason to believe that the probability distribution of the rate of return on the portfolio possessed a positive measure of skewness, and if, furthermore, the investor was attracted to the possibility of the high rate of return that such a positive skewness indicated, we could have begun with a third-degree utility function defined over the random variable. Such a *third*-degree stochastic utility function would be transformed into an expected utility function defined over the first *three* moments of the distribution of the underlying random variable. Generalizing from this result, an nth-degree stochastic utility function can be transformed into an expected utility function defined over the first n moments of the probability distribution of the underlying random variable over which the stochastic utility function is defined.

If, then, the investor is optimizing over a second-degree, or quadratic, utility function, there is no point in examining the third or higher moments of the relevant probability distribution. Similarly, if the probability distribution is assumed to be a two-parameter distribution, such as the widely assumed normal distribution of economic and financial data, there is no point in assuming that the utility function is of higher than second degree. This provides the basis for the mean–variance theory of portfolio selection and optimization.

Given the expected utility function of Equation (6.9) and recognizing its differentiable properties, we can envisage the marginal utility of expected return by taking the partial derivative with respect to the expected-return variable:

$$\frac{\partial[E(U)]}{\partial\mu} = a - 2b\mu \tag{6.10}$$

Similarly, the marginal utility of risk, or the partial derivative with respect to σ, provides

$$\frac{\partial[E(U)]}{\partial\sigma} = -2b\sigma \tag{6.11}$$

These results indicate that the marginal utility of risk, as indicated in Equation (6.11), is everywhere negative. We say, therefore, that an individual optimizing against a utility function of this form is a consistent risk averter, or that the utility function is a consistent risk-aversion function. Other functional forms and measures of risk aversion have been defined in the extensive literature on utility functions. The illustrative form with which we have worked is frequently referred to as a Tobin function (Tobin, 1958). It would be possible to adopt an exponential utility function of the form

$$U = a - ce^{-bR} \qquad a \gtreqless 0,\ c,\ b > 0 \tag{6.12}$$

which transforms into an expected utility function (see Ford, 1983, pp. 23–4, 191–92) defined as

$$E(U) = a - ce^{-b[\mu_R - (b/2)\sigma_R^2]} \tag{6.13}$$

An interesting difference exists between the Tobin function and that in Equation (6.12). In the former case, it appears from Equation (6.10) that the marginal utility of expected return will become negative for values of expected rate of return greater than $a/2b$. In the latter case, the marginal utility of expected return is everywhere positive, and the $E(U)$ function has an upper bound of a. It is not necessary for analytical purposes, therefore, to place a limit on μ to guarantee that the marginal utility is positive as in the case of the quadratic utility function.

If it can be assumed that the marginal utility of expected return is positive, and if the utility function is a consistent risk-aversion utility function where the marginal utility of risk is everywhere negative, as in Equation (6.11), the iso-utility or indifference contours in the risk–return plane will be positively inclined as in Figure 6.3. As in the analysis of the consumer utility function, the slope of the indifference curve is defined by the negative of the ratio of the marginal utilities or the partial derivatives of the function with respect to

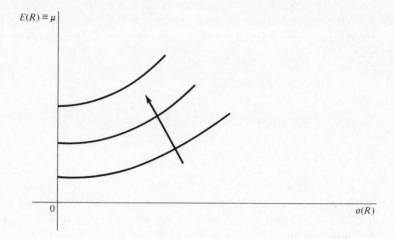

Figure 6.3

its arguments. Making use of Equations (6.10) and (6.11), this slope is defined as

$$\frac{d\mu}{d\sigma} = \frac{2b\sigma}{a - 2b\mu} \tag{6.14}$$

In Figure 6.3, the arrow indicates the direction of increasing utility. The convexity of the indifference curves can be established by taking the second derivative $d^2\mu/d\sigma^2$, which may be shown to be positive in the present example.

This analysis provides the basis for a choice between alternative portfolios depending on the probability distributions of their rates of return. If the expected values and standard deviations of portfolio rates of return are substituted into the expected utility function, the relative attractiveness of portfolios can be compared and evaluated. That portfolio will be the most attractive that offers the investor the prospect of achieving the highest attainable indifference curve. It is for this reason that decisions under uncertainty, or what we are here considering as probabilistically reducible risk, have been referred to as "choices among probability distributions" (Mossin, 1973; Hirshleifer and Riley, 1979).

Different possible degrees of risk aversion are exhibited in Figure 6.4. The indifference curves A and B shown there are derived from different utility functions, and each is a member of a different indifference map. It is imagined that the investor occupies the position marked P, holding a portfolio that promises an expected return of $E(R_p)$ and has a standard deviation of return of $\sigma(R_p)$. Moving along the risk axis to the right of P, it is readily seen that a

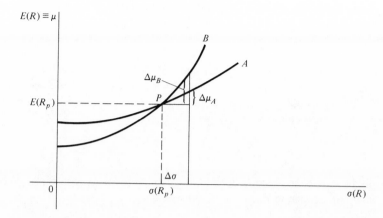

Figure 6.4

higher increment of expected return would be required if the investor were optimizing over a utility function that generated indifference curve *B* than if his utility function had generated indifference curve *A*. The utility function that gives rise to indifference curve *B* would therefore exhibit the greater degree of risk aversion.

When it is said that an investor is risk averse, this implies that his attitude to risk is such that he will reject what has been called a fair gamble. This refers to a situation in which the expected value of the outcomes of a risky prospect is equal to the amount that would have to be paid for the opportunity to acquire that prospect. For example, a lottery that offered two alternative outcomes of two dollars and zero dollars, where each outcome had a 0.50 probability of occurring, would have an expected value of one dollar. A "fair gamble" would be the exchange of the lottery prospect for its expected value of one dollar. The investor would stand to realize a net gain of one dollar if the two-dollar outcome occurred, or a net loss of one dollar in the event of the alternative outcome. But a risk-averse investor would reject such an exchange because the disutility to him of the loss would be greater than the utility he would obtain from an equivalent gain. His utility function, such as that assumed in Equation (6.5), would therefore be concave.

An alternative measure of risk aversion has been constructed by focusing on what has been called the Absolute Risk-Aversion (ARA) or the Relative Risk-Aversion (RRA) properties of the utility function. A decreasing absolute risk aversion is said to exist if an investor is prepared to increase the amount of his wealth invested in risky assets when the total amount of his wealth increases. The opposite behavior would exhibit increasing absolute risk aversion. Take, for example, a utility function defined over total wealth of the form

$$U(W) = W - cW^2 \qquad (6.15)$$

and employ the notation $U'(W)$ and $U''(W)$ to refer to the first and second derivatives of that function as defined over actual wealth outcomes. Then (see Elton and Gruber, 1984, p. 211f.; Pratt, 1964; Arrow, 1971) absolute risk aversion may be measured by

$$ARA = \frac{-U''(W)}{U'(W)} \qquad (6.16)$$

In the case of the second-degree utility function assumed in Equation (6.15), the ratio defined in Equation (6.16) would be

$$ARA = \frac{2c}{1 - 2cW} \qquad (6.17)$$

The direction of change of this ARA as wealth increases, or $d(ARA)/dW$, can be shown to be

$$\frac{d(ARA)}{dW} = \frac{4c^2}{(1 - 2cW)^2} > 0 \qquad (6.18)$$

The function therefore exhibits increasing absolute risk aversion.

Similarly, relative risk aversion has been defined with reference to the proportion of a wealth portfolio that is invested in risky assets as the total level of wealth increases. This has been defined as

$$RRA = \frac{-WU''(W)}{U'(W)} = W(ARA) \qquad (6.19)$$

An investor who places a greater percentage of his wealth in risky investments as his total wealth increases is said to exhibit decreasing relative risk aversion. By following the same procedure as before, it can be shown that the illustrative wealth utility function in Equation (6.15) exhibits increasing relative risk aversion.

By analogy, a second-degree, or quadratic, utility function such as we assumed in Equation (6.5), or the so-called Tobin function, exhibits the properties of increasing absolute and relative risk aversion. This, it should be noted, casts some doubt on the relevance in actual fact of the widespread use of this form of utility function in the literature on financial asset optimization. It would seem that contrary to the logical implications that we have just deduced, investors in general do in fact place larger amounts of their wealth in risky assets as their wealth increases, or, in other words, they exhibit decreasing absolute risk aversion. Less certainty attaches to the behavior in actual fact of relative risk aversion. But the quadratic utility functional form has been extensively used, and risky asset choice theory has been substantially based on the implicit mean–variance assumptions. Moreover, it has been shown that quadratic functional forms can be found that do exhibit more desirable risk-aversion properties (see Mossin, 1973).

Axiomatic basis of stochastic utility

The expected utility theory we have examined is derived from the work of von Neumann and Morgenstern, whose propositions regarding the axioms of choice in risky situations have influenced the vast literature that has developed in this field (von Neumann and Morgenstern, 1953).[1] In what follows, we shall specify the axioms by making direct reference to the selection of portfolios of risky assets. A particular portfolio, designated as P_i, will be described by a set of possible rate-of-return outcomes, associated with each of which is the probability of its occurrence. In Equation (6.20), the ith portfolio available to the investor is envisaged as promising n possible rates of return, R_1 through R_n, with associated probabilities p_1 through p_n. In the following discussion, the uppercase P_i refers consistently to a possible portfolio and the lowercase p_i refers to a probability magnitude.

$$P_i = [(R_1, p_1), (R_2, p_2), \ldots, (R_n, p_n)] \qquad p_i \geq 0, \sum p_i = 1 \qquad (6.20)$$

To describe the ordering of choices among the various portfolios P_i, we shall adopt the following standard notation: $P_i > P_j$ indicates that portfolio P_i is preferred to portfolio P_j, and $P_i \sim P_j$ means that the individual whose preference ordering is being considered is indifferent between portfolios P_i and P_j (see also Luce and Raiffa, 1957, Ch. 2; Hey, 1979).

Axiom 1. Axiom of completeness or comparability

Either $R_i \gtrsim R_j$ or $R_j \gtrsim R_i$ for all $i, j, = 1, \ldots, n$.

This axiom, which might be referred to also as the axiom of pairwise comparison, orders all possible pairs of the underlying rates of return on a portfolio. It states that the investor is able to describe a preference ordering over portfolio rates of return, such that his preference or indifference between all possible pairs of such rates of return can be established.

Axiom 2. Axiom of transitivity of portfolio choices

If $P_i \gtrsim P_j$ and $P_j \gtrsim P_k$, then $P_i \gtrsim P_k$.

[1] The development given here follows that in Ford (1983, p. 18f.). A somewhat condensed treatment of the same subject is contained in Henderson and Quandt (1971, p. 42f.).

This axiom states, for example, that if the ith portfolio is preferred to the jth portfolio, by virtue of its risk–return profile, and the jth portfolio is preferred to the kth, then the ith portfolio will be preferred to the kth. These relations are assumed to hold for all pairs of portfolios in the set of portfolios available to the investor.

Axiom 3. Axiom of continuity

Assume that R_1 is regarded as the most preferred rate-of-return outcome and that R_n is the least preferred. Then there exists a probability number, p_i, where $0 \le p_i \le 1$, such that

$$R_i \sim [(R_1, p_i), (R_n, 1 - p_i)] \quad \text{for all } i = 1, \ldots, n$$

This seemingly complex axiom will play a crucial part in the following construction of a utility function. It states that for each possible rate-of-return outcome R_i that may be designated (here shown on the left of the indifference sign), a combination of outcomes, and thus a portfolio choice, can be found that is indifferent to R_i. That portfolio would be made up of a combination of the most preferred and the least preferred outcomes, R_1 and R_n, as shown on the right-hand side of the indifference sign. That is, there is some probability that could be assigned to the assumedly best possible outcome, with the magnitude of 1 minus that probability assigned to the worst possible outcome, that would make the individual indifferent between a combination of those best and worst outcomes and the designated outcome R_i. The magnitude of the probability p_i that would have to be assigned for this purpose is dependent on the individual's attitude to risk and is therefore closely associated with the degree of risk aversion in his utility function.

Axiom 4. Axiom of substitutability of outcomes and portfolios

Let R_i and Q_i be possible rates of return on a portfolio. If $R_i \sim Q_i$, then $P_1 \sim P_2$, where

$$P_1 = [(R_1, p_1), (R_2, p_2), \ldots, (R_i, p_i), \ldots, (R_n, p_n)]$$

$$P_2 = [(R_1, p_1), (R_2, p_2), \ldots, (Q_i, p_i), \ldots, (R_n, p_n)]$$

This axiom makes a statement about the investor's attitude to two different portfolios, P_1 and P_2. The portfolios are understood to be the same in every respect except one. Portfolio P_1 contains a possible rate of return R_i, whereas P_2 contains a possible rate of return Q_i. All other rates of return, and also their associated probabilities, are the same for both portfolios. If the investor is indifferent between the R_i and the Q_i rates of return, and if their probabilities of occurrence are the same for both portfolios, the investor will be indifferent between the two portfolios. This axiom is also referred to as the axiom of independence of irrelevant alternatives.

Axiom 5. Axiom of monotonicity

If, given Axiom 1, $R_i \gtrsim R_j$ and if

$$P_1 = [(R_i, p_0), (R_j, 1-p_0)], \text{ and}$$
$$P_2 = [(R_i, p_1), (R_j, 1-p_1)], \text{ then}$$
$$P_1 \gtrsim P_2 \quad \text{if and only if} \quad p_0 \geq p_1$$

This axiom states that an individual who compares two portfolios containing the same possible outcomes will choose that portfolio in which the preferred outcome has the higher probability of occurring.

Axiom 6. Axiom of complexity

$$\text{If } P_j = [(R_i, p_{ij}), i=1, \ldots, n] \quad \text{for } j=1, \ldots, m$$

(that is, we suppose there exist m portfolios, P_j, each of which contains n possible outcomes, R_i, with associated probabilities p_i), and if

$$S_1 = [(P_j, s_j) \quad j=1, \ldots, m]$$

(that is, there exists a "lottery" S_1 such that one of the portfolios P_j will be the prize in the lottery, with probability s_j), and if

$$S_2 = [(R_i, p_i) \quad i=1, \ldots, n]$$

(that is, there exists a portfolio S_2 that contains n possible outcomes R_i with probability p_i), and if

$$p_i = \sum_{j=1}^{m} p_{ij} s_j \quad \text{for } i=1, \ldots, n,$$

then $S_1 \sim S_2$

This complex axiom is stating that probabilistic opportunities can be combined, depending on the probabilities specified, in such a way that an individual will be indifferent between (i) a given portfolio and (ii) a lottery in which one of the set of portfolios will be obtained as a prize. Interpretation of this rather complex case is assisted by focusing on the implicit probabilities of realizing the different possible portfolio rates of return by choosing (i) what we might call the direct route of S_2 above or (ii) the indirect route of the lottery S_1.

If the direct route of S_2 is chosen, the probability of realizing a designated rate of return, R_i, is, by definition above, p_i, which is equal, again by definition, to $\Sigma p_{ij}s_j$. Consider now the probability of realizing that same rate of return, R_i, if the indirect route of S_1 is chosen. In that case, we must consider the set of conditional probabilities involved.

The first possible way of realizing R_i is to obtain portfolio 1, P_1, as the outcome of the lottery and then to realize R_i as the outcome of that portfolio. The probability of realizing R_i by this route, then, is the product of the probability of receiving P_1 from the lottery and the probability of R_i occurring conditional on the portfolio P_1 having been obtained. A similar statement could be made regarding the probability of realizing R_i following the indirect result of each of the other possible lottery outcomes. The actual resulting probability of realizing R_i via the indirect lottery route will then be the sum of all of the products of probabilities thus obtained.

We can write, therefore, $p(R_i: S_2) = p_i = \sum_{j=1}^{m} p_{ij}s_j$ as defining the probability of R_i via the direct route, and

$$
\begin{aligned}
p(R_i: S_1) &= \sum p(P_j)p(R_i: P_j) \qquad i = 1, \ldots, n, j = 1, \ldots, m \\
&= p(P_1)p(R_i: P_1) + p(P_2)p(R_i: P_2) + \ldots + p(P_m)p(R_i: P_m) \\
&= s_1 p_{i1} + s_2 p_{i2} + \ldots + s_m p_{im} \\
&= \sum_{j=1}^{m} p_{ij}s_j
\end{aligned}
$$

thereby defining the probability of R_i via the indirect route. This, therefore, establishes the equality between the probabilities of portfolio outcome R_i by either the direct or the indirect routes. The meaning of Axiom 6, on the basis of the assumptions specified, is accordingly established.

Construction of the utility function

In the following section we shall provide a detailed example of the construction of a utility function based on behavior in accordance with the foregoing axioms. An individual will be assumed to be acting rationally when making a choice between probability distributions, or between portfolios P_i, if he acts in accordance with the axioms. This will imply that the individual will act in such a way as to maximize an ordinal utility function, where the utility of a portfolio can be written as $U(P)$ and where that utility is a weighted sum of the utilities attached to each of the possible rate-of-return outcomes contained in the portfolio. These utilities of rates of return are weighted by the probability of their realization. We can therefore write

$$
U(P) = \sum_{i=1}^{n} p_i u_i \tag{6.21}
$$

where $u_i = U(R_i)$.

Let us lay the background for that discussion as follows. We now take the least preferred and the most preferred rate-of-return outcomes and assign to them arbitrary numbers on an ordinal utility scale over which it is desired to define the utility function. We may arbitrarily assign the utility value 0 to the least preferred outcome and the utility value 1 to the most preferred, designating these outcomes R_n and R_1, respectively, as in Axiom 3. We now wish to find a way to allocate a number on the utility scale to any possible outcome between these least preferred and most preferred outcomes. Let such an outcome be designated R_i. Then we are assured by the axiom of continuity, Axiom 3, that it is possible to discover a probability magnitude such that

$$R_i \sim [(R_1, p_i), (R_n, 1 - p_i)] \tag{6.22}$$

In accordance with the axioms, the individual is indifferent between the designated outcome R_i, if it were available to him with certainty, and the chance of receiving either R_n or R_1 with probabilities $1 - p_i$ and p_i, respectively, as on the right-hand side of Equation (6.22). Both of these options must therefore be assigned the same number on the utility scale.

Suppose that in relation to R_i the probability magnitude that established the indifference in Equation (6.22) was 0.75. Then we can substitute this probability magnitude into the right-hand side of Equation (6.22) and calculate the expected utility of the distribution of outcomes described there. That expected utility will be equal to the sum of (i) the utility that has been assigned to the most preferred outcome, namely 1, times the probability of realizing that outcome, namely 0.75, and (ii) the utility assigned to the least preferred outcome, namely 0, times the probability of realizing that outcome, namely 0.25. The expected utility calculates to 0.75, and that, therefore, is the utility magnitude to be assigned to the designated outcome of R_i. In a similar way, utility magnitudes could be calculated, relying repeatedly on the axiom of continuity, for assignment to all possible values of outcomes between the least and the most preferred. In this way, a utility function will have been defined over the entire range of possible outcomes.

Once we have a utility function defined over the range of possible outcomes, it follows that the expected utility of a portfolio whose possible outcomes are described by a given probability distribution will be equal to the weighted sum of the utilities of each of the possible outcomes of the portfolio, where each such possible utility is weighted by the probability of its being realized. In other words, we have

$$U(P) = \sum_{i=1}^{n} p_i U(R_i) \tag{6.23}$$

The investor, therefore, should select that portfolio that maximizes his expected utility in this sense.

The utility function, of course, must be consistent with the preference axioms. That is, we require that

$$U(P_1) > U(P_2) \quad \text{if and only if } P_1 > P_2 \tag{6.24}$$

It can be shown from the axioms stated that this condition will be satisfied.

Example of a derived utility function

In the interest of concreteness, consider the following example of the derivation of a utility function defined over a range of possible outcomes. To change the area of application, let us imagine that a firm faces the prospect of a cash flow that may range between −$10,000 and $10,000. We desire to define the decision maker's risk-aversion utility function over that range. We use for this purpose the construction in Figure 6.5.

On the horizontal axis of Figure 6.5 we have inscribed the range of possible outcomes, and on the right and left vertical axes, respectively, we have indicated measures of probability and utility. That is, we have arbitrarily assigned the point 0 on the utility scale to the utility of −$10,000 and the point 1 to the utility of $10,000. Imagine now that we desire to assign a point on the utility scale to the amount of $6,000. We proceed, in the manner of the previous discussion based on the axiom of continuity, to visualize a so-called reference lottery in which there are only two possible outcomes equal to the worst outcome of the possible cash flow being examined, or −$10,000, and the best possible outcome, $10,000.

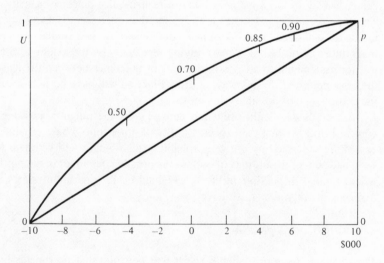

Figure 6.5

We can deduce what would have to be the probability of success in the reference lottery, that is, the probability of receiving the $10,000 outcome, to make the expected value of the lottery equal to $6,000. This so-called break-even probability follows from the equation

$$p(10,000) + (1-p)(-10,000) = 6,000 \qquad (6.25)$$

The desired value of p is 0.80. Similarly, the probability of success in the reference lottery that would make the expected value of the lottery equal to, say, $4,000 is 0.70. If the probability of success in the reference lottery is 0.30, its expected value will be equal to $-$4,000. In this way, we can build up a locus of "breakeven probabilities" that indicate the probabilities of success at which the expected value of the lottery will equal any designated amount within the range of possible outcomes of the cash flow, $-$10,000 to $10,000. This locus of breakeven probabilities will coincide with the diagonal of Figure 6.5.

We now suppose that the individual has received a certain cash flow of $6,000, and we ask him what would have to be the probability of success in the reference lottery to make him indifferent between retaining the $6,000 and surrendering it for a ticket in the lottery. He knows, of course, from the foregoing that the expected value of the lottery will be precisely equal to his $6,000 if the probability of success is 0.80. If, however, he exchanged his $6,000 for the lottery ticket, he would stand to gain a further $4,000 but would stand to lose $16,000, equal to the $6,000 he surrendered for the lottery ticket plus the $10,000 he would have to pay if the "lose" rather than the "win" result of the lottery occurred. Being a risk averter, as we shall suppose, the individual would state that he would require a probability of success greater than the breakeven probability to make him indifferent between his $6,000 and the lottery. Let us suppose that after a certain amount of questioning, meditation, and answering, the individual stated that the indifference would be established, and he would be prepared to exchange his $6,000 for the lottery ticket, if the probability of success were 0.90.

In the same way, we might establish that the individual would be indifferent between the sum of $4,000 and the lottery, not if the probability of success were simply the breakeven probability of 0.70 but were, say, 0.85. If the individual had received zero dollars and he were invited to exchange it for the lottery ticket, or, that is, to accept a free ticket in the lottery, we can similarly ascertain the probability of success that would make the exchange possible. If, of course, the individual did accept the lottery ticket, he would stand to gain $10,000 but would also stand to lose $10,000. His risk aversion would, presumably, cause him to require a probability of success greater than the breakeven probability of 0.50. Let the required probability be 0.70. Finally, as an example on the other side of the range of possible outcomes of the cash flow, we might imagine that an amount of −$4,000 had been received, or that a loss or a debt of $4,000 had been incurred. If the individual were to exchange that amount for a lottery ticket, the lottery organizer would, in exchange, be agreeing to relieve him of his debt of $4,000. If he were successful in the lottery, his net gain would be $14,000, equal to the sum of the $4,000 debt of which he had been relieved and the $10,000 prize in the lottery. But if the "loss" outcome of the lottery occurred, he would realize a net loss of $6,000, equal to the $10,000 he was now required to pay to the lottery less the $4,000 debt of which he had been relieved. His risk-aversion characteristics again will probably make him require a probability of success greater than the breakeven probability of 0.30. We can suppose it is 0.50.

In Figure 6.5, these required probabilities of success in the reference lottery are shown above the relevant magnitudes on the horizontal axis. The same procedure may be followed with relation to any other magnitude in the cash flow range between −$10,000 and $10,000. If, then, these probabilities are joined as in the figure, we have what we shall call a locus of "indifference probabilities." It will be clear that the concavity of the indifference probability locus is due to the degree of risk aversion in the mind of the individual whose utility function is being derived. Moreover, the greater the degree of risk aversion, the greater will be the concavity in the indifference locus. If the individual were risk indifferent, he would have been satisfied at every point of the foregoing to exchange given amounts of cash for the lottery ticket so long as the breakeven probabilities were operative. The locus of indifference probabilities would then be linear and would coincide with the locus of breakeven probabilities. Finally, if the individual were a risk lover rather than a risk averter, his indifference probability locus would be strictly convex, or would swing down along the southeast of the breakeven probability locus in Figure 6.5.

We are now ready for the final step that transforms the indifference probability locus into the desired utility function. Suppose, for example, that we wish to assign a utility number to the cash flow outcome of $6,000. We have just seen that the individual is indifferent between $6,000 and the lottery with a probability of success of 0.90. This indifference, then, requires us to assign to the amount of $6,000 the same utility number as represents the expected utility of the lottery with a probability of success of 0.90. That may be calculated as follows:

$$E[U(L)] = 0.90U(\$10,000) + 0.10U(\$-10,000)$$
$$= 0.90(1) + 0.10(0)$$
$$= 0.90 \tag{6.26}$$

The utility number to be assigned to the amount of $6,000 is therefore 0.90. In a similar way, utility numbers may be derived for any amount within the range of cash flows between −$10,000 and $10,000. By assigning the arbitrary numbers of 0 and 1 to the limits of the range of possible cash flows, we have been able to read the indifference probability locus against the right vertical axis, or the probability axis, of Figure 6.5 and to read the same locus as the derived utility function against the left vertical axis, or the utility axis. This convenient result, of course, is due only to the arbitrary assignment of the utility range that we made. Any other numbers could have been assigned, as the utility function we have derived is, as we have indicated, an ordinal function.

If the assumptions contained in the axioms we have defined are satisfied, and if individual behavior reflects the statement of the axioms or is in that sense rational behavior, the axioms permit us to conceive of a utility function of the general form shown in Equation (6.5). There, as in the instance we have just examined, the degree of concavity reflects the degree of risk aversion in the mind of the decision maker.

Uniqueness of the utility function

A significant difference exists between the ordinal utility function in terms of which we discussed consumer behavior earlier in this chapter and the utility function we have now derived. The former, we have seen, is unique up to a monotonically increasing transformation. But in the present analysis it is possible to envisage monotonically increasing transformations that, if they were applied to the investor's utility function, would not preserve a consistent ranking of portfolios. As a simple case, consider the following example, based on the information in Table 6.1. Column 2 of the table shows the utilities assigned to the range of values indicated in the first column, thereby describing an arbitrarily assigned ordinal utility function U_1. In column 3 are shown the utility magnitudes that would apply if a monotonically increasing transformation of the first utility function were adopted, that is, $U_2 = (U_1)^2$.

Let us suppose that two investment opportunities exist: S_1, which offers a

Table 6.1 *Ordinal utility functions*

Dollars	U_1	$U_2 = (U_1)^2$
0	10	100
2	40	1,600
4	65	4,225
6	85	7,225
8	100	10,000
10	110	12,100

50 : 50 chance of receiving $2 and $10, and S_2, which offers a 60 percent chance of receiving $4 and a 40 percent chance of receiving $8. From the second column of Table 6.1, describing U_1, the expected utilities of S_1 and S_2 are

$$E[U(S_1)] = 0.50U(\$2) + 0.50U(\$10)$$
$$= 0.50(40) + 0.50(110)$$
$$= 75 \qquad (6.27)$$

$$E[U(S_2)] = 0.60U(\$4) + 0.40U(\$8)$$
$$= 0.60(65) + 0.40(100)$$
$$= 79 \qquad (6.28)$$

It follows that S_2 will be preferred to S_1 on the basis of its higher utility ranking.

If the two investment opportunities are evaluated against utility function U_2, the utility assignments are 6,850 for S_1 and 6,535 for S_2. The order or ranking will now be reversed, and S_1 will be preferred to S_2. Thus we see that a monotonically increasing transformation of the original utility function over the range of monetary values specified in the example may fail to be order preserving.

It can be shown, however, that a monotonic *linear* transformation of the ordinal utility function will preserve the preference ordering in several important respects. Let us suppose a utility function of the form that provides, in accordance with Axiom 3, $U_B = p_i U_A + (1 - p_i)U_C$ for some p_i. Recalling that Y is a monotonic linear transformation of X if $Y = a + bX$, with $b > 0$, we can transform the utility function U to the function

$$U^* = a + bU \qquad (6.29)$$

It follows from this that $U = (U^* - a)/b$, or $U = cU^* + d$, where $c = 1/b$ and $d = -a/b$. We can say, therefore, that U_B in the present example transforms into $cU_B^* + d$. Following the example, we can therefore write

$$cU_B^* + d = p_i(cU_A^* + d) + (1 - p_i)(cU_C^* + d)$$
$$= p_i cU_A^* + (1 - p_i)cU_C^* + d \qquad (6.30)$$

from which it follows that

$$cU_B^* = p_i cU_A^* + c(1 - p_i)U_C^* \qquad (6.31)$$

and therefore

$$U_B^* = p_i U_A^* + (1 - p_i)U_C^* \qquad (6.32)$$

This demonstrates that the monotonic linear transformation of the original utility function given in Equation (6.29) provides the same results as the original utility function and is therefore itself a utility function.

The utility functions provided by the von Neumann–Morgenstern analysis that we have followed up to this point, although they are in a basic sense ordinal, have to be regarded as cardinal in a restricted sense. They partake of the same limitations of ordinal measures that the consumer utility functions contain. They do not permit interpersonal comparisons of utility or permit the statement that an outcome providing a utility of, say, 70 is preferred twice as much as an outcome with a utility measure of 35. This follows, of course, because the choice of the origin of the utility scale is arbitrary. The von Neumann–Morgenstern utility numbers do, however, provide an interval scale such that the differences between the utility numbers are meaningful. This follows from the fact that a monotonic linear transformation preserves the relative magnitudes of differences between the numbers on the original utility scale. That is, if the difference $U_C - U_B$ is greater than $U_B - U_A$ on an original scale, the same relative magnitudes of differences will be preserved under the monotonic linear transformation. Under a monotonic linear transformation, also, the sign of the rate of change of marginal utility, or the second derivative of the utility function, is invariant.

The von Neumann–Morgenstern "ordinal–cardinal" utility function, at the same time as it permits this comparison of utility differences, also permits the calculation of expected utilities in the sense in which we explored that earlier in this chapter. It thus leads to the decision criterion of expected utility, and it facilitates decision making under risk or the discrimination between stochastic objects of choice.

The firm's choice of output under selling price uncertainty

An application of the expected-value concept discussed in this chapter is found in the firm's choice of its optimum output when uncertainty attaches to the price at which that output can be sold.[2] A brief digression on this problem will consolidate our understanding of many of the main points at issue in the following chapter. We assume that in a simple static model the firm is required to choose its output level x before the selling price p is known but on the understanding that the price will be determined in a perfectly competitive market. The firm's total cost function is assumed to be known as

$$TC(x) = A + C(x) \tag{6.33}$$

where A represents the fixed costs and $C(x)$ is the variable-cost function. The firm's decision maker possesses a utility function defined over profits, π, where

$$\pi = px - A - C(x) \tag{6.34}$$

---

[2] The argument in the text is based on Sandmo (1971) as reported in Ford (1983, p. 173f.).

As in the preceding sections of this chapter, the probability distribution of the selling price is assumed to be assigned by the decision maker and is denoted by $f(p)$.

We can then make use of the expected utility therorem to specify the firm's expected utility of profit as

$$E[U(\pi)] = \int_0^\infty U[px - A - C(x)] f(p) \, dp \tag{6.35}$$

where p is assumed to be nonnegative, as it represents the market price of the output commodity.

By differentiating Equation (6.35) with respect to x, we find the first-order condition for a maximum value of $E(U)$. This is accomplished by first differentiating the utility term under the integral sign, applying the chain rule in doing so, to yield

$$\frac{dE[U(\pi)]}{dx} = \int_0^\infty U'(\pi)\left[(p - C'(x)\right] f(p) \, dp \tag{6.36}$$

Equation (6.36) will be recognized as describing the expected value of the term under its integral sign to the left of the probability function [analogous to Equation (5.4) of Chapter 5]. We can therefore write, as the first-order maximization condition,

$$E\left[U'(\pi)\{p - C'(x)\}\right] = 0 \qquad C'(x) > 0 \tag{6.37}$$

If, further, we differentiated Equation (6.36) with respect to x, we should have the second-order condition for the utility maximum:

$$E[\overset{-}{U''(\pi)}\{\overset{+}{p - C'(x)}\}^2 - \overset{+}{U'(\pi)}\overset{?}{C''(x)}] < 0 \tag{6.38}$$

In the second-order condition in (6.38), the signs above the elements of the expected value indicate the signs they can be assumed to take. The sign on $U''(\pi)$ will be negative in the case of a risk-aversion utility function, as developed at length earlier in this chapter. The sign on the squared term is, of course, positive. That on $U'(\pi)$ will be positive under the axiom of monotonicity. But it follows that the sign on $C''(x)$ will not necessarily have to be positive in order to establish the negativity condition of the overall expression in (6.38). Under certainty, of course, the positivity of the second derivative of the cost function would have been necessary, as is established in the usual textbook case.

A principal conclusion can now be derived from this model. In the case of uncertainty, it can be shown that

$$E(p) \gtreqless C'(x) \quad \text{according as } U''(\pi) \lesseqgtr 0 \tag{6.39}$$

That is, the output volume will be such, if the decision maker is a risk averter, that the expected price is greater than the marginal cost.

We can explore this condition in the following way. First, we take the expected value specified in Equation (6.37). Here we have the expectation of a product term. It will be helpful, therefore, to return to the basic discussion of expected values and covariances in Chapter 5 and observe the following.

Let us assume that X and Y are random variables and that we desire to specify the expected value of their product, or $E(XY)$. Recalling a similar development in Chapter 5, we can write

$$X_i = E(X) + d_x \quad \text{and} \quad Y_i = E(Y) + d_y$$

Then

$$\begin{aligned} E(XY) &= E[\{E(X) + d_x\}\{E(Y) + d_y\}] \\ &= E[E(X)E(Y) + E(X)d_y + E(Y)d_x + d_x d_y] \end{aligned}$$

Placing the first expectational operator within the square brackets and recalling that $E(d_x)$ and $E(d_y)$ both equal zero and that $E(d_x d_y)$ provides the covariance between X and Y, it follows that

$$E(XY) = E(X)E(Y) + \text{Cov}(XY) \tag{6.40}$$

We can then apply this procedure to specify the expected value indicated in Equation (6.37) as required above. It follows that

$$\begin{aligned} E[U'(\pi)\{p - C'(x)\}] = E[U'(\pi)][E(p) - C'(x)] \\ + \text{Cov}[U'(\pi), p] - \text{Cov}[U'(\pi), C'(x)] \end{aligned} \tag{6.41}$$

In order to justify the conclusion stated in (6.39), let us note that if, say, $U''(\pi)$ as stated in that conclusion is negative, the covariance between $U'(\pi)$ and p in Equation (6.41) will be negative and that between $U'(\pi)$ and $C'(x)$ will be positive. These results hold because if, for example, the price of output increases, thereby increasing the profit level under the assumed conditions of perfect competition, the marginal utility of profit will diminish because of the negativity of the second derivative of the utility function. Therefore, the covariance between the price level and the marginal utility of profit will be negative as stated. Similarly, if, for any given price level, the level of marginal cost should increase, this will diminish the profit level and thus imply an increase in the marginal utility of profit. Thus the covariance between the marginal cost and the marginal utility of profit will be positive as stated.

These conditions, taken together, imply that when the marginal utility of profit is diminishing, or $U''(\pi) < 0$ in (6.39), or the firm's decision maker is a risk averter, the last two terms on the right-hand side of Equation (6.41) will be negative. In order to establish the maximum condition in Equation (6.37), therefore, the first term on the right-hand side of Equation (6.41) must be positive. That implies, however, that $E(p)$ must be greater than $C'(x)$. This, then, establishes the condition specified in (6.39) as the results of the price uncertainty case, as opposed to that of the general textbook case of perfect competition under price certainty.

This means that if $E(p)$ should equal the fixed price that would have ruled in the market under conditions of certainty, the output will be lower under uncertainty [in order to make $E(p) > C'(x)$] if the firm's decision maker is a risk averter, that is, if $U''(\pi) < 0$. If the decision maker is risk netural, the outputs would be the same under both certainty and uncertainty, and if he is a risk lover, with $U''(\pi)$ positive, the output will tend to be higher under uncertainty.

CHAPTER 7

Financial asset markets and the cost of money capital

The problem of money capital, we have argued, needs to be integrated into the theory of the firm at as early a stage as possible. To employ the categories that the neoclassical theory inherited from Marshall, it needs to be incorporated before the beginning of the short-run, rather than after the end of the long-run, analysis. Otherwise, money capital has no analytically integrative significance for the theory of the firm at all.

Moreover, the notion of money capital, together with that of the money capital availability constraint, imports into the theory of the firm the realities of uncertainty and the lack of perfect expectation and foresight. The cost of money capital is very much an uncertainty concept. It takes up the questions of intertemporal valuation and the specification of risk-adjusted discount rates, or the rates of return required by the risk-averting suppliers of money capital at which future income streams should be reduced to their economic values. Behind the neoclassical development of these concepts lies a highly developed theory of the money capital or financial asset market. The cost of capital depends, in that body of analysis, on the prices of risky assets and the rates of return they provide when equilibrium conditions in the asset market are satisfied.

The apparatus we need in order to consider this equilibrium theory of prices and yields has been almost completely assembled in the preceding chapters. The theory is heavily indebted to the thought forms of the probability calculus. It interprets the rates of return on the securities that represent claims to the firm's income stream as random variables describable by subjectively assigned probability distributions. In order to examine the theory and its implications, we set aside for the present the doubts we have raised as to whether the probability calculus is as applicable in economics as it is in other fields of enquiry. In this chapter we shall examine the neoclassical development and shall return to alternative constructions in Part III.

Assumption content of the equilibrium theory of financial asset prices

The theory of financial market equilibration is a development of the two-asset portfolio theory noted in Chapter 5. In expanding this to consider the general n-asset case, we shall develop a static theory of the equilibrium market prices of a given stock of financial assets. These may be imagined, for example, as the common stock securities of nonfinancial corporations, such as those listed on the New York Stock Exchange. The existing theory has enjoyed considerable development beyond the essentials we shall examine in what follows. But it is not necessary or desirable for our present purposes to attempt a full exposition of the nuances and extensions that have entered the literature.[1]

The theory is seen as a "general equilibrium model of the pricing and allocation of the given supply of securities . . . (which) describe(s) the characteristics of a situation in which investors' combined demand is equal to the supply for every security" (Mossin, 1973, p. 64). The analysis proceeds in the tradition of general equilibrium theory. In fact, Fama and Miller, two of the most articulate and influential architects of the theory, have observed that "we use the term 'market equilibrium' in recognition of the fact that we always work conditional on an assumed equilibrium in the markets for labor and consumption goods. . . . In essence, we examine the characteristics of capital market equilibrium, given a general equilibrium, that is, simultaneous equilibrium in all markets" (1972, p. 279n.). In the application of the theory to the financial decisions of the firm, it is generally assumed that "the market is always near equilibrium" and that "the market will move toward equilibrium if a disequilibrium condition sets in" (Bierman and Hass, 1973, p. 230).

The asset market theory in its standard Sharpe–Lintner–Mossin form is based on the following further assumptions.

1. All investors in the financial asset market are single-period (all having the same single-period time horizon) expected utility of end-of-period wealth maximizers who choose among alternative portfolios of asset opportunities on the basis of the mean (expected value) and variance of the rate of return. All individuals are optimizing over risk-aversion utility functions.
2. All investors can borrow or lend an unlimited amount of funds at an exogenously given risk-free rate of interest, R_F.
3. All investors have made identical estimates of the means, variances, and covariances of returns among all available assets.

---

[1] See the references in Chapter 5 to the work on the foundations of the theory by Markowitz, Sharpe, Lintner, Arrow, Tobin, and Hicks. Important development and application is contained in Fama and Miller (1972) and Mossin (1973). More recent developments are contained in Weiss (1984) and his rejoinder to Vickers (1984). A highly valuable discussion of what he terms "the orthodox approach" is contained in Ford (1983, Ch. 1). See also a number of more advanced treatments of related issues in the papers included in Levy and Sarnat (1977). Note there the paper by Arditti and Levy, which extends the analysis beyond the two-moment, or the mean–variance, case considered in this chapter. Further expansion of the theory is contained in Elton and Gruber (1984), and applications to the firm's cost of capital and capital expenditure decisions are provided in Brealey and Myers (1984).

4. All assets are perfectly divisible and are marketable free of transactions costs.

5. There are no taxes.

6. All investors are price takers in a perfectly competitive asset market.

7. The total quantity of all assets in the opportunity set is given and fixed, each such asset being uniquely defined, as implied by assumption 3, by a universally agreed, subjectively assigned probability distribution of returns.

8. Each individual enters the market with a given wealth endowment, which he proceeds to distribute over the asset opportunity set in a manner that is optimal in the utility-theoretic sense.

9. No changes occur in the asset opportunity set during the single-market period, it being assumed that corporate firms neither issue new securities nor withdraw previously outstanding securities from the market.

Only brief comments need be made on the assumptions at this point. The first assumption recalls the analysis of probability distributions and utility theory in Chapters 5 and 6. The second assumption is analogous to that included in the development of the separation theorem in Chapter 3, where it was assumed that both firms and the owners of firms could borrow or lend at a given and exogenous market rate of interest.

The separation theorem in what follows depends also on the third assumption, that of "homogeneous expectations." This, it will become clear, is necessary in order to obtain from the theory a uniquely definable, "utility-free," optimum portfolio of risky assets. Attempts have been made to dispense with the assumption of homogeneous expectations, for example by Lintner (1969; see also Jensen, 1972, p. 390), but in such cases theoretical complications of a high order follow.

The assumption of perfect financial asset markets is expressed in both the perfect divisibility and marketability of assets and in the unlimited borrowing and lending opportunities at a risk-free rate of interest. Difficulties inhere in the assumption of given and uniform borrowing and lending rates, as they do also in connection with the givenness of the asset opportunity set. In the movement and change that continually occurs in the economy, firms also change. They expand, merge, decline, and die, and the volume and kinds of their capital securities outstanding also change, with traceable implications for financial investors' market opportunities.

Similar observations might be made regarding the assumption of the givenness of investors' wealth endowments, and the notion that transactions always take place in the asset market at equilibrium prices. The possibility of "false trading," or the consummation of market transactions at nonequilibrium prices, is assumed away (see Hicks, 1946, p. 127; Vickers, 1975, 1978). If false trading did occur, redistributions of endowments would take place prior to the achievement of market equilibrium, and this could conceivably have further expectations-inducing effects.

But at this stage we are interested in the validity of the conclusions that follow from the assumptions of the theory. The determination of equilibrium asset prices will provide the equilibrium yields, or the market's required rates of return, on those assets. It is in this form that the theory leads to a description of the firm's cost of money capital.

Portfolio asset choice

The economic value of the ownership or equity capital in the firm is defined by the present discounted value of the firm's expected time vector of residual earnings. Using notation employed up to this point, the value of the firm can be written as $V = \pi/\rho$. We now need to develop an explanation of what it is that determines the discount rate or the capitalization rate, ρ, in this valuation formula.

Generalizing from the two-asset portfolio case in Chapter 5 and making use of the relations between expected values, variances, and covariances between rates of return on financial assets, we define the expected rate of return and risk on an n-asset portfolio. In the following development, we shall use the symbols R_i and R_j to refer to the rates of return on the ith and the jth assets or securities in a portfolio, and R_p will refer to the portfolio rate of return. The weights attached to the portfolio assets, here referred to as x_i, x_j, will represent the proportion of the total portfolio value accounted for by the ith and jth assets. The portfolio weights will therefore sum to unity. The expected value, variance, standard deviation, and covariance notation will be recognized from preceding arguments, and the coefficient of correlation between pairs of asset returns will again be denoted by ρ_{ij}. For the n-asset portfolio,

$$E(R_p) = \sum_{i=1}^{n} x_i E(R_i) \qquad \sum_i x_i = 1 \tag{7.1}$$

$$\sigma^2(R_p) = \sum_{i=1}^{n} x_i^2 \sigma^2(R_i) + 2 \sum_{i=1}^{n} \sum_{j>i}^{n} x_i x_j \rho_{ij} \sigma_i \sigma_j \tag{7.2}$$

or

$$\sigma(R_p) = \left[\sum \sum x_i x_j \sigma_{ij} \right]^{1/2} \tag{7.3}$$

It is possible to generate, in the case of this n-asset opportunity set, an efficient boundary that is of the same nonlinear kind as the two-asset opportunity locus derived in Chapter 5 under the assumption that the underlying

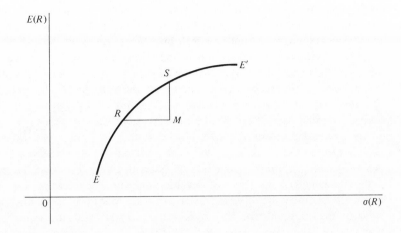

Figure 7.1

asset returns were less than perfectly correlated. We saw then that the form of such an opportunity locus depended on the form of the covariance matrix describing the relations between the asset returns. That is, it depended on the magnitude and sign of the covariances, or the coefficients of correlation, between all possible pairs of assets that were candidates for inclusion in the portfolio. The n-asset opportunity set therefore generates the nonlinear boundary of the form depicted by the curve EE' in Figure 7.1.

The locus EE' in Figure 7.1 is referred to as the efficient portfolio opportunity boundary. Every point on that locus dominates attainable portfolios interior to the opportunity set. The risk–return plane is populated by a set of points, each of which describes the risk–return coordinates of a separate asset opportunity or an achievable portfolio combination of assets. Point M, for example, is one such point and indicates that an asset is available that provides an expected return and standard deviation of return described by the intercepts to the axes from that point. Every portfolio on the boundary between R and S dominates portfolios in the interior of the segment RMS, in the sense that it offers a higher expected rate of return for a specified degree of risk, or a lower degree of risk for a given expected return. In this sense, the boundary EE' is itself undominated.

The efficient locus EE' is objectively calculable in the manner we shall indicate immediately below once we are given the forms of the subjectively assigned probability distributions of the underlying asset returns and the relevant covariance matrix. The locus EE' can then be regarded as the *objectively attainable* asset market risk–return trade-off. But it is, of course, objectively attainable only in the sense that the actions of market participants consistent with their assumed probability beliefs about asset returns will clear the asset market in the manner we shall investigate. If those beliefs should be falsified, market movements of a new and different kind will point to a new and differently specified market clearing condition. The slope of the EE' locus at any point, $dE(R)/d\sigma(R)$, describes the *objectively attainable marginal rate of transformation* between risk and return. Any point on the locus is accordingly a potential equilibrium point for the investor.

We solve the problem of asset choice by setting out to minimize Equation (7.3) subject to Equation (7.1). We specify a required rate of return and then determine the portfolio combination of assets that would provide the minimum attainable risk, or standard deviation of return, at the same time as it offers the specified rate of return. To discover this portfolio, it is sufficient to solve for the magnitudes of the x_i weights that would provide the desired asset combination. We visualize the constrained minimization problem in the form

$$\min_{x_i} \; \phi = \left[\sum_i \sum_j x_i x_j \sigma_{ij} \right]^{1/2} + \lambda_1 \left[E(R_p) - \sum_i^n x_i E(R_i) \right]$$

$$+ \lambda_2 \left[1 - \sum_j x_i \right] \qquad x_i \geq 0 \text{ for all } i \tag{7.4}$$

The first constraint on the right-hand side of Equation (7.4) anchors the solution to a specified rate of return, and the second constraint takes account of the fact that the weights must sum to unity. If a portfolio rate of return, $E(R_p)$, is specified in the first constraint and the solution values of the x_i are calculated, the resulting portfolio will be described by a point on the efficient portfolio locus such as EE' of Figure 7.1. By varying the level of $E(R_p)$ to which this first constraint is anchored, the entire portfolio locus can be generated (see Sharpe, 1963, 1970, for computational procedures, and Elton and Gruber, 1984, Chs. 5–7).

The meaning to be attached to the risk of an asset needs further clarification in this context. An asset's *own*, or *intrinsic*, risk has been defined in terms of the variance of the subjectively assigned probability distribution of that asset's rate of return. But when we take account of the contribution that that asset makes to the portfolio's covariance matrix, we must envisage also what we shall term the asset's *portfolio membership risk*. It is this latter concept that we shall have in mind when the risk of an asset is referred to in the following analysis. The risk of an asset is measurable, then, by the contribution a unit of that asset makes to the risk of the portfolio of which it is a member, or by $\partial\sigma(R_p)/\partial x_i$.

There will be occasion to use in what follows two other equivalent expressions for the same idea. Thus,

$$\sigma(R_p) = \left[\sum\sum x_i x_j \sigma_{ij}\right]^{1/2}$$

$$= \frac{\sigma^2(R_p)}{\sigma(R_p)}$$

$$= \frac{\sum\sum x_i x_j \sigma_{ij}}{\sigma(R_p)}$$

$$= \sum x_i \frac{\sum x_j \sigma_{ij}}{\sigma(R_p)}$$

from which it follows that

$$\frac{\partial \sigma(R_p)}{\partial x_i} = \frac{\sum x_j \sigma_{ij}}{\sigma(R_p)} \tag{7.5}$$

From a different viewpoint, the covariance between an asset's return and the return on the portfolio can be written as

$$\mathrm{Cov}(R_i, R_p) = \mathrm{Cov}\left(R_i, \sum x_j R_j\right) = \sum x_j \mathrm{Cov}(R_i, R_j)$$

Substituting this into the numerator of Equation (7.5) provides

$$\frac{\partial \sigma(R_p)}{\partial x_i} = \frac{\mathrm{Cov}(R_i, R_p)}{\sigma(R_p)} \tag{7.6}$$

We then have three formulations of the risk of an asset:

$$\text{Risk of asset} = \frac{\partial \sigma(R_p)}{\partial x_i} \tag{7.7}$$

$$= \frac{\sum x_j \sigma_{ij}}{\sigma(R_p)} \tag{7.8}$$

$$= \frac{\mathrm{Cov}(R_i, R_p)}{\sigma(R_p)} \tag{7.9}$$

Risk-free asset opportunity

Consider again the concave portfolio opportunity locus. If the investor was required to invest his entire wealth endowment in the opportunity set of risky assets, he would be confronted with the task of deciding which of all the efficient portfolios he should choose from the points on the efficient boundary. But in fact, the investor may not be constrained to invest only in risky assets. It is assumed by the theory that he may place a part or the whole of his wealth endowment in a risk-free asset yielding a riskless rate of return R_F. As shown in Figure 7.2, let us imagine that an investor was to divide his

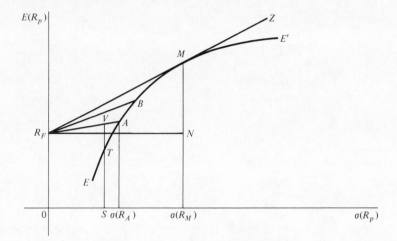

Figure 7.2

investable endowment between the risk-free asset yielding a return of R_F and portfolio A, which promises a return of $E(R_A)$, not shown in the figure, and presents a degree of risk $\sigma(R_A)$. The investor's return on his overall wealth portfolio, assuming a proportion w was placed in the risk-free asset, would be

$$E(R_p) = wR_F + (1 - w)E(R_A) \tag{7.10}$$

Similarly, his overall portfolio risk would be

$$\sigma^2(R_p) = (1 - w)^2\sigma^2(R_A) \tag{7.11}$$

or

$$\sigma(R_p) = (1 - w)\sigma(R_A) \tag{7.12}$$

Differentiating Equations (7.10) and (7.12) with respect to w and dividing the first such result by the second yields

$$\frac{dE(R_p)}{d\sigma(R_p)} = \frac{E(R_A) - R_F}{\sigma(R_A)} \tag{7.13}$$

In adopting this procedure, we have specified (i) the rate at which the portfolio expected return would be changed, in this case reduced, by an increase in w, or in the relative importance of the risk-free asset [by taking the derivative of Equation (7.10) with respect to w], and (ii) the rate at which the portfolio risk would be affected by the same action [by taking the derivative of Equation (7.12) with respect to w]. The implicit relation between these changes in the portfolio expected return and risk, consequent upon the change in w, is described by Equation (7.13). It represents the manner in which the investor may take advantage of the risk–return trade-off that is available in the asset market. If the relative importance of the risk-free asset in the portfolio is increased in the manner we have just envisaged, this would imply a reduction in the portfolio risk and also, as the development leading to Equation (7.13) indicates, a reduction in the portfolio expected rate of return.

Alternatively, we may solve Equation (7.12) for w to obtain

$$w = \frac{\sigma(R_A) - \sigma(R_p)}{\sigma(R_A)}$$

and substitute this into Equation (7.10) to obtain

$$E(R_p) = \left[1 - \frac{\sigma(R_p)}{\sigma(R_A)} \right] R_F + \frac{\sigma(R_p)}{\sigma(R_A)} E(R_A) \qquad (7.14)$$

Differentiation of this equation with respect to $\sigma(R_p)$ provides the result shown in Equation (7.13). Further, rearrangement of Equation (7.14) yields the result shown in Equation (7.15) that defines the slope of the attainable locus $R_F A$:

$$E(R_p) = R_F + \left[\frac{E(R_A) - R_F}{\sigma(R_A)} \right] \sigma(R_p) \qquad (7.15)$$

Given the risk–return characteristics of portfolio A, this provides a linear opportunity locus. The slope coefficient of that locus, defined by the bracketed term in Equation (7.15), is analogous to what will emerge below as the market price of risk implicit in the asset market portfolio opportunities. The existence of this opportunity implies that the *new* portfolio locus $R_F A$ *dominates* that portion of the previously existing locus EE' that lies to the southwest of A. In exchange for a risk exposure of $0S$, for example, the EE' locus offers an expected return of ST, whereas the new linear locus offers a prospective return at that risk level of SV, indicating a dominant portfolio.

The introduction of the risk-free asset opportunity has therefore transformed the efficient portfolio boundary from EE' to an *effective* efficient opportunity locus of $R_F AE'$. If, in the same way, the investor were to contemplate combinations of the risk-free asset and portfolio opportunity B, he could achieve a dominating locus of $R_F B$ and an effective opportunity locus of $R_F BE'$. By experimenting in a similar fashion with other possible risky asset portfolios, the investor could discover an *optimum portfolio of risky assets* with which the risk-free asset could be combined. Such a portfolio is designated as M in Figure 7.2. At that point, the linearized locus is tangential to the previously existing EE' boundary. The investor's effective opportunities are then described by R_FME'. Such an attainable locus is dependent, of course, on the specified risk-free rate, R_F. A different risk-free rate would generate a different opportunity locus and a different optimum portfolio of risky assets. But we have not at this stage considered what, in a general equilibrium asset market context, will determine that risk-free rate (see Vickers, 1975). Considerations of general economic conditions and monetary policy are clearly relevant. The risk-free rate will be dependent also on the volume of borrowing and lending that market participants desire to undertake at that rate.

To the extent that the investor is allocating his wealth between the risk-free asset and the optimum portfolio of risky assets M, he is *lending* at the risk-free rate of interest. Depending on his decision as to the proportion of his wealth that he should lend at that rate, he will settle at a point on the linear segment R_FM. But suppose also that the investor could *borrow* at the same risk-free rate. Then he could increase his expected return even further, at the same time undertaking additional risk, by borrowing at the risk-free rate and investing the proceeds in the risky portfolio M. In such an event, he would settle somewhere on the MZ portion of what is now a completely linearized opportunity locus R_FMZ. This locus may now be referred to as the Capital Market Line.

It should be recalled that in this analysis we are dealing with an *equilibrium* theory of financial asset prices and yields. Every investor in the market is contemplating the selection of an optimum portfolio from the given asset opportunity set and will similarly be concerned to discover the optimum combination of the risk-free asset, promising the given return of R_F, and the optimum risky asset portfolio M. What are being discovered in such relations as those summarized in Figure 7.2, then, are the conditions that will exist when full general equilibrium conditions are satisfied in the asset market.

This requires us to make a careful interpretation of the linear portfolio opportunity locus we have derived, such as R_FMZ. It is, in a sense, objectively attainable, in the manner in which we previously referred to the efficient set boundary EE' as objectively attainable. But in both cases, that objectivity is based on the existence of underlying investor preferences that determine their demands for securities in the asset market and influence the determination and expectations of market prices and yields. Moreover, it would be a mistake to interpret the locus R_FMZ as a *trading* opportunity locus in a disequilibrium opportunity sense, along which investors could move once it had been established. Rather, that locus describes simply the conditions that exist and the relations between risks and rates of return that exist when equilibrium conditions are satisfied. The theory of equilibrium asset prices, in other words, is not competent, in the form in which it has been developed, to make any statement about trading processes. It is a theory, not of trading behavior, but of equilibrium relations.

We have assumed, in order to exhibit the results of this financial market theory, that all participants in the market hold the same expectations regarding the risk–return profiles of the asset opportunities. Every investor who holds risky assets will in that case choose to invest part of his wealth in portfolio M, and we may then refer to this as the market portfolio. This portfolio's expected return and risk will be referred to in what follows as $E(R_M)$ and $\sigma(R_M)$, respectively. This risk and return profile of the market portfolio will be the outcome of the supply and demand forces of asset market equilibration that establishes the final asset prices. These, in turn, establish the asset yield relations that define the final opportunity locus. The slope of that locus, which defines the market risk–return trade-off that exists *when full equilibrium conditions are satisfied,* will be referred to as the market price of risk.

The market portfolio M must be made up of *all* the assets in the risky opportunity set, and the proportion each asset occupies in the portfolio must equal the ratio of its market value to the total market value of all the assets combined. It is impossible for an asset, say the jth asset in the set, to account for a proportion of the total market value of all risky assets that is different from the proportion of the value of their risky investments that all investors combined place in that asset. In full equilibrium, all the assets will be held by willing holders, the amounts borrowed will be offset by amounts lent, and net borrowing will be zero (see Sharpe, 1970, p. 82).

Asset market equilibrium condition

Consider now the portfolio selection or the optimum-asset choice problem confronted by a representative investor and summarized in Equation (7.4). Differentiating this objective function with respect to x_i and x_j and setting the partials equal to zero for first-order optimization conditions yields

$$\frac{\partial \phi}{\partial x_i} = \frac{\partial \sigma(R_p)}{\partial x_i} - \lambda_1 E(R_i) - \lambda_2 = 0 \tag{7.16}$$

$$\frac{\partial \phi}{\partial x_j} = \frac{\partial \sigma(R_p)}{\partial x_j} - \lambda_1 E(R_j) - \lambda_2 = 0 \tag{7.17}$$

It follows from Equations (7.16) and (7.17) that

$$\frac{\partial \sigma(R_p)}{\partial x_i} - \lambda_1 E(R_i) = \frac{\partial \sigma(R_p)}{\partial x_j} - \lambda_1 E(R_j) \tag{7.18}$$

or that

$$E(R_j) - E(R_i) = \frac{1}{\lambda_1} \left[\frac{\partial \sigma(R_p)}{\partial x_j} - \frac{\partial \sigma(R_p)}{\partial x_i} \right] \qquad (7.19)$$

From the mathematical interpretation of Equation (7.4), λ_1 describes the partial derivative of the minimand function with respect to the constraint variable to which the λ_1 is attached, or $\lambda_1 = \partial \sigma(R_p)/\partial E(R_p)$. Understanding, as summarized in the preceding sections, that every investor will choose to invest part of his wealth in the market portfolio when the market equilibrium conditions are satisfied, we can now investigate the nature of the portfolio optimization conditions at the optimum risky portfolio point M. In the further development of the conditions in Equations (7.16)–(7.19), and in the interpretation of the equilibrium solution value of λ_1, we can replace $E(R_p)$ and $\sigma(R_p)$ by $E(R_M)$ and $\sigma(R_M)$.

The solution value of λ_1 at the optimization point can be linked to the fact that $\partial \sigma(R_M)/\partial E(R_M)$ is the reciprocal of the slope of the Capital Market Line, $R_F M$, in Figure 7.2. This latter magnitude, $MN/R_F N$ in the figure, can then be interpreted as the market price of risk. It is equal to $[E(R_M - R_F]/\sigma(R_M)$, and it indicates the increment of return the market is providing in equilibrium for a unit change in portfolio risk.

Focusing now on the relations that exist when the market portfolio is held, we may substitute this equivalent expression for λ_1 in Equation (7.19) and perform the following operation. First, multiply the resulting equation by x_1 and record the result. Then multiply the equation by x_2 and record the result. Proceed in a similar fashion, multiplying the equation by each of the x_i. We then have a total of n such new equations. If all of these n equations are added, the following result is obtained:

$$\sum_i x_i E(R_j) - \sum_i x_i E(R_i) = \frac{E(R_M) - R_F}{\sigma(R_M)} \left[\sum_i x_i \frac{\partial \sigma(R_M)}{\partial x_j} - \sum_i x_i \frac{\partial \sigma(R_M)}{\partial x_i} \right] \qquad (7.20)$$

We recall now that $\sum x_i$ in the first term on the left-hand side of Equation (7.20) equals unity, so that the term as a whole equals $E(R_j)$. In the second term on the left-hand side, each x_i is multiplied by its corresponding $E(R_i)$, as the summation takes place over the index i, and the term as a whole therefore equals the expected return on the market portfolio, $E(R_M)$. Similar interpretations attach to the $\sum x_i$ on the right-hand side of Equation (7.20).

Now in making a further interpretation of Equation (7.20), we may substitute for the first term inside the brackets on the right-hand side the equivalent expression in Equation (7.9). For the final term inside the brackets we may substitute the equivalent expression in Equation (7.8). Making the substitutions, we obtain

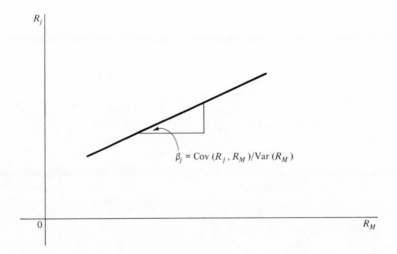

Figure 7.3

$$E(R_j) - E(R_M) = \frac{E(R_M) - R_F}{\sigma(R_M)} \left[\frac{\text{Cov}(R_j, R_M)}{\sigma(R_M)} - \frac{\Sigma x_i \Sigma x_j \sigma_{ij}}{\sigma(R_M)} \right] \quad (7.21)$$

The last term inside the brackets in Equation (7.21) can be recognized as the variance of return on the market portfolio divided by its own standard deviation, or simply the standard deviation of the market portfolio return. This equivalence permits us to remove the brackets from Equation (7.21), with the following result:

$$E(R_j) - E(R_M) = R_F - E(R_M) + \left[\frac{E(R_M) - R_F}{\sigma(R_M)} \right] \frac{\text{Cov}(R_j, R_M)}{\sigma(R_M)} \quad (7.22)$$

Equation (7.22) may then be simplified to provide

$$E(R_j) = R_F + [E(R_M) - R_F] \frac{\text{Cov}(R_j, R_M)}{\sigma^2(R_M)} \quad (7.23)$$

To make an interpretation of the final term on the right-hand side of Equation (7.23), and focusing on the expression $\text{Cov}(R_j, R_M)/\sigma^2(R_M)$, consider the relationship shown in Figure 7.3. Here we have envisaged the regression of the rate of return on the jth asset on the rate of return earned on the market portfolio. The regression coefficient in such a relationship may be written as the covariance between the two variables divided by the variance of the independent variable. The regression coefficient is then defined precisely by the

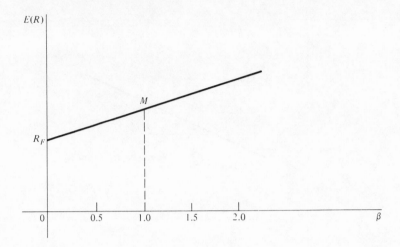

Figure 7.4

ratio we now observe on the extreme right-hand side of Equation (7.23). This magnitude has attracted a precise designation in the theory of capital asset market equilibrium and is referred to as the jth asset's beta coefficient. It is written as β_j.

With this in hand, we can make a final interpretation of Equation (7.23) by substituting into that equation the regression coefficient we have just defined. In doing so, we are defining the market's required rate of return on the jth risky asset when full general equilibrium conditions are satisfied:

$$E(R_j) = R_F + \beta_j[E(R_M) - R_F] \tag{7.24}$$

We conclude from Equation (7.24) that the market's required rate of return on the jth risky asset, for example the shares of common stock of the jth firm in the risky asset set, will be equal to the risk-free rate of interest plus a risk premium. That risk premium is equal to the asset's beta coefficient multiplied by the market risk premium, or the excess of the return on the market portfolio over the risk-free rate. If the first R_F on the right-hand side of Equation (7.24) is transposed to the left-hand side, it follows that in market equilibrium the risk premium on the jth asset will be equal to that asset's beta coefficient muliplied by the market risk premium.

This result can be further interpreted with the aid of Figure 7.4.

Consider the principal result of the theory described in Equation (7.24). If we envisage the market rate of return, $E(R_M)$, on the left-hand side of that equation, it follows that the "market beta" must be equal to 1. We depict this as point M in Figure 7.4. This figure shows the equilibrium relationship that exists between the beta coefficient and the expected rate of return on a security. Such a relationship, which can be referred to as the Security Market Line, must be linear, as will be clear from an inspection of Equation (7.24). We have, by definition of the underlying relations, two available points on this line: (i) the coordinates of M described by the expected return on the market portfolio and the value of β equal to 1 and (ii) the risk-free rate R_F. We are therefore able to describe the locus. This Security Market Line implies that the beta coefficient now appears as a fundamental measure of the asset risk.

This result may be further interpreted as follows. We have seen that by combining securities in a portfolio, and by taking advantage of the form of the covariance matrix that describes the risk relation between securities, it is possible to diversify in such a way and to such an extent as to reduce the portfolio risk to a minimum attainable level. But there is, of course, a limit to that attainable risk reduction. The proportion of a security's total risk that can be diversified away, or eliminated by diversification, is frequently referred to as unique risk or unsystematic or residual risk. This implies that there remains a systematic risk, also referred to as market risk, that cannot be diversified away.

It is this remaining systematic risk, reflecting the manner in which a security's return fluctuates in relation to the market rate of return, that is captured and described by the security's beta coefficient. It follows that securities whose risk–return profile places them to the northeast of M on the Security Market Line in Figure 7.4 are more risky than the market portfolio, and those to the southwest of M are less risky. These relationships will be seen to be directly relevant to the specification by the asset market equilibrium theory of a firm's cost of capital. It follows from the preceding development also that the beta coefficient of a portfolio of securities will be a weighted average of the beta coefficients of the securities in the portfolio, where the weights are described by the proportions of the total portfolio value represented by each security.

Nonstandard results of the equilibrium asset pricing theory

It is beyond our present objectives to consider the large number of critical amendments that have been made to, and the advances that have been made beyond, the standard form of the capital asset pricing model that we have considered in the foregoing [see the extensive bibliographies in Elton and Gruber (1984)]. But a minimal comment will be made on two points.

Consider again the basic result of the theory presented in

$$E(R_j) = R_F + \beta_j[E(R_m) - R_F] \tag{7.25}$$

This result, it will be recalled, was derived on the assumption that unlimited

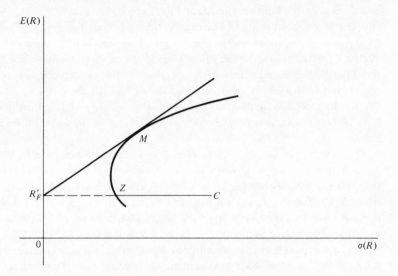

Figure 7.5

borrowing and lending opportunities at a risk-free rate were available to investors. This is reflected in the first term on the right-hand side of Equation (7.25). If, however, no such borrowing and lending opportunities are available, the analysis can be cast in an alternative form that yields comparable results for equilibrium security prices and yields, and therefore for a firm's cost of capital (see Black, 1972; Elton and Gruber, 1984, Ch. 12).

We restate the meaning of the Security Market Line in Figure 7.4 by observing that it passes through the two points of (i) the market portfolio point M and (ii) the rate-of-return ordinate corresponding to an asset or portfolio whose beta coefficient is zero. We can envisage the available rate of return on such a "zero-beta" portfolio and ask what determines its magnitude. Let us approach this question by considering Figure 7.5. The location of the market portfolio, or the optimum portfolio of risky securities, was observed to depend on the location of the risk-free rate at which borrowing and lending were assumed to take place. Let us then observe the actual market portfolio and note its risk–return profile and its location as described by point M in Figure 7.5. It is then possible to define, by making use of the linear locus tangential to M, the ordinate R'_F. This can be interpreted as the risk-free rate such that if investors *could* borrow and lend at that rate, they would hold the market portfolio. Such a rate and such an opportunity as represented by R'_F do not, of course, under the present assumptions, exist. But there do exist portfolios that provide a prospective rate of return equal to R'_F. If R'_F were available, the expected return on the jth risky asset could, in accordance with our previous results, be defined as

$$E(R_j) = R_F' + \beta_j[E(R_m) - R_F']$$ (7.26)

Consider then an asset such that its rate of return $E(R_j)$ is equal to R_F'. In that case, the value of the final term on the right-hand side of Equation (7.26) would have to be zero. This implies that the beta coefficient of any such asset or portfolio must be zero. We may therefore define R_F' as the equilibrium market rate of return on the zero-beta portfolios that could be chosen from the asset opportunity set. Such portfolios, lying within the opportunity set, are described by the ZC portion of the line $R_F'ZC$ in Figure 7.5.

The equilibrium condition where borrowing and lending opportunities at a risk-free rate are not available can therefore be described by replacing the risk-free rate in Equation (7.25) by the rate available on a zero-beta portfolio, R_z. The equilibrium required rate of return on the jth risky asset then becomes

$$E(R_j) = R_z + \beta_j[E(R_m) - R_z]$$ (7.27)

Given this result, the analysis and application to the firm's cost of capital can proceed as before. We shall return to the detailed specification of that cost of capital below.

A final point of amendment to, or rather an extension of equilibrium asset theory beyond, the standard form of the capital asset pricing model can be noted without extended analysis (see Ross, 1976, 1977, 1978). This development, referred to as the Arbitrage Pricing Theory (APT), explains that in full generalized asset market equilibrium the expected return on a risky asset can be related to a number of fundamental "factors" as expressed in

$$E(R_j) = a + b_1 I_1 + b_2 I_2 + b_3 I_3 + \cdots + b_n I_n$$ (7.28)

where the I_i, $i = 1, 2, \ldots, n$, refer to the factors or indexes on which the return on a risky security depends. The APT in fact bypasses the problem and theory of efficient portfolio construction we have examined in this chapter. It looks directly to the determinants of the asset's price and effective rate of return. The theory argues that if the existing risk premium on an asset is lower than is implied by the relationship envisaged in Equation (7.28), the asset can be considered to be overpriced. Investors would then sell the asset and engage in an "arbitrage" action by buying an alternative asset to replace it in their portfolios. Similarly, the asset would be purchased if its available risk premium were higher than the norm specified in Equation (7.28), and other assets would be sold in the rush to purchase it. This arbitrage activity in the risky asset market would, it is presumed, maintain market equilibrium and permit a direct approach to be made to estimating the asset's equilibrium rate of return. This again could then be incorporated into the analysis of the firm's cost of money capital.

A utility-theoretic interpretation

The foregoing development has concentrated on the means and variances of the risky asset opportunities, and as such it exposes the essence of what we have referred to as the mean–variance theory of asset portfolio optimization. We can therefore exploit an alternative way of integrating this body of theory with the mean–variance utility functions we examined in the preceding chapter.

The investor's mean–variance utility function may be written in the form $U = U[E(R_p), \sigma(R_p)]$. Its first-order optimization condition with respect to the jth asset in the investor's portfolio, where x_j now represents the proportion of his *total wealth* placed in the jth risky asset, is

$$\frac{\partial U}{\partial E(R_p)} \frac{\partial E(R_p)}{\partial x_j} + \frac{\partial U}{\partial \sigma(R_p)} \frac{\partial \sigma(R_p)}{\partial x_j} = 0 \tag{7.29}$$

It follows that

$$\frac{\partial E(R_p)}{\partial x_j} = -\frac{\partial U/\partial \sigma(R_p)}{\partial U/\partial E(R_p)} \frac{\partial \sigma(R_p)}{\partial x_j} \tag{7.30}$$

The first term on the right-hand side of Equation (7.30), the negative of the ratio of the partial derivatives of the utility function, is recognizable as the investor's marginal rate of substitution between risk and return. This must be equal in equilibrium to the market price of risk or the slope of the Capital Market Line. Using previous notation, we may make use of the market price of risk at the point of utility optimization, and the condition described in Equation (7.30) may be written as

$$\frac{\partial E(R_p)}{\partial x_j} = \frac{E(R_M) - R_F}{\sigma(R_M)} \frac{\partial \sigma(R_p)}{\partial x_j} \tag{7.31}$$

The investor's overall wealth allocation problem is now solved by placing a proportion of his wealth equal to $\sum x_j$ in a *risky* asset portfolio and the balance, $1 - \sum x_j$, in a risk-free asset yielding a return as before of R_F. The investor's expected return and risk exposure then become

$$E(R_p) = \sum x_j E(R_j) + \left(1 - \sum x_j\right) R_F \tag{7.32}$$

and

$$\sigma(R_p) = \left[\sum\sum x_i x_j \sigma_{ij}\right]^{1/2} \tag{7.33}$$

Differentiation of Equations (7.32) and (7.33) with respect to x_j provides

$$\frac{\partial E(R_p)}{\partial x_j} = E(R_j) - R_F \tag{7.34}$$

and

$$\frac{\partial \sigma(R_p)}{\partial x_j} = \frac{\sum x_i \sigma_{ij}}{\sigma(R_M)} \tag{7.35}$$

We recall, in the final term of Equation (7.35), that the portfolio on which interest can be focused when equilibrium conditions are satisfied is once again the market portfolio.

Equations (7.34) and (7.35) may then be substituted into the utility optimization condition in Equation (7.31) to provide

$$E(R_j) - R_F = \frac{E(R_M) - R_F}{\sigma(R_M)} \frac{\sum x_i \sigma_{ij}}{\sigma(R_M)} \tag{7.36}$$

In the final term of this equation, the risk of the jth asset in the portfolio is recognizable from the result established in Equation (7.8). From Equation (7.36), using Equation (7.9),

$$E(R_j) - R_F = [E(R_M) - R_F] \frac{\text{Cov}(R_j, R_M)}{\sigma^2(R_M)} \tag{7.37}$$

This states again that when general equilibrium conditions are satisfied, the market's required risk premium on the jth risky asset will be a linear function of the risk premium on the market portfolio. The final term on the right-hand side of Equation (7.37) again incorporates the jth asset's beta coefficient.

Wealth allocation separation theorem

We recall that from the point of view of the individual investor the financial asset market is assumed to satisfy the requirements of a perfectly competitive market. We assume that conditions in the market are such that the optimum portfolio of risky assets has been determined at point M in Figure 7.2, reproduced as point M in Figure 7.6. It then follows that the investor's decision as to the division of his wealth endowment between this risky portfolio and the risk-free asset will depend on the form of his utility function, in particular on the degree of risk aversion it exhibits. If, for example, the form of the indifference curves is such that the relevant point of tangency is established at M in Figure 7.6, the individual would place his entire wealth in the risky portfolio.

If, on the other hand, the utility function exhibited a higher degree of risk aversion and established tangency at point S, the investor would divide his wealth between the risky portfolio and the risk-free asset. The rate of return on his total wealth position in that case, and the overall risk to which he would be exposed, would be described by the intercepts on the axes (not shown in

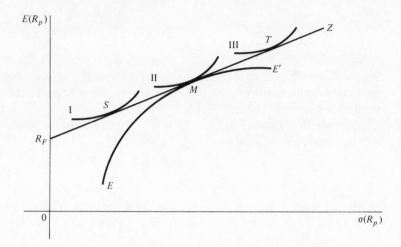

Figure 7.6

the figure) adjacent to S. If the investor, instead of investing in the risk-free asset and thereby *lending* at the given interest rate R_F, were to *borrow* at that rate and invest the proceeds in the risky portfolio, he might optimize at point T on the $R_F MZ$ opportunity line. This could occur if his utility function exhibited a somewhat lower degree of risk aversion. The investor would then be increasing his expected return above that obtainable on the market portfolio M, but he would be increasing the degree of risk to which he was exposed. His expected return and risk are indicated by the intercepts on the coordinate axes adjacent to point T.

This, therefore, establishes the wealth allocation separation theorem. The investor's final decision regarding the distribution of his wealth endowment is *separable from* the decision as to the structure of the optimum portfolio of risky assets. The result is dependent on the assumption that all investors can borrow or lend any desired amount at an exogenously given risk-free rate of interest in perfect money capital markets. But a number of difficulties arise.

The assumption of perfection in the asset market may not provide a reasonable basis from which to begin an analysis of the trading that takes place in it. There may be quasi-monopsonistic and monopolistic phenomena on the respective sides of the market, and neither transactions nor the gathering of information may be costless. Furthermore, the risk-free rate is likely to be unstable. To the extent, also, that trading takes place in the market at non-equilibrium prices, the windfall gains and losses that occur can be expected to have endowment-redistribution and expectations-inducing effects. Finally, the supply of financial assets, for example the debt and equity capital securities of firms, is not likely to be stable, as firms change, grow, merge, expand, decline, and die.

But the final results of the orthodox theory, at least in the form in which we have exhibited it, are such that when equilibrium conditions are satisfied, three situations obtain. First, and assuming we can rule out a corner solution in which the investor's entire wealth would be placed in the risk-free asset, all investors will hold the *same* portfolio of risky assets. Some of every asset will be held by every investor. Moreover, there would be no reason, in the idealized world of the general equilibrium asset theory, for an individual to retain sole proprietorship of a firm. He could reach a higher utility level by exchanging part, perhaps most, of his ownership for other components of the market portfolio and realizing the benefits of asset diversification. These results, of course, are demonstrably false as a description of the world. The whole advantage of the theory, therefore, as claimed by adherents to the equilibrium-theoretic tradition, rests in the extent to which the results generated by the abstractions contained within it provide reasonable and usable approximations to the rates of return actually observed on risky securities.

Second, the proportionate distribution of investor's wealth will depend on the degree of risk aversion in their assumed mean–variance utility functions. Third, all investors will exhibit the *same* subjective marginal rate of substitution between risk and return, equal to the slope of the objectively determined linearized market opportunity locus, or the objectively attainable marginal rate of transformation between risk and return. This may be further conceptualized as the market price of risk.

The cost of money capital

The foregoing analysis implies that the measure for which we have been searching, the specification of the firm's cost of equity capital or of ρ in the economic valuation equation, is now defined by the asset market's equilibrium required rate of return on the firm's equity capital security. It is defined precisely in Equation (7.24). We should note carefully, however, that this result and this specification follow only so long as we are committed to the presumed validity and relevance of the asset market equilibrium theory from which it was derived.

The principal result of the theory, and therefore the principal implication for the firm's cost of money capital, has to do with the nature of the covariation between the rate of return on the risky asset, in this case the common stock of the jth firm, and the rate of return being earned on the market portfolio. The analysis is concerned with what we designated at an earlier stage as the "variability risk" in the income stream generated by the risky asset.

The total variability of an asset's rate of return can be separated into what we have called "systematic risk," or "market risk," on the one hand and "unsystematic," or "unique," risk on the other. The latter can be diversified away by an investor who combines the asset with other assets in a portfolio. But the market or systematic risk cannot be diversified away, for it remains by virtue of the fact that asset returns move together with the asset market in general, being linked to the market fluctuations by the asset's beta coefficient.

We need to consider more precisely, however, what it is that contributes to or determines the overall variability of equity capital rates of return. We recall the argument in Chapter 2 regarding the leverage structures of the firm and the manner in which the operating and financing structures contribute to the instability of the firm's residual income stream. That overall instability, we saw, was due to both external forces and economic developments bearing on the firm and to internal structural forces that determined the manner in which the firm's income stream behaved in reaction to external events.

The integrated view of the firm's production, real capital investment, and financing structures that we examined in Chapters 2 and 4 enables us to isolate for analytical purposes what we might call a first-stage or operational leverage effect. Given that variations occur in the general level of economic activity, this will cause fluctuations in a firm's sales revenue. But then, in reaction to those developments, magnified fluctuations will occur in the firm's net operating income stream. The extent to which this will happen will depend on the incidence of fixed operating costs that have to be deducted from gross revenue before the net operating income is determined. Such fixed operating costs stem, we have seen, from the decision to employ durable real capital assets in the firm. The resulting instability at the operating income level has been referred to as a reflection of operational leverage.

This instability or risk may be referred to as "business risk" or "operating risk." In speaking of business risk, we are envisaging the character or quality of the operating income stream that is generated by the total asset investment at work in the firm. We saw, in the examples we gave in Chapter 2, that two firms of the same size, in the same industry, with the same total asset investment, and subject to the same variations of economic fortunes may have adopted different financing methods. They may have different debt-to-equity ratios in their financing mix or in the structure of the liabilities sides of their balance sheets. The possibility of different financing methods gave rise to different possible degrees of financial leverage and led, as a result, to different potential degrees of instability in the firm's residual income stream.

The instability in a firm's residual income stream, or in the rate of return earned on its residual equity, is thus due to (i) general external economic fluctuations, (ii) the firm's operating structure, and (iii) the firm's financing structure. We can expect that the overall risk in the firm's rate of return on equity will depend on the force of, and the interaction between, these several sources of instability. We can expect the residual earnings of firms with different operating and financing structures to exhibit different degrees of relationship with the rate of return earned on the asset market as a whole. In other words, firms with different operating and financing structures can be expected to exhibit different beta coefficients.

This points to a fuller specification of the functions determining the required rates of return on a firm's debt and equity securities, or its costs of debt and equity capital. Let us designate the business or operating risk in the firm by the symbol θ and the further degree of risk induced by financial leverage as δ. We shall employ the symbol TMC to refer to the total money capital employed by the firm. We can then write the cost of debt and equity capital, respectively, as

$$r = r(\theta, \delta, \text{TMC}) \tag{7.38}$$

$$\rho = \rho(\theta, \delta, \text{TMC}) \tag{7.39}$$

The total money capital variable is included here as a size variable to capture what might be economies of scale in the use of the financial markets, even though in the analysis in this chapter, under the assumption of perfect money capital markets, no such economies of scale apply.

In our discussion of the firm's constrained optimization in Chapter 4, we referred to these debt and equity costs as $r = r(K, D)$ and $\rho = \rho(K, D)$, concentrating on the firm's money capital decision variables. But that constrained optimization analysis did take extensive account of the determinants of the firm's operating structure, and it is necessary to bear in mind also, therefore, the impact of such structural decisions on the money capital financing costs we now envisage. We shall return to the question of the cost of money capital in the next chapter.

CHAPTER 8

The cost of money capital: further analysis and controversy

One of the principal conclusions we reached in Chapter 4 was related to the description of the firm's cost of money capital. We specified there the full marginal costs of debt and equity capital, and these were related to the full marginal cost of relaxing the money capital availability constraint. Equation (4.47) in Chapter 4 instanced an equilibrium or an optimization relation between these full marginal costs. We begin our discussion of the cost of capital in this chapter by considering those concepts further. In doing so, we adopt a quite different analytical stance from that of the preceding equilibrium asset market theory. There we examined the implications of *general* equilibrium in *perfect* financial markets. In what follows, we shall be initially concerned with questions of *partial* equilibrium in conceivably *imperfect* markets. We shall return to some general equilibrium considerations in later sections of this chapter.

Illustration of the full marginal cost of relaxing the money capital availability constraint

The following example illustrates the empirical meaning of the full marginal cost of increasing the amount of money capital available to the firm by raising an increment of debt capital. It provides an instance of the concept first introduced in Equation (4.31). It will be useful to keep in mind throughout the discussion the fundamental definition of the firm's cost of money capital.

Definition

The cost of money capital is the minimum required rate of return that must be earned on investing marginal money capital in the firm in order not to cause a dilution of the owners' economic wealth position.

Let us suppose that a firm, with a given total asset investment and a given debt-to-equity financing mix, is generating a residual income stream that provides the common stockholders with earnings of $3 per share. If the owners' required rate of return is 10 percent, the market value of the shares of common stock will be equal to $3 capitalized at 10 percent, or $30. Suppose now that the firm decides to undertake an investment project that is financed by a new issue of debt capital. This issue of debt will increase the degree of leverage in the firm's financing structure, and as a result of their increased risk exposure the owners' required rate of return will be assumed to rise from 10 to 12.5 percent. If there were no change in the residual earnings per share, the market value of the shares would fall from $30 to the equivalent of $3 capitalized at 12.5 percent, or $24. This reduction in market value, or in economic value, is referred to as a dilution of the owners' economic position. This could be expected to happen if the project in which the new debt capital is invested generated only sufficient earnings to pay the interest on the debt. In order to prevent this dilution, the new debt capital, when it is put to work in the firm, must generate a level of earnings greater than the cost of the interest on the debt. After the new investment and financing has occurred, the residual earnings must increase by such an amount that when the new earnings per share are capitalized at the new higher capitalization rate, the value of the common stock will be at least as high as it was before. If, as in the example, the capitalization rate rose from 10 to 12.5 percent, the earnings per share would need to rise from $3 to $3.75 in order to prevent dilution. The following example will explore this set of relationships more fully.

The firm's constrained objective function, analogous to Equation (4.28), may be stated as

$$\max_{x_i, K, D} \phi = \frac{1}{\rho(K, D)} \begin{array}{l}[p(Q)f(X) - a'X - r(K, D)D](1-t) \\ + \lambda[K + D - b'X]\end{array} \tag{8.1}$$

where $f(X)$ describes the production function of the firm in vector notation, X describing an n-element factor input vector. Similarly, a' refers to a factor cost vector (meaning by this the operating flow cost as previously examined), and b' describes a vector of money capital requirement coefficients. In Equation (8.1), the firm's net income, contained in the first square brackets on the right-hand side, is multiplied by the complement of the tax rate, t, to define the residual net after-tax income actually available to the owners. The remaining variables are defined as previously.

To trace out the effects of marginal debt financing, we examine the partial derivative of Equation (8.1) with respect to the debt variable D:

$$\frac{\partial \phi}{\partial D} = -\frac{\pi(1-t)\partial \rho}{\rho^2} \frac{\partial \rho}{\partial D} - \frac{1}{\rho}\left[r + \frac{D}{\partial D}\frac{\partial r}{\partial D}\right](1-t) + \lambda = 0 \tag{8.2}$$

It follows from Equation (8.2) that

$$\left[r + \frac{D}{\partial D}\frac{\partial r}{\partial D}\right](1-t) + \frac{V}{\partial D}\frac{\partial \rho}{\partial D} = \rho\lambda \tag{8.3}$$

Dividing throughout by $1 - t$ yields

$$r + D \frac{\partial r}{\partial D} + V \frac{\partial \rho}{\partial D}\left[\frac{1}{1-t}\right] = \rho \lambda' \qquad (8.4)$$

where λ' equals the marginal productivity measure multiplied by a tax step-up factor to express it on a before-tax basis. The tax step-up factor, which also appears on the left-hand side of the equation, is the reciprocal of 1 minus the firm's tax rate.

Both sides of the optimization condition in Equation (8.4) are expressing the firm's marginal cost of debt capital, and the left-hand side exhibits in more detail the "full marginal cost of relaxing the money capital availability constraint." The first two terms taken together describe the derivative of the firm's interest burden with respect to debt, $\partial[r(K, D)]/\partial D$, or the increase in the interest burden that results from the increased use of debt. We refer to this magnitude $(r + D \, \partial r/\partial D)$ as the firm's marginal *direct* cost of debt. Recognizing the first term, r, as the interest rate that has to be paid on the marginal debt itself, the marginal direct cost of debt will be greater than the interest cost of the marginal debt. This is because the higher interest rate on debt capital that results from the increase in the debt-to-equity financing ratio will have to be paid, not only on the new debt now being issued, but also on the previously existing debt when that matures and has to be refinanced.

Recalling the foregoing discussion of the equity owners' position, the minimum rate of return that must be earned on the marginal debt capital must exceed this marginal direct cost of debt by an amount sufficient to offset any tendency to a dilution of the market value of the equity. Consider, therefore, the following example. The magnitudes are hypothetical and no doubt exaggerated, but they exhibit the nature of the causation involved. Employing a time subscript of zero to refer to the firm's situation before the new financing and investment and subscript 1 to refer to the situation after the new financing, let us assume the following situation:

$D_0 = \$3$ million (the market value of debt capital)
$V_0 = \$6$ million (the market value of equity)
$W_0 = D_0 + V_0 = \$9$ million (the total market value of the firm's capital securities)
$r_0 = 0.05$
$DI_0 = \$150,000$ (debt interest)
$\rho_0 = 0.10$
Number of equity shares outstanding $= 100,000$
Earnings per share $(EPS_0) = \$6$
Market value per share $(S_0) = \$6/0.10 = \$60$

Table 8.1 *Income statement data* ($000)

	Before new financing	Required position after new financing	Incremental data
Operating income	$1,350	$1,800	$450
Less debt interest	150	300	150
Earnings before tax	1,200	1,500	300
Less tax	600	750	150
Net income (Residual equity earnings)	600	750	150
Earnings per share	$6	$7.5	$1.5
Market value per share	$6/0.10 = $60	$7.5/0.125 = $60	

Marginal debt financing $(\Delta D) = \$2$ million
$r_1 = 0.06$
$DI_1 = \$300,000$ (after refinancing all maturing debt)
$\rho_1 = 0.125$
$t_0 = t_1 = 0.50$

In this situation, the full marginal cost of debt as defined on the left-hand side of Equation (8.4) quantifies as

$$0.06 + \frac{3(0.01)}{2} + \frac{6(0.025)}{2}\frac{1}{1-0.50} = 0.06 + 0.015 + 0.15$$
$$= 0.225 \qquad (8.5)$$

The full marginal cost of debt, or the required rate of return on a before-tax basis necessary to establish economic viability, is 22.5 percent. To reinforce the understanding of these relationships, consider the pro forma income statement of the firm in Table 8.1.

The data in Table 8.1 imply that the residual earnings per share of equity after tax would increase by $1.50, sufficient to increase earnings per share to $7.50. When this amount is capitalized at the new higher capitalization rate of 12.5 percent, the market value per share of $60 can be maintained, and no equity dilution will have occurred. But this will occur only if the operating income of the firm increased by $450,000, or by 22.5 percent of the new $2 million investment, precisely the gross before-tax required rate of return or the full marginal cost of the debt as specified in Equation (8.5).

Weighted average cost of capital

Leaving aside now the question of computation, and ignoring the technical adjustment for the firm's tax rate, we recall the firm's full marginal cost of equity that was brought into relation with the full marginal cost of debt in Equation (4.47). At the firm's optimum structural planning point, both these full marginal costs were equal to the magnitude $\rho\lambda$, which therefore emerged as the firm's optimum planning discount factor or valuation rate.

We consider now whether any traceable relation exists between this planning discount factor and the more familiar concept of the firm's weighted average cost of capital. It will be shown that the two are in fact equal to one another when the firm has been brought to its optimum size and structure. At that point, and when all parts of the interdependent planning nexus have been brought to their optimum solution values, the weighted average cost of capital will be equal to both the full marginal cost of debt and the full marginal cost of equity. It can therefore be employed for valuation purposes at the margin. This will, in fact, provide a potential linkage with the results of the general equilibrium-theoretic analysis. But it follows from the full set of optimum conditions that this is admissible only when the firm has chosen its mutually determined optimum levels of output, factor usages, asset investments, and financing sources. The reasons for this will be clarified in the following argument.

Consider the following notation: V, π, and ρ refer, as before, to the market value, profits, and capitalization rate applicable to the owners' equity, and D, F, and r refer to the market value, interest earnings, and market yield (average rate of interest) on the debt capital of the firm. In the planning model of the firm with which we are working, the market value and the book value of the debt will be equal. This is because we are supposing that following any change in the amount of debt, or in the average rate of interest on the debt, all of the firm's previously existing debt, as in the foregoing numerical illustration, is refinanced at the new rate of interest. Finally, W and O refer to the total capitalized value, W, of the net operating income of the firm, O, and the relationship O/W will provide a measure of i, the effective rate of capitalization at which the total earnings of the firm are being valued in W. The total value of W, moreover, will be equal to the sum of D and V.

These definitions imply the following relations.

$$V = \pi/\rho \qquad \pi = \rho V \tag{8.6}$$

$$D = F/r \qquad F = rD \tag{8.7}$$

$$W = O/i \qquad O = iW \tag{8.8}$$

If, at any planning point, a set of security values and income statement items are observed and described as in the foregoing list, the following definitional statements can be made.

$$i = \frac{O}{W} = \frac{F + \pi}{W} \tag{8.9}$$

whence

$$i = \frac{rD}{W} + \frac{\rho V}{W} \tag{8.10}$$

From Equation (8.10), the overall capitalization rate, i, which may now be referred to as the average cost of capital, is seen to be a weighted average of the costs of debt and equity capital, r and ρ, respectively. Each such capital cost is weighted by the relative importance of the corresponding capital in the total market value of the firm's securities.

In the optimization model, the debt and equity capital costs were assumed to be functionally related to the amounts of debt and equity capital measured at book values (as book values represent the decision variables confronting the firm[1]). Equation (8.10) may therefore be written as

$$i = r(K, D)\frac{D}{W} + \rho(K, D)\frac{V}{W} \tag{8.11}$$

We are interested now in the combination of debt and equity capital at work in the firm, D and K, that will afford the minimum attainable value of i when the firm is at its optimum capital usage point. We accordingly differentiate Equation (8.11) partially with respect to D and K, setting the partial derivatives equal to zero, and noting that $W = D + V$. We note also that because we are investigating these relationships at the optimum planning point, we are at the situation at which, as seen in Equation (4.51), dV/dK is equal to unity. Employing this fact, $\partial W/\partial K$ may be replaced in what follows by $\partial W/\partial V$. Differentiation of Equation (8.11) yields

$$\frac{\partial i}{\partial D} = \frac{D}{W}\frac{\partial r}{\partial D} + r\left[\frac{W - D}{W^2}\right] + \frac{V}{W}\frac{\partial \rho}{\partial D} - \rho\frac{V}{W^2} = 0 \tag{8.12}$$

[1] An additional reason for using book values rather than market values as functional arguments is that the use of market values introduces a bias due to the fact that they reflect business risk (on which we shall comment further later) as well as financial risk. This implies that market values may vary, quite independently of financial risks, in reaction to changes in business risk, as the latter induces changes in the debt and equity required rates of return or capitalization rates. See Barges (1963), Turnovsky (1970, p. 1065), and Herendeen (1975, p. 125).

$$\frac{\partial i}{\partial K} = \frac{D}{W} \frac{\partial r}{\partial K} - r \frac{D}{W^2} + \frac{V}{W} \frac{\partial \rho}{\partial K} + \rho \left[\frac{W-V}{W^2} \right] = 0 \tag{8.13}$$

Multiplying Equation (8.12) by W and rearranging yields

$$r + D \frac{\partial r}{\partial D} + V \frac{\partial \rho}{\partial D} = r \frac{D}{W} + \rho \frac{V}{W} \tag{8.14}$$

Similarly, Equation (8.13) yields

$$\rho + D \frac{\partial r}{\partial K} + V \frac{\partial \rho}{\partial K} = r \frac{D}{W} + \rho \frac{V}{W} \tag{8.15}$$

Equations (8.14) and (8.15) together imply that when full optimization conditions are satisfied, the full marginal cost of borrowing and the full marginal cost of equity are both equal to the weighted average cost of capital.

It is instructive to compare the results in Equations (8.14) and (8.15) with Equations (4.47) and (4.48). Combining the equations, it follows that

$$r < \rho\lambda = i < \rho \tag{8.16}$$

The relationships we previously hypothesized as relevant to the optimum structure of the firm continue to hold. The average rate of interest on the debt is less than the weighted average cost of capital (which, at the structural optimum, is equal to the full marginal cost of relaxing the money capital availability constraint), and this is in turn less than the cost of equity capital. Moreover, it follows from Equation (8.16) that

$$\lambda = \frac{i}{\rho} < 1 \tag{8.17}$$

a result corresponding to that reached in Equation (4.48).

The question of business risk

We have defined business risk in terms of the degree of instability in the firm's net operating income. It might be measured by the standard deviation of the probability distribution of that operating income, or, to establish a "risk class" of firms of different size, by the coefficient of variation of that distribution (see Modigliani and Miller, 1958). If the firm did not employ any debt capital, all of the net operating income would become the property of the equity holders, and the measure of business risk would in that case be synonymous with the comparable dispersion parameter of the distribution of equity earnings, or, in some formulations, earnings per share of common stock. But in the presence of debt financing the concept of business risk must be referred consistently to the operating income. That, as we have noted, provides an indication of the income-generating ability of the total asset investment at work in the firm, irrespective of how that investment has been financed.[2]

We may assume that both the suppliers of debt capital and the residual equity holders are risk averse and that the respective cost of money capital functions contain business and financial risk arguments in the following general form[3]:

$$r = r(\theta, \theta L) \qquad r_1 > 0, r_2 > 0 \tag{8.18}$$

$$\rho = \rho(\theta, \theta L) \qquad \rho_1 > 0, \rho_2 > 0 \tag{8.19}$$

Equation (8.18) states that the rate of interest on debt capital depends directly on the business risk, here referred to as θ, and that it is directly related also to the debt-to-equity, or financial leverage, ratio, here described as $L = D/K$. Not only does the interest cost increase with financial leverage, however, but also its positive response to that variable increases with the degree of business risk. Notationally, r_1 on the right-hand side of Equation (8.18) refers to the partial derivative of the interest cost function with respect to the first variable in the function. Similarly, r_2 refers to the partial derivative with respect to the second variable. Comparable notation is employed in conjunction with the equity cost function in Equation (8.19). The equity cost function may be interpreted in terms analogous to those implicit in the specification of the cost of debt capital.

If money capital is invested in the firm in such a way as to increase the degree of business risk, both the interest rate on debt capital and the equity owners' required rate of return can be expected to increase. The investment, therefore, must generate an income stream that is somewhat larger than that necessary to pay simply the interest cost of the marginal debt capital that might have been used in the financing. We saw earlier in this chapter that in order to specify the full marginal cost of debt, account needed to be taken of (i) the additional earnings necessary to provide for the incremental interest costs when previously existing debt has to be refinanced at a new higher interest rate (this was specified as $D \, \partial r/\partial D$) and (ii) the further additional earnings necessary to increase the residual equity owners' income sufficiently to offset any tendency for their economic position to be diluted; this was specified as $V \, \partial \rho/\partial D$. Similarly, we now have to bear in mind the impact on

[2] See Turnovsky (1970), where business risk is defined in terms of the variability of the net equity earnings even when those earnings reflect a deduction for interest payments on debt capital and even though, as a result, the variability of the residual equity earnings will in that case reflect instabilities due to financial risk as well as business risk. Turnovsky's paper is an important discussion of the issues raised by the original Vickers model and it throws significant light on some of the comparative static properties of the argument.

[3] This form is suggested by Turnovsky (1970), though, as indicated, the business risk argument here refers to the dispersion of the net operating income of the firm, not the residual equity income as Turnovsky envisages.

the firm's internal required rate of return on investment in income-generating assets due to the influence of $\partial r/\partial \theta$ and $\partial \rho/\partial \theta$.

Moreover, not only will the incidence of business risk change the money capital costs in the manner we have just observed but also it opens up a possible relation between the degree of business risk and the degree of financial leverage, or the optimum financing mix, in the firm. Firms that confront a high degree of business risk and employ a high degree of operational leverage may be reluctant to increase the residual owners' risk further by adding to that operational leverage a significant degree of financial leverage.

Modigliani–Miller hypotheses: weighted average cost of capital revisited

We have observed that the firm's weighted average cost of capital is usable as an investment decision criterion only when the firm has been brought to an optimum structural position. It is not valid or reliable at infra-optimum planning stages. But the weighted average concept has gained wide currency in the finance literature and in business practice. This has been due in large part to the seminal arguments of Modigliani and Miller, who have demonstrated that *under well-specified assumptions* and for a specified risk class of firms the weighted average cost of capital is invariant with respect to the firm's financing mix. If, of course, such an average cost of money capital is invariant, its marginal value is equal to the average value, and it is thereby established as a valid decision criterion. The traditional theory of finance, on the other hand, argues that the assumptions necessary to establish the Modigliani–Miller invariance cannot be expected to hold in fact, and an alternative construction of the money capital cost theory is presented.

For purposes of the following analysis, recall the definitions contained in Equations (8.6)–(8.8). From these definitions, the weighted average cost of capital was derived in Equation (8.10). The notional capitalization rate defined there as i, the effective rate at which the total income stream of the firm is capitalized in the total market value of the firm's capital securities, is not an observable variable in the financial asset or money capital market. The data that *are* observable are the r and the ρ capitalization rates, depending on market asset values and implicit required rates of return in the debt and equity sectors of the money capital market. Consider the equity capitalization rate, ρ:

$$\rho = \frac{\pi}{V} = \frac{O - F}{V} = \frac{i(D+V)}{V} - \frac{rD}{V} \tag{8.20}$$

From this it follows that

$$\rho = i + (i - r)D/V \tag{8.21}$$

This appears to present us with the proposition that the equity capitalization rate is a linear function of the debt-to-equity financing ratio, D/V, in the firm. In fact, Equations (8.10) and (8.21) contain the two principal propositions in capital financing theory that were presented in the celebrated Modigliani and Miller paper and have become the source of a very extensive debate.[4] But care must be taken in the interpretation of the average capital cost and the equity capitalization rate formulas derived in these equations. These expressions are merely *definitional statements* implicit in the structure of things observable *at a given moment in time*. They do not, as they stand, provide a *theory* of the cost of capital or of the owners' required rate of return. To move from the definitional propositions to a theory of money capital costs, it is necessary to introduce a set of behavior postulates to describe the ways in which participants in the financial markets actually behave in conditions of change. Or we may put this important point in other terms. So far as the Modigliani–Miller theorems specify conclusions similar to those in our definitional Equations (8.10) and (8.21), they are, in their framework of analysis, deduced as equilibrium conditions; and when equilibrium conditions are satisfied, no further change or movement with the objective of improving one's economic position is possible.

We must therefore avoid any statement about the manner in which a firm may be able to *move along* the apparent functional relation described, for example, in Equation (8.21). The equation serves only to identify the relation that would exist *if conditions of equilibrium in the financial asset market were also assumed to exist*. If we can assume that *perfect markets* exist, that no transactions costs or taxes are incurred, and that both firms and individuals can borrow at an externally given market rate of interest, the following argument regarding a *possible* market equilibrating activity can be posited.[5]

---

[4] Modigliani and Miller (1958). See also, for an early but highly valuable summary of the debate, Robichek and Myers (1965) and, for an up-to-date view, Brealey and Myers (1984, p. 357f., and references cited there, especially Durand, 1952; Hamada, 1969; and Fama, 1978). The paper by Hamada, which we shall refer to again below, demonstrates the consistency between the Modigliani–Miller propositions and the results of the financial asset market theory that we examined in Chapter 7.

[5] The assumptions invoked in this sentence should be carefully noted, as the violation of any one or more of them will be sufficient to invalidate the Modigliani–Miller equilibrium conclusions that will be deduced in what follows in the text. For a discussion of transactions costs and market imperfections, see Baumol and Malkiel (1967). See also the highly insightful discussion of the Modigliani–Miller theorem in Nickell (1978, Ch. 8), where a U-shaped average cost of capital curve is derived similar to that described in Figure 8.2 below (Nickell, 1978, p. 177). Moreover, Nickell demonstrates the contribution to the shape of this cost of capital curve made by the risk of bankruptcy, an issue we have not examined. As to the general perspective we have adopted on the money capital markets, Nickell observes that "the assumption of 'perfection' for a capital market in a world of uncertainty is clearly liable to lead to absurdity. . . . Capital markets are inherently imperfect and . . . these imperfections are nontrivial in their effects" (p. 167). The upshot of Nickell's analysis is to confirm the fundamental proposition we examined in a preliminary fashion in Chapter 4 and to which we shall return in Part III,

166   **II The neoclassical tradition**

Table 8.2

	Firm *A*	Firm *B*
Total assets	$10,000	$10,000
Internal rate of return	10%	10%
Net operating income	1,000	1,000
Market value of equity	10,000	6,000
Market value of debt	—	5,000
Total market value of firm's securities	10,000	11,000

Let it be supposed that two firms, *A* and *B*, of the same size and operating in the same industry in the same economic environment both earn the same rate of return on the total capital invested and that they both exhibit the same degree of risk in their operating income streams. They differ only in the financing mix they have adopted. We shall suppose that firm *A* has financed its asset investments completely from equity capital sources and that firm *B* has financed 50 percent of its requirements by means of debt capital. We shall assume that for both firms the internal rate of return on capital employed, or the ratio of the net operating income to the book value of the assets, is 10 percent. Finally, both the firm and its security holders can borrow at 4 percent, the total value of the assets is $10,000, and no account is taken for the present of either corporate or personal taxes.

Our objective is to demonstrate that on the assumption of a smoothly functioning investor arbitrage mechanism in an assumedly perfect capital asset market, the total market value of the securities of the levered firm *B* cannot diverge permanently from the total market value of the unlevered firm *A*. If it is possible to substantiate the claim that the total market values of the respective firms' securities, *W*, must be equal, then for a given total income stream, *O*, the ratio of *O/W* must be the same for both firms. The weighted average cost of capital for both firms, or $i = O/W$, will then also be equal. It would be able to be said, then, that the weighted average cost of capital to the firm is invariant with respect to its financing mix.

Suppose that a "temporarily anomalous" situation exists in the financial asset market and that the securities of the levered firm *B* are overvalued relative to those of firm *A*. In that event a supposed arbitrage mechanism would correct the anomaly and restore the equality of market values.

Table 8.2 indicates the sense in which firm *B* is assumed to be overvalued.

namely, "the (firm's) financing decision and the investment decision are interdependent" (p. 178).

Table 8.3 *Investor alternative income positions*

	Income from 10 percent ownership	
	Firm *A*	Firm *B*
Firm net operating income	$1,000	$1,000
Less debt interest at 4%	—	200
Residual equity income	1,000	800
of which 10% equity income =	100	80
Less interest on personal debt	16	—
Net portfolio income	84	80

Because of the anomalously high market value of its equity, the total market value of the firm, $11,000, is greater than the comparable unlevered firm's value of $10,000. Let us imagine that an owner of 10 percent of the common stock of the relatively overvalued firm *B* can sell his shares and purchase a 10 percent ownership of the relatively undervalued unlevered firm *A*, or, that is, that he can "arbitrage" in the firms' common stock securities. Given that such an investor will obtain $600 from the sale of his 10 percent ownership in firm *B* and that he requires $1,000 to acquire the contemplated 10 percent ownership of firm *A*, he will need to borrow the difference of $400 on his personal account, conceivably against the collateral security of the equity stock of firm *A* that he is about to acquire. Such borrowing, it has already been assumed, can be made at the same rate of interest as that at which debt capital is available to the firms. Consider, then, the income accruing to the investor from his alternative positions (Table 8.3).

Table 8.3 indicates that by selling his 10 percent ownership of the levered firm *B* and purchasing a corresponding proportionate ownership of the unlevered firm *A*, the investor can increase his income prospects from $80 to $84. But as the market arbitrage proceeds, the selling pressure can be expected to reduce the market value of the firm *B* security, and the corresponding buying pressure will increase the value of firm *A*. The motivation for arbitrage will disappear when the divergence of market values between firm *A* and firm *B* has been eliminated, and a common market value will then have established an equality of average capital costs. The operating income stream, *O*, being given for the two firms, and the *W*'s having been brought into equality, the $i = O/W$ must be the same for each of the firms.

A good many reasons can be adduced why things may not work out as smoothly as we have just supposed. Doubts may be expressed as to the ability of individuals and firms to borrow on comparable terms, or as to whether the investor, by thus substituting "home-made leverage" in his personal portfolio for what was previously a levered position by reason of the financial leverage in firm B's capital structure, has in fact maintained a strictly comparable risk exposure. The assumption of zero transactions costs and the assumed absence of corporate and capital gains taxes could also be questioned.

But leaving these details aside, we can note two aspects of the argument that give it a kinship with the static equilibrium asset pricing theory presented in Chapter 7. These have to do with the assumption of an exogenously given and fixed market rate of interest and that of perfect financial market conditions. Additionally, if all firms in a given "risk class" exhibited the same average cost of capital, $i,$ this would provide an empirical vindication of the analytical proposition that the financing cost is invariant with respect to the financing mix. A basis would thereby be provided for a reliance on the posited linear form of the equity cost function described in Equation (8.21).

We take note at this point of the methodological difference between the foregoing and the so-called traditional way of looking at things. The latter, as we observed at the beginning of this chapter, takes a *partial* equilibrium approach under assumptions of conceivably *imperfect* markets rather than a *general* equilibrium approach under assumptions of *perfect* capital markets. We recall the two definitional equations in terms of which we are conducting the argument:

$$i = r\frac{D}{W} + \rho\frac{V}{W} \tag{8.22}$$

and

$$\rho = i + (i - r)\frac{D}{V} \tag{8.23}$$

It may be claimed that the cost of equity capital described in Equation (8.23) is what it is because the weighted average cost of capital, $i,$ as defined in Equation (8.22), is constant. But it might be said, on the contrary, that the empirically observable equity and debt costs provide the basis *from* which deduction about capital costs can proceed and that the average cost function is the conclusion *to* which we argue. Then the cost of a firm's debt capital will be whatever it is observed to be by virtue of the supply and demand conditions in the debt capital sector of the money capital market, taking account of the degree of risk aversion in the attitudes of the suppliers of debt capital funds. Similarly, the cost of equity capital will reflect conditions in the equity capital sector of the money capital market.

The differences of viewpoint can be illustrated by the functional relations depicted in Figures 8.1 and 8.2.

Figure 8.1 depicts the essence of what has become known as the "net

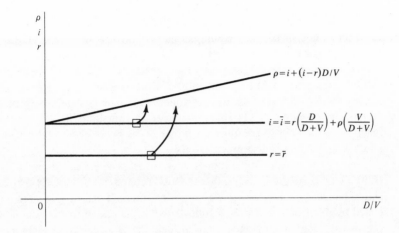

Figure 8.1

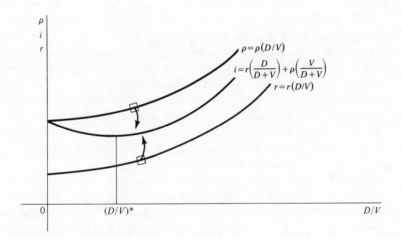

Figure 8.2

operating income theory'' of the firm's capital structure and money capital costs. It is also referred to as the ''economic entity theory,'' and it reflects the Modigliani–Miller analysis. The theory states that the value of the firm, meaning by that the total market value of the firm's capital securities, is equal to the total net operating income stream capitalized at a capitalization rate equal to the weighted average cost of capital. It is defined by W in the preceding derivation, where $W = O/i$. As we have seen, for a given income stream, O, and a constant capitalization rate or weighted average cost of capital, i, the economic value of the firm is uniquely determined as W. The capitalization rate, i, is constant for a given firm, or risk class of firms, independent of the degree of financial leverage in the capital structure. In Figure 8.1, the financial leverage ratio, defined as the ratio of debt to equity capital measured at market values, is shown on the horizontal axis. The cost of equity capital, derived in Equation (8.21) and reproduced in Equation (8.23), is a linear function of the debt-to-equity ratio, provided, as is assumed, that the rate of interest on the debt is also given and fixed.

This way of looking at the money capital cost problem has been called the entity theory because it argues that the total economic value of the firm as an entity depends, in the manner we have seen, on the total income stream generated by the firm as a whole. It follows that if the rate of interest on the debt is given at r, and the market value of the debt therefore equals the debt interest payments capitalized at the rate of r percent, the value of the equity is simply the difference between the total entity value, W, and the value of the debt, D. On one view, the value of the equity is a residual derived from the relation $V = W - D$. On another view, the cost of equity capital is a derived residual. For given the value of i, the weighted average cost, and r, the cost of debt, the value of ρ is deduced in the manner of the preceding analysis. This direction of relationship or causation has been indicated in Figure 8.1 by the arrows, which are intended to depict the initial statements or suppositions *from* which the causation proceeds and the conclusion *to* which it leads. It should be borne in mind in evaluating this line of approach that the analytical postulate of the constancy of the overall capitalization rate, i, has been vindicated, assumedly, by the empirical demonstration of the market arbitrage mechanism that we discussed earlier in this chapter.

Figure 8.2 presents the alternative approach to the money capital cost and capital structure problem. It is frequently referred to as the "traditional theory." The theory assumes, as shown in the debt cost function in the figure, that the rate of interest on debt will be determined by the market conditions in the debt capital sector of the money capital market. It is shown in the figure as an increasing function of the financial leverage ratio, and unlike the entity theory, it sees no reason to assume that the interest rate on the debt will be constant.

Similarly, the cost of equity capital is depicted in Figure 8.2 as depending on conditions in the equity capital sector of the money capital market and is shown as an increasing function of the financial leverage ratio. No necessary, or a priori, form can be prescribed for this function, which, like the debt cost function, is here an approximation to the fuller specification that takes account of the business as well as the financial risks in the firm. Moreover, the form of the equity cost function will depend on the degree of risk aversion inherent in the attitudes of the suppliers of equity capital funds. If it is argued that both the debt cost and the equity cost are determined by money capital market conditions, it follows that the weighted average cost of capital will be, in fact, the weighted average of these separately determined debt and equity costs. Again the arrows in Figure 8.2 are designed to indicate the initial statements or conditions *from* which the relationship proceeds and the conclusion *to* which it leads.

While, on one view, then, this approach argues from the debt and equity capital costs to the weighted average cost of capital, on another view it argues from the observation of the market value of the debt, D, and the market value of the equity, V, to the total market value of the firm's securities, W. Against the entity theory's $V = W - D$, we can therefore set the traditional theory's $W = D + V$.

Adjustment for the firm's tax liability

In an earlier section of this chapter an adjustment was made to the firm's constrained objective function to acknowledge the effect of the liability to taxation on residual net income. The entity theory accomplishes an adjustment for taxes in the following manner. Using established notation, the tax deductibility of interest on debt capital implies that

$$\pi = (O - F)(1 - t) \tag{8.24}$$

and the total after-tax earnings generated for the security holders becomes

$$\begin{aligned} \pi + F &= (O - F)(1 - t) + F \\ &= O(1 - t) + tF \end{aligned} \tag{8.25}$$

Substituting $F = rD$ from Equation (8.7), and defining W_L as the total market value of the securities of the levered firm and $L = D/W_L$ as the degree of financial leverage in the firm's capital structure, the total market value, W_L, is obtainable by capitalizing the total net earnings of the security holders as shown in Equation (8.25). The entity theory at this point argues that the portion of that earnings stream defined as $O(1 - t)$, or what would be the net after-tax earnings if no debt capital were employed, should be capitalized at a capitalization rate applicable to an all-equity firm, or at an equity rate of ρ that would in that case be the same as i, the average cost of capital. The remaining portion of the total income stream in Equation (8.25), it is argued, should be capitalized at the rate of interest actually being paid on the debt. Making these substitutions, the value of the firm is definable as

$$W_L = \frac{O(1 - t)}{i} + tW_L L \tag{8.26}$$

Equation (8.26) permits the derivation of the average cost of capital of the levered firm, i^*, after taking account of the tax effect. Rearrangement of the equation leads to

$$i(1 - tL) = \frac{O(1 - t)}{W_L} = i^* \qquad (8.27)$$

The tax adjustment thus effectively reduces the cost of capital to the firm (see Bierman and Hass, 1973, p. 170, note 7, for an alternative view of this tax adjustment effect). By virtue of the tax deductibility of interest payments on the firm's debt capital, the total market value of a levered firm will, on the given assumptions of an arbitrage activity in perfect financial markets, exceed the market value of a comparable unlevered firm by tW_LL, representing the present capitalized value of the annual tax saving realized by the firm.

Entity theory of the firm's capital structure and the equilibrium theory of financial asset markets

In the foregoing analysis a number of references have been made to financial asset market equilibrium. It should be no surprise that the results of the Modigliani–Miller entity theory can be demonstrated to be consistent with the general equilibrium conditions of the financial asset market theory developed in Chapter 7. A close kinship is established by the assumptions of perfect financial markets and an externally given market rate of interest. The principal result of the financial asset pricing model can, in fact, be transformed into the equity cost function in Equation (8.23). But this, of course, confirms that this widely espoused functional description of the cost of equity capital is subject to the same criticisms and reservations as the equilibrium asset market theory from which it can be derived (see Hamada, 1969; Haley and Schall, 1973, Chs. 7, 8, to which the following argument is indebted).

In the following development, we assume again that firm A is completely equity financed with a market value of V_A, and the expected rate of return on its equity ownership is

$$E(R_A) = E(X_A)/V_A \qquad (8.28)$$

In this expression X_A refers to the annual stream of benefits resulting from holding the shares of common stock, here interpreted as a random variable.

In the case of the levered firm B, which is otherwise comparable with A, its borrowing will be assumed to take place at a given rate of interest R_F. Referring to its debt outstanding as D_B and ignoring the firm's liability to taxes, the expected rate of return on the equity is

$$E(R_B) = \frac{E(X_A) - R_F D_B}{V_B} \qquad (8.29)$$

We recall the principal result of the equilibrium theory of financial asset prices, stated in Equation (7.23) as

$$E(R_j) = R_F + [E(R_M) - R_F] \frac{\text{Cov}(R_j, R_M)}{\sigma^2(R_M)} \qquad (8.30)$$

We now let $\mu = [E(R_M) - R_F]/\text{Var}(R_M)$, and rewrite Equation (8.30) in the form

$$E(R_j) = R_F + \mu \, \text{Cov}(R_j, R_M) \qquad (8.31)$$

Expressing Equations (8.28) and (8.29) in corresponding notation and making use of Equation (8.31) yields

$$\frac{E(X_A)}{V_A} = R_F + \mu \, \text{Cov}(R_A, R_M) \qquad (8.32)$$

and

$$\frac{E(X_A) - R_F D_B}{V_B} = R_F + \mu \, \text{Cov}(R_B, R_M) \qquad (8.33)$$

In Equations (8.32) and (8.33), the final terms on the right-hand sides may be written in the following equivalent forms:

$$\text{Cov}(R_A, R_M) = \text{Cov}\left[\frac{X_A}{V_A}, R_M\right] \qquad (8.34)$$

$$= \frac{1}{V_A} \text{Cov}(X_A, R_M)$$

and

$$\text{Cov}(R_B, R_M) = \text{Cov}\left[\frac{X_A - R_F D_B}{V_B}, R_M\right]$$

$$= \frac{1}{V_B} \text{Cov}(X_A, R_M) \qquad (8.35)$$

Substituting these equivalences into Equations (8.32) and (8.33) provides

$$E(R_A) = R_F + \frac{\mu}{V_A} \text{Cov}(X_A, R_M) \qquad (8.36)$$

and

$$E(R_B) = R_F + \frac{\mu}{V_B} \text{Cov}(X_A, R_M) \qquad (8.37)$$

It is known from previous development that the rate of return on the levered equity shares of firm B can be expected to exceed the rate of return on the unlevered equity shares of firm A. We therefore subtract $E(R_A)$ from $E(R_B)$, or Equation (8.36) from (8.37), to yield

$$E(R_B) - E(R_A) = \mu \operatorname{Cov}(X_A, R_M) \frac{V_A - V_B}{V_A V_B} \tag{8.38}$$

If, now, Equations (8.32) and (8.33) are solved for $E(X_A)$ and the results equated, it follows that

$$V_A[R_F + \mu \operatorname{Cov}(R_A, R_M)] = V_B \left[\mu \operatorname{Cov}(R_B, R_M) + R_F \frac{V_B + D_B}{V_B} \right] \tag{8.39}$$

In this expression, we can substitute the equivalences in Equations (8.34) and (8.35) to provide

$$V_A \left[R_F + \frac{\mu}{V_A} \operatorname{Cov}(X_A, R_M) \right] = V_B \left[\frac{\mu}{V_B} \operatorname{Cov}(X_A, R_M) + R_F \frac{V_B + D_B}{V_B} \right] \tag{8.40}$$

From Equation (8.40), it follows that

$$V_A R_F = V_B R_F + D_B R_F \tag{8.41}$$

which implies that

$$V_A = V_B + D_B \tag{8.42}$$

The significant result in Equation (8.42) states a principal conclusion of the asset pricing model from which it has been derived. It is that *when the full equilibrium conditions are satisfied,* the total market value of the levered firm B, shown as the sum of the market values of its equity and debt capital on the right-hand side of Equation (8.42), will be equal to the market value of a comparable unlevered firm, as shown on the left-hand side of the equation. This is the same result as was established previously under the assumptions of a smoothly functioning arbitrage mechanism in a perfect financial market. The total market values of comparable levered and unlevered firms, according to this vision, must be equal and invariant with respect to their financing mix.

Making use of this result, Equation (8.38) implies that

$$E(R_B) - E(R_A) = \mu \operatorname{Cov}(X_A, R_M) \frac{D_B}{V_A V_B} \tag{8.43}$$

Inspection of Equation (8.36) indicates that *in the generalized equilibrium the asset market model has in view,*

$$\mu \operatorname{Cov}(X_A, R_M) = [E(R_A) - R_F]V_A \tag{8.44}$$

and Equation (8.44) may then be substituted into Equation (8.43) to yield

$$E(R_B) - E(R_A) = [E(R_A) - R_F] \frac{D_B}{V_B} \tag{8.45}$$

Rearranged, Equation (8.45) provides

$$E(R_B) = E(R_A) + [E(R_A) - R_F] \frac{D_B}{V_B} \tag{8.46}$$

The conclusion in Equation (8.46) states that *in full general equilibrium conditions* the rate of return on the levered firm's equity will be equal to that on the unlevered firm's equity plus a risk premium. This risk premium is equal to the market's risk premium on the unlevered firm's equity $[E(R_A) - R_F]$ multiplied by the financial leverage ratio in the levered firm. This statement can be compared with the previous conclusion derived from the Modigliani–Miller entity theory of capital costs and stated in Equation (8.23). It is reproduced for convenience of comparison:

$$\rho = i + (i - r)D/V \tag{8.47}$$

By comparing Equations (8.46) and (8.47), it is seen that both bodies of analysis lead to the same conclusion. The equilibrium-theoretic analysis of a perfect money capital market provides the same result for the cost of equity capital as the entity theory of money capital costs under the assumption in the latter theory of a freely functioning market arbitrage mechanism.

Growth of the firm and the cost of equity capital

The value of a share of common stock has been defined up to this point as the present discounted value, or the present capitalized value, of the future expected earnings accruing to the owner of the stock. In our optimization model, the value of the equity has been stated as $V = \pi/\rho$, where π refers to the residual income accruing to the owners and ρ describes the owner's required rate of return or capitalization rate.

This analysis, however, has been cast for the main part in a static mold. The different approaches to the money capital and valuation problem that we have discussed have also been developed from the same static perspective. We did observe, in the introductory discussion of the firm's economic position and performance statements in Chapter 2, that not all of the residual earnings of the firm may actually be paid to the owners in the form of dividends. Part may be retained and reinvested in the firm, and the market value of the ownership stock may increase as a result, as the future prospective income stream rises and reflects the earnings on the reinvested capital.

The valuation formula we have used may be accommodated to the possibility of the growth of the firm that results from such reinvestment. Let us first restate the economic value of a share of common stock as the present discounted value of the future stream of cash flow benefits that the owner of the stock expects to receive. The value of a share of stock may be defined as

$$P_0 = \frac{D_1}{1+k} + \frac{D_2}{(1+k)^2} + \frac{D_3}{(1+k)^3} + \cdots \tag{8.48}$$

where the series of terms in the summation extends to infinity. Each term in the series in Equation (8.48) expresses the present discounted value of a dividend payment, where D_t describes the dividend to be received in year t. The value of the share of stock can be stated alternatively as

$$P_0 = \sum_{t=1}^{\infty} \frac{D_t}{(1+k)^t} \tag{8.49}$$

or, when time is taken as a continuous variable,

$$P_0 = \int_0^{\infty} D_t e^{-kt} \, dt \tag{8.50}$$

If the dividend remains constant each year, integration of Equation (8.50) yields the result

$$P_0 = D/k \tag{8.51}$$

and by transposition it follows that the required rate of return on the stock, k, is equal to the dividend yield, or

$$k = D/P_0 \tag{8.52}$$

This formulation for k can be regarded as the firm's cost of equity capital in the static nongrowth case.

If, however, earnings are retained and reinvested, it is necessary to make an assumption, for valuation purposes, regarding the rate of growth of earnings that can be expected in the future. Let us assume, therefore, that the firm expects a growth rate of g percent per annum. If we assume also a constant dividend or payout ratio, the dividends will also grow at g percent per annum. Then, taking D_0 to represent the current or most recent dividend, the dividend expected in year t in the future will be describable as

$$D_t = D_0(1+g)^t \tag{8.53}$$

if discontinuous growth is assumed, or

$$D_t = D_0 e^{gt} \tag{8.54}$$

under assumptions of continuous growth.

The present discounted value of the dividend stream then follows as

$$P_0 = \sum_{t=1}^{\infty} \frac{D_0(1+g)^t}{(1+k)^t} \tag{8.55}$$

or, under assumptions of continuous growth and discounting, as

$$P_0 = \int_0^\infty D_0 e^{gt} e^{-kt} \, dt$$

$$= \int_0^\infty D_0 e^{-(k-g)t} \, dt \tag{8.56}$$

Integration of Equation (8.56) provides the value of the share of stock under the specified growth rate asumptions:

$$P_0 = \frac{D_0}{k-g} \tag{8.57}$$

It follows by transposition of Equation (8.57) that the required rate of return, or the cost of equity capital, can be specified as

$$k = D_0/P_0 + g \tag{8.58}$$

The cost of equity is now equal to the dividend yield on the common stock plus the assumed growth rate.[6]

Variable growth rates and the cost of equity capital

It is unlikely, however, that a firm's earnings and dividends will grow at a constant rate forever. A firm may expect a supernormal growth rate of g_s to be realized for, say, n years into the future, but after that the growth rate will fall to a normal rate of g_n. Again we can determine the value of the share of common stock by taking the present discounted value of the expected stream of dividends. But now it is necessary to proceed in two stages. First, the present value of the first n years' dividends may be stated in the familiar way as

$$PV_0 = \sum_{t=1}^{n} \frac{D_0(1+g_s)^t}{(1+k)^t} \tag{8.59}$$

To this must be added the present discounted value of the dividends that are expected to be received subsequent to year n. These can be discounted back to the year n by applying the same valuation principle:

$$PV_n = \sum_{t=1}^{\infty} \frac{D_n(1+g_n)^t}{(1+k)^t} \tag{8.60}$$

This expression will be recognized, however, as a perpetual dividend stream commencing at the beginning of year $n+1$. Applying the formula for a perpetual growth stream derived in Equation (8.57), the valuation element in Equation (8.60) can be expressed as

---

[6] The analysis of growth stock valuation was first developed by Williams (1965 [1938]) and rediscovered by Gordon and Shapiro (1956). The model presented in the text has become widely known as the Gordon model (see also Gordon, 1962, Ch. 4, and Vickers, 1966).

$$PV_n = \frac{D_n}{k - g_n} \tag{8.61}$$

Equation (8.61) provides the present value *at year* n of the stream of dividends that is expected to be received subsequent to that date. In order to obtain the present value *now* of that stream, the value at year n, PV_n in the equation, must be further multiplied by the factor $1/(1+k)^n$.

Bringing these elements together, the value of the share of stock under the variable growth rate conditions assumed can be written as

$$P_0 = \sum_{t=1}^{n} \frac{D_0(1+g_s)^t}{(1+k)^t} + \frac{D_n}{k - g_n} \frac{1}{(1+k)^n} \tag{8.62}$$

The required rate of return on the firm's equity can be estimated as the solution value of the discount factor, k, in Equation (8.62) that equates the right-hand side with the present value, P_0, or the current market price at which the share of stock can be acquired. In principle, any number of variations of growth rates could be assumed in this way, and an implicit discount factor could be calculated to provide an indication of the firm's cost of equity capital.

Comparison of equity capital costs

From the various perspectives and the controversies related to the firm's cost of equity capital, we can summarize the following five points of view or alternative definitions. In each case, the symbol k is intended to refer to the cost of equity capital.

i. Nongrowth firm (ignoring the implicit debt cost effect) — $k = D/P$ [Equation (8.52)]

ii. Dividend growth at an assumed constant rate — $k = D_0/P_0 + g$ [Equation (8.58)]

iii. Dividend growth at assumed variable rates — $k =$ solution value in Equation (8.62)

iv. Equity capital required rate of return implied by the financial asset market equilibrium theory — $k = i + (i - r)D/V$ [Equations (8.23) and (8.47)]

v. Full marginal cost of relaxing the money capital availability constraint — $k = \rho + D\dfrac{\partial r}{\partial K} + V\dfrac{\partial \rho}{\partial K}$ [Equations (4.46) and (4.47)]

It should be noted that the equity capital costs specified in Equations (i), (iv), and (v) make no allowance for growth, whereas those in Equations (i), (ii), and (iii) make no allowance for risk or uncertainty. For purposes of judging the economic worthwhileness of a proposed investment expenditure, the firm would be advised to estimate the cost of capital from more than one approach or set of assumptions in order to envisage a range within which the cost might fall.

CHAPTER 9

The investment expenditure project

The cost of money capital, understood in one or another of the ways examined in the preceding chapter, serves as a criterion of the economic worthwhileness of investing in the firm. The addition of money capital to the firm, or the retention within it of the money capital that presently exists and may be transferable to other economic uses, may depend, of course, on a number of considerations. Investment may be made in order to protect or increase market shares and in anticipation of economic growth, to effect cost reductions or take advantage of technological change, or to maximize the size of the firm because of the benefits that might thereby accrue to the management. But wisdom dictates, when account is taken of the long-run viability and economic position of the firm, that regard should be paid to the fact that money capital is a scarce resource and that a cost has to be paid for its employment. A balance should be struck between that cost and the economic values or benefits that the employment of money capital can generate.

Investment decision criterion

The basic notations relevant to money capital investment decisions were encountered in Chapter 3. The investment decision requires, in the terms summarized there, that the prospective increment of economic value be no less than the amount of marginal money capital it is proposed to employ. Alternatively, the investment criterion was stated in terms of the anticipated rate of profit, or the internal rate of return, that can be earned on the investment. In those terms, a decision to invest requires that the prospective rate of return should be no less than the cost of the money capital employed.

Much depends, in the investment decision, on the proper formulation of both the prospective cash flow streams and the cost of capital used to ascertain their discounted value or to function in other ways as the decision criterion. In this chapter we shall look briefly at both these issues. But it will not be possible or necessary to take up the large number of technical questions or computational methods that abound in the business finance literature (see, for example, Archer, Choate, and Racette, 1983, Chs. 6–10, and Brealey and Myers, 1984, Chs. 7–12).

180

Relevant cost of capital

Consider the basic valuation Equation (9.1), where S_t refers to the periodic net incremental cash flow attributable to the investment project and m refers to the firm's cost of money capital. The other variables are as defined in Equation (3.7) of Chapter 3, and we ignore for the present the possible liquidation value of the project, J_n, at the end of its economic life:

$$V = \sum_{t=1}^{n} S_t(1+m)^{-t} \tag{9.1}$$

Our task now is to specify the appropriate magnitude of the money capital cost, m, in the equation. We can consider the following possibilities.

First, if the firm is employing only equity or common stock capital, it is concerned only with the cost of equity capital at the margin of capital employment. That money capital cost may be estimated in one of the ways summarized in equations (i), (ii), or (iii) in the concluding section of Chapter 8.

Second, it may be desired, in ways again that we have summarized in Chapter 8, to take more explicit account of the risks involved in money capital investment. Such risks may emanate from the forces that determine the instability in the firm's operating income stream (taking account of operational leverage) or from the manner in which the employment of debt capital induces a prospective instability in the residual equity income stream (taking account of financial leverage). The relevant cost of capital, then, will depend on two different possible analytical perspectives that might be adopted.

First, if an analytical commitment is made to the apparatus of the general equilibrium theory, and if, as a result, it is imagined that the financial asset market reflects, at any time, conditions that closely approximate equilibrium, the cost of the equity portion of the money capital employed by the firm may be defined by the equilibrium required rate of return on the firm's equity capital. This was derived in Equation (7.24) as

$$E(R_j) = R_F + \beta_j[E(R_M) - R_F] \tag{9.2}$$

This describes the rate of return that, at the point of observation and in the assumed asset market equilibrium conditions, investors require in order to induce them to hold the common stock or equity securities of the jth firm. It therefore specifies the rate of return that the firm must be able to generate on its equity capital if new investment and financing is undertaken. Only by doing so will it leave the equity holders as well off as they would be if no such investment and financing were to occur.

If, however, the firm also employed debt capital or had a levered financial structure, it would need to adjust that equity capital cost in order to arrive at the rate of return that must be earned on its marginal investment project. The relevant cost of capital would in that case be approximated by taking a weighted average of the debt and equity capital costs. In doing so, the cost of debt capital would be weighted by the proportion of the total market value of the firm's capital securities accounted for by the debt capital, and the equity capital cost as described in Equation (9.2) would be weighted by the proportion of equity capital in its total capital employed. The rationale for making use of such a weighted average cost of capital under assumed market equilibrium conditions was examined at some length in Chapter 8.

But such a weighted average cost of capital is, as we have said, at best an approximation to the relevant money capital cost involved. Care must be taken to consider whether the risk inherent in the proposed investment project is comparable with the overall risk of the firm into which it is being incorporated. If the risk of the new project is estimated to be the same as that of the existing firm, the existing weighted average cost of capital may be used directly as the relevant capital cost. But if, on the other hand, a more risky project is contemplated, it will be necessary to increase the required rate of return, and thereby the effective cost of capital, to take account of those higher risks. A rigorous adherence to the cost-of-capital concepts implicit in the equilibrium asset theory requires the conclusion that "the true cost of capital depends on the use to which the capital is put" (Brealey and Myers, 1984, p. 165).

We recall at this point the concept, developed at length in Chapter 7 and reproduced in Equation (9.2), of the firm's beta coefficient. The logic of the equilibrium asset market theory requires the firm to estimate the beta coefficient of any contemplated investment project and to define a unique cost of capital for each project. In Equation (9.3), the cost of capital for the ith project is referred to as r_i, the project's beta coefficient as β_i, the expected rate of return on the market security portfolio as $E(R_M)$, in the same manner as in Chapter 7, and the risk-free rate of interest that also entered the development of Chapter 7 is referred to as R_F:

$$r_i = R_F + \beta_i[E(R_M) - R_F] \tag{9.3}$$

In this manner, the asset market equilibrium theory takes account of the risk inherent in any contemplated investment project. Moreover, a further and most important conclusion, from the perspective of that theory, is arrived at from the same direction of argument. This can be observed briefly as follows.

Given that separate project betas can thus be calculated, it can be shown that in a perfect financial asset market, such as is assumed in the equilibrium theory, where extensive opportunities exist for investment portfolio diversification in the manner we have examined, there is no reason why a firm should diversify into different kinds of investment projects. Theoretically, separate investment projects could be established as separate firms, and ownership claims to them could be marketed in the financial asset market. Investors could then make their own diversification by combining such claims in optimum-security portfolios. This conclusion derives from what has become known as the "Value Additivity Principle." This states, in effect, that a firm that holds only the two assets A and B would find that the market value placed on the firm would be precisely the sum of the valuations placed by the market on the assets A and B separately. Values are additive, and the total market value of all such assets must therefore be independent of the firm that legally owns them. Diversification at the level of the firm is accordingly unnecessary and can, indeed, diminish the potential economic welfare of investors by reducing what would otherwise be opportunities for investor portfolio diversification (see Brealey and Myers, 1984, pp. 132–35, 408, 728–30). The logic of this line of argument is that in the last analysis no reason exists for the existence of firms at all. They can, on this view of things, be conceptualized simply as bundles of contracts or legal claims, and in the perfect world of the equilibrium theory the justification for the reality of firms must be found in decidedly nonfinancial reasons.

In our search for the cost of capital that should be used in investment decisions, it might be preferred to view the question from an alternative, or a partial equilibrium, imperfect capital market perspective. In that case, the question arises as to whether, at the point at which the investment decision is being contemplated, the firm can be understood to have been brought to its optimum size and its optimum production and financing structures. If that should be so, then as exhibited in Chapter 8, there is reason to believe that the weighted average cost of capital can again be employed as the investment decision criterion. For the weighted average cost of capital is then equal to both the full marginal cost of debt and the full marginal cost of equity. It is equal, in other words, to the full marginal cost of relaxing the firm's money capital availability constraint.

But a further question of risk remains. It is necessary to adjust the costs of debt and equity capital for an estimate of the ways in which those capital costs will be affected by any change in the overall risk exposure of the firm if the proposed investment is undertaken.

There may be reason to believe, on the other hand, that the firm has not, prior to the new investment and financing, been brought to an optimum structural position. Its money capital cost decision criterion must then be of the kind we examined in Chapter 4 as relevant to such an infra-optimum stage. That capital cost was interpreted as the full marginal cost of relaxing the money capital availability constraint. In Equation (4.47) of Chapter 4, we specified both the full marginal cost of debt and the full marginal cost of equity. The former, for example, was stated as

$$\text{FMCD} = r + D\ \partial r/\partial D + V\ \partial\rho/\partial D \qquad\qquad (9.4)$$

In Chapter 8 also an example was given of how the cost of capital should be adjusted to take account of all of the potential effects on capital costs induced by changes in the financial leverage ratios in the firm's financing structure. Then in Equations (7.38) and (7.39) of Chapter 7 it was observed that a further adjustment of prospective capital costs may need to be made to take account of changes in the so-called business risk of the firm. This latter point was commented on further in Chapter 8.

These observations on the cost of capital, whether they envisage the implications of the general equilibrium asset market theory or the partial equilibrium analysis of the firm, still need to be carefully adjusted to take account of the future possible rate of growth of the firm and the incremental risks that might be entailed. We have given some examples in Chapter 8 of the cost of equity capital for a growth firm, depending on whether growth is anticipated to occur at a constant or a variable rate. In such cases, and assuming again that the firm is understood to be expanding along an optimally structured growth path, a weighted average cost of capital may be calculated by incorporating the appropriate equity cost expression in the capital cost formula.

We shall return to the question of the possible growth of the firm in Part III, where reference will be made to the use of internally generated funds, or retained earnings, as a source of money capital. Because retained earnings constitute a source of equity capital that is a substitute for external issues of new equity shares, the cost of external equity serves as an approximation to the cost of retained earnings. A possible difference in costs arises for a technical reason that need not detain us at this point. This follows from the fact that if earnings are distributed to the equity holders in the form of dividends, the recipients will have to pay tax on them at their effective income tax rates. But if earnings are retained, the equity holders will receive the benefit, if all develops according to plan and the retained earnings are invested effectively by the firm, in an appreciation in the market value of the shares of common stock. The equity holders may realize part of that capital appreciation by selling off a part of their equity holdings. In that event, they would be required to pay tax, not at the income tax rate, as in the case of dividends, but at a lower capital gains tax rate. This difference in potential tax liability may reduce the effective cost of retained earnings relative to the cost of new equity issues.

Investment project expected cash inflows

Investment project valuation also requires a careful specification of the cash flows that the activity is expected to generate during its economic life. This is referred to in the S_t variable in Equation (9.1). Such cash flows should be adjusted to take account of anticipated inflation in input and output price levels. If future selling prices are expected to rise along with some general inflation factor, care should be taken to adjust future labor and other input costs by an appropriate amount also. A more extensive examination can be inspected in the business finance literature we have referred to. We shall conclude this chapter with some minimal comments on ways in which the risks in investment activities might be taken into account.

Probabilistically reducible risk and investment decisions

Let us suppose that the elements of the cash inflow vector, S_t, are not uniquely definable but are regarded as random variables describable by subjectively assigned probability distributions. We can envisage a separate probability distribution for each cash flow element. The distributions may or may not be identical for different periods. We conceive, then, of the expected value and the standard deviation of each such cash flow element. Our problem now is that of finding the present discounted value of a time vector of expected cash flows and defining the degree of risk associated with them. Consider first the present valuation as indicated in Equation (9.5):

$$E(V) = \sum_{t=1}^{n} E(S_t)(1+m)^{-t} \tag{9.5}$$

Since the economic value is now functionally dependent on a series of random variables, that economic value must itself be interpreted as a random variable. The expected value of the implicit probability distribution of the economic value is then definable as the weighted sum of the expected values of the cash flow components. The decision criterion may then be set as

$$E(V) \gtreqless C \tag{9.6}$$

But this leaves unexamined and unspecified the degree of risk involved in the investment. We need therefore to determine the variance or the standard deviation of the economic value of the project. This, however, will depend on what we assume regarding the correlation between the successive elements of the cash flow stream. We may consider three different possibilities.

First, the cash flow elements may be assumed to be independent, or the covariance between every pair of cash flow elements may be zero. The variance we are searching for can then be interpreted simply as a weighted sum of the variances of the cash flow elements. In Equation (9.7), which reinterprets the expected economic value of the project, we have made use of the notion of the weighted sum of the expected values of the cash flows. We let $(1 + m)^{-1} = 1/(1 + m) = w$, and the expected economic value of the project is then interpretable as

Table 9.1 *Conditional probability analysis of project cash flows*

Period 1		Period 2		
Cash flow ($)	Probability	Cash flow ($)	Conditional probability	Joint probability
		50	0.40	0.10
100	0.25	100	0.40	0.10
		200	0.20	0.05
		100	0.20	0.10
200	0.50	200	0.60	0.30
		400	0.20	0.10
		200	0.20	0.05
400	0.25	400	0.40	0.10
		700	0.40	0.10

$$E(V) = \sum_{t=1}^{n} w^t E(S_t) \qquad (9.7)$$

In the case of independent cash flows, the variance of the economic value can be specified as

$$\text{Var}(V) = \sum_{t=1}^{n} w^{2t} \text{Var}(S_t) \qquad (9.8)$$

Second, the elements of the cash flow stream may be perfectly correlated. Again an analytical specification of the variance of the economic value is possible:

$$\text{Var}(V) = \left[\sum_{t=1}^{n} w^t \sigma(S_t) \right]^2 \qquad (9.9)$$

This case of perfect correlation of annual cash flow elements may be interpreted to mean that if an increase of 5 percent were envisaged in any given cash flow element, every other cash flow element would be expected to increase by the same percentage.

Third, the analytical specifications of the variance in Equations (9.8) and (9.9) may not be possible because the cash flow elements may be neither independent nor perfectly correlated. The relation $-1 < \rho_{ij} < 1$ may apply to the correlation between the ith and the jth cash flow elements. An application of conditional probability arguments is then necessary.

In Table 9.1, the first period's cash flow is described by a subjectively assigned probability distribution. Then the second period's cash flow is described, not by a uniquely specified probability distribution, but by as many

Table 9.2 *Probability distribution of cash flow sequences*

Cash flow sequence (from Table 9.1) ($)		Probability of realizing cash flow sequence
Period 1	Period 2	
100	50	0.10
100	100	0.10
100	200	0.05
200	100	0.10
200	200	0.30
200	400	0.10
400	200	0.05
400	400	0.10
400	700	0.10
	$\sum = \overline{1.00}$	

conditional probability distributions as there are possible outcomes in the first period. The same process can be continued for any number of periods. Any given period's cash flow will be described by as many conditional probability distributions as there are possible outcomes in the preceding period. In the example of Table 9.1, the third period's cash flow would be described by nine conditional probability distributions. The magnitudes in the final column of Table 9.1 are obtained by focusing on the different possible cash flow sequences. For example, the first possible such sequence is $100 in the first period followed by $50 in the second period. The joint probability of realizing this sequence, or 0.10, is given by the product of the probabilities attached to each of the elements in the sequence.

In this way, it is possible to build up a probability distribution of cash flow sequences. We note that the probability magnitudes in the final column of Table 9.1 sum to unity, thus providing the probability distribution described in Table 9.2.

It is not necessary to take the details further. If each possible cash flow sequence in Table 9.2 is discounted back to the present at a discount factor equal to the firm's cost of money capital, those discounted values may be set beside the probability magnitudes in the final column of Table 9.2 to provide a probability distribution of the economic value of the investment project. Then the expected value and the standard deviation of that distribution may be computed by familiar procedures. Those data will then provide estimates of the expected economic value of the project and the degree of risk inherent in it, and they may be used to establish decision criteria in the manner we have previously envisaged.

By the various procedures examined in this section it is possible to apply the probability calculus to estimate the expected values and risks in investment activities. Similar procedures could be used in connection with other distributional variables, or variables that are assumed for analytical purposes to be describable by subjectively assigned probability distributions, though the detailed applications would, of course, be different in different cases. For example, the rates of return on investment projects could be interpreted as random variables, or the rate of return on a firm's common stock could be similarly interpreted, as was done at some length in Chapter 7 in the discussion of the equilibrium theory of financial asset prices and yields.

In all such cases, notably in the investment project valuation and decision problem, the attractiveness of the project and the choice decision can be further examined in ways that are now familiar. Given the estimate of the expected value and variance (or standard deviation) of the economic value, those data describing the project could be substituted into a utility function defined over the same two moments of the probability distribution in the manner we developed in Chapters 6 and 7, thereby providing a utility-theoretic approach to decision criteria. Alternatively, the investment decision criterion may be simply stated as in Equation (9.6), subject to the proviso that the estimated risk does not exceed a specified critical level. The risk measure may be stated in terms of the coefficient of variation of the economic value, or the relative standard deviation as described by the ratio of the standard deviation and the expected value.

Other approaches to risk analysis in investment activities, such as sensitivity analysis, are widely used and are discussed in the business finance literature we have referred to.

PART III

Postclassical perspectives

CHAPTER 10

Neoclassicism and an alternative perspective

The place of money capital in the theory of the firm is interdependent with the analysis of production, pricing, and investment. The preceding chapters of Part II have examined these issues from the perspective of received traditions in the theory. But that analysis, though it has shed considerable light on the financing problem and the specification and usefulness of the cost of money capital, was shackled by the heavy weight of the neoclassical assumptions that it carried. In this chapter we shall look briefly at some of the logical and methodological difficulties inherent in the neoclassical apparatus of thought. Our discussion will not be exhaustive, and it will be designed principally to prepare the way for the alternative perspectives we shall consider in the remaining chapters of this part.

Production and factor employment

Consider first the production problem of the firm. The neoclassical theory proceeds on the assumption that it is possible to specify a production function in such a way that there exists an infinite divisibility of factor inputs and a continuous substitutability between them. The implicit factor relations that exist by virtue of their substitutability are described in terms of the isoquants in the factor input plane. Any such isoquant describes a locus of factor combinations capable of producing a specified level of output. Or more technically, the isoquant describes the set of factor combinations that produce the same output when the factors are combined in their technically most efficient way. The slope of the isoquant, such as we employed in Chapter 4, exhibits the marginal rate of technical substitution between factors.

Difficulty arises from this point of view when the capital factor is considered. In what respect, and with what analytical implications, it needs to be asked, is capital to be considered a factor of production? If capital is considered simply in money value terms, the well-known problem arises of defining capital, or at least of measuring its magnitude. For a value cannot be placed on capital until a rate of return, or a discount factor of the kind we have employed in the preceding chapters, has been calculated. When that is done, such a discount factor can be used to value capital by applying the discount factor to the prospective income streams that capital is expected to generate and thereby determine their present capitalized value. This then provides the implied value of the capital factor. But if capital as a factor of production cannot be valued until the exercise that searches for its optimum employment level has been completed and its rate of return has been determined, no meaning can attach to the concept of the marginal productivity of capital. No datum is therefore discoverable with which other factors' marginal productivities can be compared. No possibility exists, therefore, of defining a marginal rate of technical substitution between factors or the ratio of the marginal productivities of the factors. The latter, it has been seen, is, nevertheless, a central concept in the neoclassical production theory.

In the model presented in Chapter 4 this difficulty was alleviated by distinguishing between real capital and money capital. Money capital, it was observed, was not to be regarded as a factor of production. Rather, it served as a constraint that defined the firm's command over factors of production and the other assets that were required in order to establish and maintain an effective production process. Real capital, on the other hand, was regarded as a factor of production. But the real capital factor in the production function was understood to be not the real capital assets that the firm acquired, such as machine tools, for example, but rather the flow of real capital asset services per period of time. In this sense, the production function was considered a flow – flow relation, associating flows of product output with the flows of factor services as inputs to production. This construction, with its emphasis on the flow of real factor services, avoids the circularity of what otherwise exists as the capital valuation problem. But even this procedure fails to come to grips adequately with the realities to which the problems and theory of the firm should be addressed.

The preceding device retains the assumption that a continuous substitutability between factors exists. In doing so, it retains the possibility that varying returns to scale may also exist and may be reflected in ranges of decreasing returns and an upward sloping supply curve for the firm. In actual fact, large numbers of firms produce under conditions that do not permit them to exploit the possibilities of varying factor proportions and factor substitutability. Their production possibilities reflect fixed-factor combinations or fixed technological coefficients of production. This condition would appear to apply in large sections of the manufacturing sector where the relations between machines and the labor hour inputs necessary to operate them are technologically fixed. Of course, technological change or the adoption of new ways of doing things can alter those technological coefficients, and degrees of factor substitution may be able to be achieved in long-run structural decisions. It is precisely that recognition of the long run that justified our argument in Chapter 4 that an ab initio structural planning decision was relevant. But the realities to which the theory of the firm needs to be addressed frequently require, in the light of fixed-factor proportions and constant technological production coefficients, the assumption of constant rather than varying returns to scale. In that case, the firm's average cost curve will be horizontal rather than upward sloping, and within normal operating ranges the supply curve will also be horizontal or perfectly elastic.

Output markets and competitive conditions

This implies that the neoclassical assumption of perfect competition in perfect markets may not be adequately descriptive of the firm's realities. If firms are not atomistic competitors in perfectly competitive markets, they will possess, in the general case, varying degrees of price-making power. Firms are not then primarily price takers. The selling price at which their products are offered will be determined by the cost structures that set the level of their horizontal supply curves. Variations in product demand will then most likely be reflected in variations in the level of output, or possibly in inventory accumulation or decumulation by the firms, rather than in changes in selling prices. A further principal difficulty of the neoclassical analysis, therefore, particularly in the form in which it establishes the notion of an economywide general equilibrium, is its assumption that prices are everywhere determined by supply-and-demand conditions. Price formation, on the contrary, may be such that industrial firms exhibit production and output variations at fixed prices, at least within normal operating ranges, rather than the generally conceived price flexibility.

Theory of utility

Central to the neoclassical theory also is the notion of utility that we have examined at some length. The theory, it has been seen, has expanded the utility analysis from the more familiar consumer utility or indifference theory to the construction of investors' utility functions defined over risk and rate-of-return characteristics. We labeled that extension of analysis stochastic utility, and we have observed that assumptions of differing degrees of risk aversion may be introduced into it. Powerful use has been made of the resulting apparatus within the neoclassical equilibrium theory. But a problem arises in this body of analysis if there is reason to believe that the utility functions might not be stable over time, or if the arguments over which utility functions are defined vary, or vary in their relative importance, as changes occur in other economic variables with which utility is brought into relation. This implies that the widespread analytical use of the indifference curves that are generated by utility functions may not be capable of serving the highly important function required of them in determining equilibrium situations. For that reason, it will be necessary to suggest in the final chapter of this part a way of coming to grips with economic decisions that does not make the same kind of reliance on the notion of static utility optimization.

Logic of constrained optimization

On the production side, the neoclassical theory visualizes the firm as deciding on its optimum production levels against the constraint of specified cost conditions. Or it might be viewed as deciding on minimum cost production levels against a production function constraint. On the consumer side, a similar analytical process is envisaged. The consumer or the consuming household is understood to optimize the choice of commodity combinations in such a way as to maximize attainable utility or satisfaction against an income or expenditure constraint. Neoclassical theory is therefore substantially a theory of the economic activity of decision-making units that maximize, or optimize, certain well-specified objective functions in the presence of definable constraints. Methodologically, it is a theory of constrained optimization or the discovery of constrained extrema of relevant maximand or minimand functions.

We made use of this methodology in introducing into the firm's decision nexus in Chapter 4 a money capital availability constraint. This alerted us to the manner in which firms must take account, in interpreting and specifying their money capital costs, of the full effects that follow from the introduction of new money capital. The relations we adduced remain highly significant for the firm's money capital decision. But it would be a mistake to imagine, as we acknowledged at that earlier stage, that optimization decisions can proceed on the assumptions that all determinant functions are as precisely and uniquely defined as our initial argument might appear to posit. The general nature and directions of the causal relations might thereby be established. But care must be taken to observe the manner in which, in the ever-changing uniqueness of decision points in historic time, the determination of the relevant outcomes on the level of money capital employment also varies.

Historic time, uncertainty, and knowledge

The reintroduction of the realities of historic time brings into focus a further principal difficulty of the neoclassical theory. It is essentially a timeless theory. It is static and has not been able to accommodate effectively the realities of actual time and its unidirectional historic passing. To the extent that the future is considered, the uncertainties inherent in it have generally been abolished by interpreting future-dated variables as random variables and assuming that their values can be described by subjectively assigned probability distributions. By this sleight of hand, the problem of knowledge, or more particularly of ignorance and unknowledge, has been assumed away. This means that the neoclassical theory has placed heavy demands on credibility by the manner in which its assumptions as to knowledge have been fitted into its scheme of perfect market and perfectly competitive analysis. Perfect market theory has generally carried along with it the assumption of perfect knowledge or perfect foresight. To the extent that assumptions of this kind have been modified by the theory, and to the extent that analyses of imperfectly competitive conditions have been proposed, the assumption has been retained that whereas precise knowledge of future-dated variables might not be available, at least the future could be corraled by positing the form of the probability distribution that described future possible events and outcomes. But such an assumption of the form of a probability distribution is an assumption of knowledge. The realities of uncertainty and of ignorance are thereby assumed away, and decision makers are assumed to be incapable, in an ultimate sense, of being surprised.

General equilibrium postulates

The neoclassical theory has made much of the notion that its conclusions regarding production and consumption optimization could be incorporated into a general equilibrium analysis. Having explained the determinants of consumer behavior and the behavioral decisions of producing firms, and assuming that at any time the total availability of resources in the economy is given, all decision makers could be understood to make optimizing decisions in such a way that all markets, for both product outputs and factor inputs, would clear at optimal prices and volumes. General market clearing is in this way taken to be symptomatic of, and descriptive of, the general equilibrium situation that guarantees a full employment of all available resources, including labor, and a maximum economic welfare. The unemployment problem is solved by assuming it away. The general equilibrium scheme provides full employment by definition. Or at least whatever unemployment exists is interpreted to be voluntary unemployment. All suppliers are on their supply curves. The possibility of involuntary unemployment is eliminated by the underlying assumption that suppliers of labor, for example, will have decided, along with all other decision makers, on their optimum supply. This will be determined by their utility functions that include as determinant arguments the supply of effort and the level of income received.

In actual fact, not all markets clear continuously at optimum price and volume levels. Coherence in such a generalized sense might not occur. Market failures exist, and the imperfections and rigidities that potentially give rise to them need to be accommodated in any scheme of analysis of the market system.

An alternative theory of money capital investment

For our present purposes, the considerations we have raised will influence our understanding of the problems the firm faces in deciding on its employment of money capital. In the remaining two chapters of this part we shall focus on two main issues. First, we shall suggest in the following chapter how a more relevant theory of the firm and its money capital investment problem may be constructed. This will imply an examination, from analytical perspectives somewhat different from those adopted up to this point, of the interdependence we have already emphasised, namely, that between the firm's production, pricing, investment, and financing decisions. In particular, we shall take account of the potentially high degree of concentration of outputs among small numbers of imperfectly competitive or oligopolistic firms rather than the widespread distribution of outputs among large numbers of perfectly competitive or atomistically competitive firms. Pricing and production policies will be related to such competitive structures. In the light of that, reasons will be adduced why incremental money capital investment in the firm will be required, and the conditions under which money capital may be obtained will be examined. In this connection, we shall be able to rely on the basic notions of the costs of money capital that we have already adduced, understanding that full adjustments to such capital costs will need to be made for the incidence of the risks introduced by the operational and financial leverage structures of the firm. We shall be able to make use also of the notion already examined of the rate of return that incremental investment in the firm might be expected to generate. But in that connection, an advance will be made beyond the basic money capital cost argument we have considered so far. We shall pay particular attention to the firm's use of internally generated funds, or retained earnings, as a source of money capital. It will be seen that the decision as to desirable money capital investment and the need to generate a sufficiently high level of internal cash flow to accommodate those investment requirements will be relevant to the interpretation of the firm's cost structure and the setting of its output price level.

Uncertainty and potential surprise

Finally, we shall examine in Chapter 12 the ways in which, in all of the decision situations we envisage, account may be taken of the real uncertainties that abound. Uncertainty will not be collapsed into what we have referred to as probabilistically reducible risk. We shall introduce in that connection the notion of a potential surprise function to replace the probability calculus on which, in the preceding chapters, the neoclassical apparatus has made such heavy reliance.

CHAPTER 11

Production and the place of money capital

An adequate theory of the interdependence between the firm's production, pricing, investment, and financing requires an examination of both its short-run and long-run behavior. A model of the firm's production decision will not only reflect its selling price consistent with the chosen level of output but will also explain why that price is set at a level adequate to accomplish two objectives. First, net revenues after the deduction of operating costs must be sufficient to provide an acceptable or required rate of return on the money capital invested in the firm. This rate of return must be available after the deduction from revenues of the periodic allocation to a capital asset replacement fund if, in the manner we have emphasized, the firm is to maintain its capital intact. Second, the cash flow generated by the firm will bear a relation to its regular capital investment expenditures. Part of the money capital necessary to finance that investment will be obtained, as a policy decision, from internally generated cash flows. The level at which the firm's selling price is set, as a markup over costs, will therefore need to be large enough to generate those required investable funds. The remaining part of the capital budget will be financed by making new capital issues in the external capital market.

The availability of money capital is brought into relation with the demand for investable funds by the money capital supply-and-demand curves in Figure 11.1. The horizontal axis of Figure 11.1 describes the investment expenditure, I_t, undertaken in a given time period t. The vertical axis describes, first, the cost of money capital, r, at which the requisite money capital funds are available and, second, the prospective internal rate of return on investment projects at the margin, or the marginal efficiency of investment, k. The curve labeled D describes the firm's demand for money capital. By using such analytical methods as those summarized in Equations $(3.11) - (3.13)$, it is possible to calculate the expected true rate of profit, or the internal rate of return, that can be earned on each investment project contemplated by the firm. This true rate of profit will be the discount factor that makes the present discounted value of the project's expected cash inflows equal to the capital outlay on it. If the investment opportunities are ranked by order of their expected rates of return, the cumulative investment opportunities schedule will provide the marginal efficiency of investment relation, D, shown in Figure 11.1. The

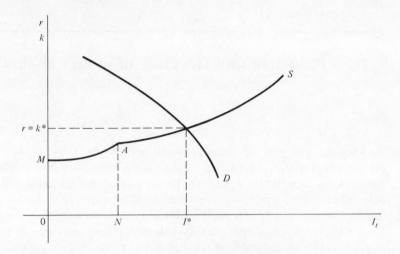

Figure 11.1

larger the level of contemplated investment expenditure, the lower will be the expected rate of return on the marginal, or the last added, project.

Consider now the supply-of-funds curve, or the marginal-cost-of-money-capital curve, MS in Figure 11.1. Note that a kink appears at point A. The portion of the curve extending from the vertical axis to point A describes the supply of money capital funds from internally generated sources. That is shown in the figure as a positive function of the effective cost of funds, r. The AS portion of the supply curve describes the rate at which, and the money capital costs at which, investable funds are available from the external capital market.

The cost of internally generated funds or retained earnings is shown in the figure to be lower than that of externally available capital. In the discussion of the investment project decision in Chapter 9, it was observed that the cost of retained earnings will approximate that of new equity issues, or the rate of return required by the equity holders. This followed from the fact that the retention of earnings is a substitute for new equity issues, as both are sources of equity capital. But the equity holders might enjoy a tax advantage from earnings retention compared with the distribution of dividends. The retention of earnings, provided the funds retained are invested effectively by the firm, can be expected to lead to an increase in the market value of the equity shares. An investor could realize part of that increased value by selling off part of his holding, thereby making himself subject to capital gains tax on the realized capital appreciation. That gains tax, however, will in general be lower than the personal income tax that would have been paid on the receipt of dividends. This relative tax advantage of retained earnings might therefore reduce their effective cost marginally below the cost of new equity funds. Moreover, new equity issues carry further costs that are avoided in the use of retained earnings. A new issue of equity will frequently require the new shares to be sold at a fractionally lower price than the current market value of the existing shares, such an underpricing being necessary to guarantee the successful flotation of the issue. Also, a certain amount of underwriting costs will be incurred. No such costs exist in the case of retained earnings, and this, together with the tax advantage, suggests a lower effective cost of internally generated funds.

The retained earnings portion of the supply-of-funds curve in Figure 11.1 has been shown as rising slightly. This reflects the possibility that increased earnings retention, implying a lower dividend distribution, may cause investors to fear that the risks in the firm's operation may be adversely affected as investment proceeds further. If that is so, the required rate of return on the equity will increase, leading to the possibility of a dilution of the value of the equity holders' investment position. We examined this kind of effect when we observed the possible impacts from the marginal use of debt capital. There is no a priori necessity for these incremental risk effects to occur in the earnings retention case. But the incremental income streams that the retained earnings will generate remain in the future; and the further in the future they are, the more risky they may appear to be. The distribution of earnings as dividends, on the other hand, provides the equity holders with immediate cash benefits. But any such risk effect depends on the quality of the investment opportunities in which the management invests its funds.

It has been argued by exponents of the equilibrium asset market theory that in perfect capital markets investors will be indifferent between dividend distributions and retained earnings (see Brealey and Myers, 1984, p. 336f.). This so-called dividend irrelevance theorem is based on the assumption that a firm's capital expenditure program has been decided upon and that earnings retention and new capital issues are then two alternative ways of financing the given capital budget. Quite apart from whatever difficulties attach to the assumptions of the perfect capital market theory, investors who might be concerned about the incremental risks associated with the investment of retained earnings may visualize a somewhat different set of relations. Rather than contemplating the use of retained earnings and new equity issues as simply alternative ways of financing a given capital budget, they may be concerned also with the way in which earnings retention may lead to investment decisions by the firm's management that would not otherwise have been taken.

The *MA* portion of the supply-of-funds curve in Figure 11.1 may also reflect an increase in the cost of internally generated funds that may occur if, as we shall examine below, the firm's selling price is raised in order to increase the availability of funds from residual cash flow sources (see Eichner, 1985, Ch. 3). This points to an examination of the relation between the firm's average cost markup, which translates those average costs into the firm's selling price, and the effective cost of changing that markup if investment or financial policies should make that desirable.

The estimation of the marginal cost of external money capital, or the costs that are described in the AS portion of the supply curve in Figure 11.1, may proceed in the manner we indicated previously. Rather than relying on the assumptions of the equilibrium asset market theory, we may look directly to the marginal costs of debt and equity funds, or a combination of them, under imperfect capital market conditions. In other words, we rely again on what we exhibited earlier as the full marginal cost of relaxing the firm's money capital availability constraint. This may or may not, we have seen, be precisely measurable by the firm's weighted average cost of capital. If there is reason to believe that the firm is proceeding along an equilibrium growth path, and if, therefore, the firm raises its incremental finance in such a way as not to cause any change in its financing mix, and if it is maintaining production structures that provide the same degree of business risk, the weighted average cost of capital will be relevant and usable. But if, on the other hand, investment is being undertaken as a means of changing the firm's growth rate, perhaps by diversifying into other sectors of the economy where higher growth rates are attainable, a careful calculation will need to be made of the new overall risks that will be involved and the new implied costs of money capital.

To the extent that firms do make new capital issues, the total supply of securities available in the financial asset market will be increased. The significance of this lies in the fact that in the exposition of the equilibrium asset market theory of Chapter 7 the assumption was made that the total supply of securities did not change. If firms do make new capital issues, the specification of the investors' asset opportunity set in the equilibrium asset market theory will be changed, and a different optimum market portfolio will be defined as a result. This will change the locus of the efficient boundary of the asset opportunity set, and it will alter, therefore, the characteristics of the Capital Market Line. This, in turn, will cause a change in the equilibrium market price of risk and a change in the effective costs of capital to all firms, or in the required rate of return on each firm's risky capital securities.

In the situation envisaged in Figure 11.1, the firm would undertake an investment expenditure of $0I^*$, of which $0N$ would be financed from internally generated cash flows and the balance, NI^*, would be financed by new capital security issues. Our task now is to develop a model of the firm in

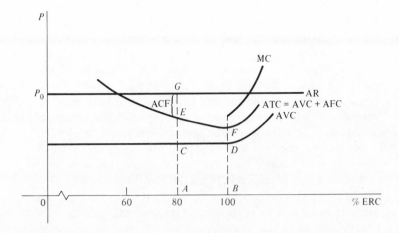

Figure 11.2

which the underlying determinants of these relations can be brought into clearer focus.[1]

Operating characteristics of the firm

Let us imagine a firm whose production decisions are made on the basis of a fixed technological coefficient production relation. It will combine factor inputs in fixed and, in the short run, well-defined and unalterable proportions. We now depart from the earlier neoclassical assumptions of infinitely divisible and continuously substitutable factors of production. We may imagine that the firm is, in the expressive language of Eichner (1976), a "megacorp." It will conceivably arrange its production apparatus in such a way as to install a number of plant segments, each of which will operate with fixed factor combinations and will exhibit, as a result, a cost level dependent on its optimally attainable productivity. That will be determined by the technological character and efficiency of the particular vintage of capital equipment it contains. The operating characteristics of the firm can then be depicted in Figure 11.2.

The horizontal axis of Figure 11.2 describes the Engineer Rated Capacity

---

[1] The following sections are heavily indebted to Eichner (1976, 1985), whose work has profoundly significant implications, not only for the theory of the firm and its financing, but also for problems in macrodynamic theory and policy. Figures 11.2, 11.3, and 11.4 and the analysis to which they are related are essentially an interpretation of Eichner's work, and full acknowledgment is due to his important conceptual and terminological inventions. See also the related and highly insightful discussion in Wood (1975).

(ERC) of the firm's production apparatus. For production levels below 100 percent of ERC, the average variable cost per unit of output remains constant. This follows from the fact that the firm, as suggested, will be likely to maintain a number of plant segments, each of which will be brought into operation or taken out of operation as the firm desires to alter its total level of production. Each such production segment, however, will have been designed to operate at maximum efficiency, or at a lowest attainable average cost level, depending on its given vintage and technological characteristics. If it is called into operation, it will normally be operated at that optimum level of intensity. In this manner, the firm will be able to maintain a fairly constant level of overall average variable costs per unit of output. Or, perhaps, the average variable-cost curve depicted in Figure 11.2 might rise as the firm nears its 100 percent ERC, as older and less efficient plant segments are brought into operation in order to achieve the desired level of output. In the general case, a firm may aim to operate at a usual intensity of, say, 80 percent of its ERC as shown in the figure. Plant design may be such as to incorporate a target standard excess capacity. This, in turn, will provide the firm with the degree of production flexibility it may imagine it needs in order to satisfy the requirements of the output fluctuations it expects to encounter during normal business fluctuations.

The average fixed cost per unit of output will, of course, decline as the level of output increases. When this is added to the average variable cost, the average total cost curve, ATC, is defined as in Figure 11.2. The marginal cost, which will again be constant (and equal to the average variable cost) at output levels below 100 percent of ERC for the reasons previously adduced, will rise if output is pushed beyond the 100 percent ERC level.

The level at which the firm plans to operate can be referred to as its Standard Operating Ratio (SOR). It will be possible for the firm to determine at its planning stage the average fixed cost, average variable cost, and average total cost at the SOR level. The firm then faces the decision as to the price at which it should offer its output for sale. At that point, it must bear in mind that if it is going to maintain its share of its output market, it must plan to grow at the expected growth rate of the industry of which it is a member. This may be determined by estimates of the growth rate for the economy and by the likelihood that new entrants to the industry might succeed in reducing the firm's attainable market share. If, however, the firm is to retain its market share, and if it is to maintain the established degree of real capital intensity in its production arrangements, it will need to expand its capital stock each period at a rate equivalent to its expected overall rate of growth. This, then, will provide the firm with an estimate of its desired or target rate of incremental investment per period.

Of course, other reasons may exist for incremental capital investment in the firm. Investment may be made for purposes of achieving cost reductions, to install technologically more efficient or newer vintage capital equipment, or to diversify into new sectors of industry. The latter possibility introduces some potentially important analytical considerations. First, the firm may desire to diversify into a more rapidly expanding industry in order to increase its overall rate of growth. Or it may wish to diversify as a means of maintaining its growth rate if, for any reason, the attainable rates of growth in its currently established industry have slackened. But second, the suggestion that diversification might be desirable contradicts a significant conclusion of the equilibrium asset market theory. That theory implies that firms cannot accomplish anything positive for investors by undertaking diversification and that, indeed, the best interests of investors are served by leaving them to accomplish their own diversification by combining portfolio assets in the manner we have examined.

In any event, the firm will decide, given the cost relations exhibited in Figure 11.2, the size of the markup it will add to its average total cost, as estimated at its SOR production level, to determine its selling price. The price it sets and announces to the market will then be defined as its average total cost multiplied by a markup percentage. We define the markup percentage as m and derive the relation between average total cost C and the selling price P:

$$m = (P - C)/C, \tag{11.1}$$

whence

$$P = (1 + m)C \tag{11.2}$$

The apparent simplicity of this relation should not be allowed to conceal its significance. When production volumes are maintained at the SOR level on which the cost estimates and the selling price decisions were based, the firm will be realizing its target rate of return on the total money capital it employs. An alternative way of referring to its desired markup factor, then, is to say that it will mark up its average costs, and thereby set its selling price, in such a way as to realize a target rate of return on capital at its standard operating volume. The basic reason it does this, it should be borne in mind, is that it can thereby expect to realize also the internally generated cash flow it plans to use for financing its annual investment budget.

If, in the course of business fluctuations, the demand for its product should increase, the firm's production can be increased above its SOR level without any change in its selling price. This, of course, is quite contrary to the vision of market price and volume changes implicit in the neoclassical view of industrial operations. In the present case, we have the prospect of price rigidity and volume flexibility. But at the same time, if the output volume is increased in the manner envisaged, there will be an increase in the residual internally generated cash flow, or in the ACF magnitude (Average Surplus Cash Flow) in Figure 11.2. In that case, a larger amount of funds will be available for investment or for distribution to the equity holders in the form of dividends. Alternatively, depending on the level of incremental investment envisaged, the higher internally generated cash flows may diminish the need for reliance on new issues of securities in the external capital market.

Moreover, if the production volume rises above the SOR level, the realized rate of return on the money capital invested in the firm will also rise above its previous target level. By the contrary argument, of course, if demand should decline and production levels fall below the SOR level, both the internally generated cash flow and the realized rate of return on capital will fall. In that event, the firm will have to decide whether it should reduce its capital budget or increase its demand on the external money capital market. Or it may, depending on whether it thought its diminished cash flow was a temporary phenomenon, increase its demands on the financial institutions for short-term loans, with a view to repaying them when the hoped for revival in demand and cash flows was realized. The extent to which that can occur, however, will depend on the creditworthiness of the firm in the short-term loan market, on the willingness of the financial institutions to supply the short-term accommodation, and possibly on the conduct of monetary policy that sets the tone and the overall availability of funds in the loan market.

The firm may not, however, enjoy complete freedom to set its selling price in the manner we have suggested by marking up its average cost to realize a target rate of return on capital. It may be a price follower in its industry, not a price leader. Its demand curve, or its unit selling price curve, shown as AR in Figure 11.2, may be set at its existing level by the industry's price leader. In that event, the firm will decide on the standard operating volume at which it should plan to produce in order to achieve its target rate of return and cash flow.

It follows that the average rate at which surplus internally generated cash flows become available differs from the marginal rate. The former is, as indicated, the difference between the selling price and the average *total* cost. But the marginal surplus cash flow is the difference between the selling price and the average *variable* cost. In conditions of rising demand, the average surplus cash flow will increase proportionately more rapidly than the marginal cash flow, with a contrary relation existing under conditions of reduced demand.

We note finally the implications of this view of the firm's operations for the degree of risk to which it is exposed. If the firm is able to maintain its established share of the market or markets in which it sells its output, its principal risk will be that associated with demand fluctuations in the industry market as a whole. Of course, there remains the risk that in the context of the growth of the economy and the industry, the firm may not be able to maintain the market share. The risk that new entrants to the industry may capture part of the firm's existing market share will be one of the factors that the firm takes into account in deciding whether or not it should make changes in the average cost markup by which its selling price is set. Moreover, there are also risks associated with fluctuations in the economy. These give rise to the fluctuations in demand that we considered above when examining their possible effects on the realized cash flows and rate of return on capital. In the event of such fluctuations, the degree of instability in the residual income stream earned for the owners will be determined by the overall degrees of what we referred to in Chapter 2 as operational leverage and financial leverage.

Money capital employment decision

The foregoing analysis implies that the incremental capital investment decision in the firm is integrated with its production and pricing decisions. The selling price at which the firm offers its output in the market will be set at that markup over cost that provides it with the internally generated cash flow it needs, along with the external financing it is prepared to undertake, to finance its capital expenditure. Let us suppose that in an established and ongoing situation the firm is generating precisely the amount of internal surplus cash flow it needs to implement its regular capital expenditure program. This, we may suppose, enables it to maintain its normally desired rate of growth, consistent with the expansion of its industry and with its established market share. We may consider, then, the possible ways in which the firm might finance a new set of investment opportunities in order to undertake a faster than previously planned expansion. How, in other words, should the incremental money capital be divided between larger internally generated cash flows and demands on the external capital market?

Given the argument summarized in Figure 11.2, a higher average surplus cash flow could be generated by increasing the markup factor, say from m as in Equation (11.2) to $m + \Delta m$. If the firm were able to operate at its previously established level of output, or at the same SOR level, the higher selling price implicit in the higher markup factor would, of course, generate higher internal cash flows. But whether the firm could maintain that production level will depend on the elasticity of demand for its output. It will actually depend on a number of such factors that we might inspect in the following way.

Consider for this purpose Figure 11.3. In Figure 11.3(a) we have shown a relation between a possible increase in the markup factor m on the horizontal axis and the expected incremental surplus cash flow per period of time, F/t, that might result from such a decision.

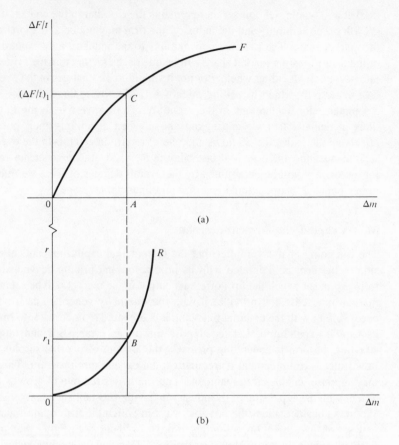

Figure 11.3

It is posited in the figure that increases in the markup factor will be likely
to increase the surplus internal cash flow at a decreasing rate. There are a
number of reasons why this might be so. First, the firm will have to consider,
in its estimate of the outcome following a change in the markup factor, the
extent to which the higher selling price will affect its position in the output
market. It must take account, that is, of the substitution effects that might
divert demand onto other competitive products, depending on the cross-
elasticities of demand that exist, as well as on the direct price elasticity of
demand for the products of the industry of which the firm is a member. If the
industry demand curve is inelastic, an increase in a selling price that is followed by the industry in general will increase the total revenue from product
sales. A price increase under conditions of elastic demand, on the other hand,

will lead to a reduction of total sales revenues. The firm that is contemplating a possible increase in its markup factor will therefore make some estimates of the likely impact of these elasticity effects, particularly as they stem from commodity cross-elasticities of demand.

Second, the firm will need to consider the likelihood that if it increases its markup and selling price, and if it increases its revenue by continuing to produce at its existing SOR production level, it will generate a larger rate of return on the capital employed in the firm. This higher rate of return might not be able to be realized permanently, of course, because the longer-run effects of its actions might offset any shorter-run benefits. The industry of which the firm is a member may be confronted in its immediate market by an inelastic demand curve, and firms in the industry may therefore be able to increase their revenues by increasing their markup factors. But in the longer run, the cross-elasticities of demand for substitute commodities could operate in such a way as to lower the industry's demand curve and thereby diminish every firm's revenue-generating prospects. But whereas attention is thus paid to the longer-run as well as the shorter-run effects, the prospect of a higher rate of return on capital may nevertheless attract new entrants to the industry. If the firm has reason to believe that such new entrants may emerge and in due course reduce its existing market share, that will also be taken into account in deciding on the wisdom of increasing the markup factor and the selling price. The extent to which such new entry problems may exist will depend, among other things, on the minimum size of the initial capital investment necessary to obtain a foothold in the industry as well as on other entry barriers such as access to input materials and complementary production resources.

We may suppose, therefore, that the firm, in facing the decision whether it should increase its markup factor and selling price with a view to increasing its internal surplus cash flow for investment purposes, considers the following possible developments over time. It may estimate that in the short run, say the next few years, it may be able to increase its surplus internally generated cash flow by a certain amount if the markup is increased. But it estimates also that after that time it will begin to experience a reduced cash flow because of the kinds of considerations we have referred to. On the basis of projected data of this kind, it can perform a cost–benefit analysis, or an economic valuation or rate-of-return analysis of the kind we considered in Chapter 3 and other places.

The anticipated ultimate reduction in the cash flow below what it would otherwise be will assume a calculable time shape. Similarly, the nearer term increase in cash flows generated in the firm will assume an estimated time shape. It is then a straightforward matter to compare the size and time shape of the ultimate cash flow reductions with the size and time shape of the im-

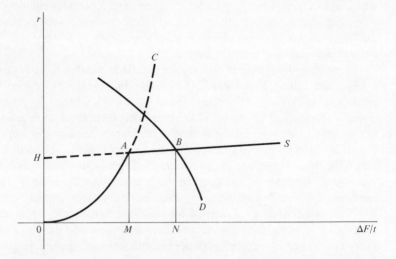

Figure 11.4

mediate cash flow benefits. The former can be regarded as the cost of realizing the latter. It is possible, therefore, to set these two estimated incremental cash flow streams, one positive and the other negative, against each other and to calculate the rate of discount that will reduce them both to the same present discounted value. The discount factor that establishes the equality will be an estimate of the effective cost of realizing the benefits defined in the relation between the two cash flow streams.

The vertical axis of Figure 11.3(a) shows the annual equivalent incremental cash inflow that, it is anticipated, would result from different possible increases in the markup factor. In Figure 11.3(b), the vertical axis depicts the effective cost of realizing those incremental cash flows by setting against the increase in the markup factor that would give rise to them the effective cost, or the effective rate of discount as described in the preceding paragraph. Taking Figures 11.3(a) and (b) together, the firm now has, on the vertical axes, estimates of both the incremental annual cash flow and the effective rate of cost associated with any specified change in the markup factor. We may then refer to the effective rate of cost as the cost of internally generated money capital. The data on the vertical axes of these figures are brought together in Figure 11.4.

Take first the curve $0AC$ in Figure 11.4. This describes an effective supply curve of internally generated money capital funds, understanding that this analysis is intended to apply to incremental possible cash flows additional to the regular ongoing capital budget expenditures that are financed from existing markup and pricing relations and the established use of external capital market sources. The curve can be expected to assume the convexity illustrated in Figure 11.4 by virtue of its derivation from Figures 11.3(a) and (b), where the concavity of the incremental funds curve in Figure 11.3(a) is married to the convexity of the effective-rate-of-cost curve in Figure 11.3(b).

Inscribed in Figure 11.4 also is an incremental supply of money capital curve, *HAS*, describing the costs at which further amounts of capital may be obtained from the external capital market. This has been drawn with a positive slope to suggest that the capital market may impose larger required rates of return or higher effective costs of money capital on the firm as its capital expenditure continues to rise. Questions of risk that we have considered at length already come into view. If, as the level of capital financing increases, the firm makes increasing use of debt capital funds, the implications of the increased financial leverage can be expected to increase the cost of equity capital as well as raise the cost of debt, imparting an upward tilt to the cost of external capital funds curve. Much would depend also on the nature of the risks attaching to the firm's proposed incremental investments if it is investing as a means of gaining entry to a new industry, in which, conceivably, it does not have a history of experience and management. Moreover, the same effects as previously will again follow from the operational leverage and financial leverage that enter the firm's production and financing structures as a result of the incremental investment and financing.

We introduce to Figure 11.4 also the firm's demand curve for incremental investable funds, understanding again that we are here describing the demand for funds over and above those provided for by the established markup and pricing policies and capital market relations. This demand-for-funds curve is juxtaposed with the effective supply-of-funds curve. The latter will be described by the internally generated cash flow curve extending from the origin to the point *A*, and thereafter by the *AS* portion of the external funds supply curve. The dotted portion of the internal funds supply curve, *AC*, is irrelevant because the cost of funds from that source has increased, beyond point *A*, above the external cost. Similarly, internally generated funds will be employed up to point *A*, as the cost of funds from internal sources is lower in that range than that of externally available money capital. The effective-supply-of-funds curve is therefore described by 0*AS* in Figure 11.4. The optimum level of incremental investment, reading from the supply-and-demand cross at point *B*, will be 0*N*. Of this amount, 0*M* will be obtained from internal sources, with the increase in the markup factor being set at the level that makes that possible, as derived from Figure 11.3(a). The balance of incremental funds, *MN* in Figure 11.4, will be obtained from the external capital market at an effective marginal cost of *NB*.

Of course, the incremental demand-for-funds curve, *D*, in Figure 11.4 could have crossed the effective supply curve $0AS$ in the segment $0A$. All of the necessary funds would then be obtained by making the change called for in the firm's markup factor and selling price, and no additional recourse would be made to the external capital market (see Eichner, 1976, 1985). It is conceivable that in the presence of temporarily surplus internally generated cash flows the firm could be a supplier of funds to the capital market.

The firm's optimum-structure decisions

The analysis we have developed in this chapter can usefully be compared with that in Chapter 4. In that earlier chapter we explored the ways in which, after refurbishing and expanding the widely accepted neoclassical theory, it was possible to conceive of a simultaneous solution to the firm's production, pricing, investment, and financing problems. The principal result of that analysis was the realization that the firm's optimum production structure was not independent of its optimum financing structure and that this carried along with it a fundamental message regarding the specification of the firm's effective cost of money capital. That was defined as the full marginal cost of relaxing the firm's money capital availability constraint. This latter concept can be carried over to the level of analysis contained in this chapter, as can also the basic notions of the valuation of income streams and the implicit rates of return on capital investment outlays. But some vital differences exist.

In the earlier neoclassical analysis, no consideration was given to the possibility of earnings retention in the firm and the division of money capital sources between internally generated funds and financing obtained from the external capital market. That question was submerged in the light of the fact that the model of Chapter 4 was designed as a long-run planning model, which could, however, be reconsidered at any desired intervals of time. No division of the total equity funds into internal and external sources was made because, as we have seen, the costs of those funds are comparable, being close substitutes for one another. In the argument of this chapter, on the other hand, that division of fund sources has been brought into critical prominence. This has been possible for a further significant reason.

In this chapter the firm has been regarded not so much as a static entity that structures itself once and for all at a point in time but as a developing structure that needs, if it is to maintain its place in a growing economy, to be continually expanding. It needs to reassess in each time period its optimum rates of capital investment and money capital usage, along with its most advisable financing sources, as well as reconsider its pricing policies, via its average cost markup policies, that make the realization of its overall goals possible.

But one final point of similarity between the methodologies of Chapter 4 and the present chapter remains. In neither of these analyses is it intended to leave the impression that the functional relations and the marginal values of outcomes, such as the comparison between the marginal efficiency of investment and the marginal effective cost of money capital in this chapter, can be specified with uniquely definable accuracy. In all of this work on the questions of the optimum structures and the decision problems of the firm, the realities of uncertainty and the relevance of the ignorance and the unknowledge that abounds impinge in ways we have not yet investigated directly on the making of management decisions. Our arguments have been designed to alert the analyst to the main directions of causation in some of the more critical relations that exist, or must be seen to exist, in the theory of the firm and its employment of money capital. In the following chapter we shall turn explicitly to the construction of a framework for decision making that addresses the uncertainties with which real historic time is inevitably pregnant.

CHAPTER 12

Uncertainty and decisions in the firm

The analytical issues of time and uncertainty have been relevant to many parts of our exposition. They throw an important light on many aspects of sequential decision making in the firm. In the traditional development of our subject, the assumptions that have been made in order to render the problems of time and uncertainty tractable have been related to the notion of equilibrium and equilibrium theorizing. In this chapter we shall reexamine a number of the interrelations that exist between these issues, and we shall bring into focus again a number of the questions that were raised in this connection in Chapter 1.

The theory of the firm has all too often been cast in a timeless, static, certainty, or certainty-equivalent mold. The capitulation of economics to the analytical priorities of general equilibrium theory has left the theory of the firm preoccupied with the description of equilibrium states of affairs. This has become paramount so far as our principal object in this book is concerned, namely the analysis of the firm's employment of money capital. Money capital costs have been conceptualized by the theory as definable by the rates of return that investors require on risky assets when equilibrium conditions are satisfied in the financial asset markets. We have suggested, on the other hand, ways of envisioning the money capital problem from the perspective of partial equilibrium and imperfect market theory. Our move in that direction comes from the recognition that the general equilibrium theory, under its perfectly competitive assumptions, has no way of explaining how decisions are made in nonequilibrium situations. That, of course, is the only kind of situation in which decisions have to be made. If equilibrium obtains, the sea is calm and the ocean is flat and all is at rest. If equilibrium does not exist, the theory has no way of telling us how we can get into equilibrium. We know it only if we are there.

The realities of time, moreover, bound us in a relative ignorance and shatter the comfortable epistemological security that assumptions of certainty and certainty-equivalents provide. Knowledge cannot be known before its time. But reality forces upon us the unavoidable moments of economic decision, and in them we form *imaginative perceptions of the possibilities* that the future contains. We inherit at our decision moments an accumulated knowledge and awareness and all the epistemological baggage that uniquely identifies us.

212

We bring to those moments our particular complex of resources, endowments, skills, and capacities. We inherit a knowledge, or at least our private interpretation, of the fact situations that have structured the course of history that antedates our decision point. Our realization, or our imagination, of what fills out the bounded horizons of possibilities for the future is constrained by an awareness of the economic institutions that delimit our actions and color their outcomes.

In such conditions our decisions are made. But in economic affairs we can never be sure of where we are going to be, or where, if we take certain actions, we shall arrive as a result. We can never know the end or the conclusion to which action will actually take us. We know only where we stand in the unique decision moments in the flux of time. Our task is that of interpreting our history, our present, and our tentative future in such a way as to make, in each unique situation, our best next move. How, then, can our decision moments have decisive meaning, and how are our decisions themselves determined? Historic time enters economic analysis when the passing of it influences our grasp of the uniqueness of the decision moments at which we stand. It casts its kaleidoscopic light on the imaginative perception of possibilities for the future that offers us the skein of conceivable outcomes and actions among which we choose. In the following sections of this chapter we shall allow these perceptions to throw further light on the theory of the firm and its employment of money capital.

Possibility and economic decisions

To begin an answer to these questions, we confront an issue that has partially intruded into our previous discussions. To what extent, we have asked, can the variables that influence decisions be properly understood as distributional variables, or subject, that is, to description by assigned probability distributions? This question raises acutely the meaning and treatment of uncertainty. The matter at issue is not simply that of uncertainty as distinct from risk, though in the fashion of Knight, Keynes, Shackle, and others, we have highlighted that distinction. The issue is grounded in the fact that the human perception of *uncertainty* is bound up with the perception of the passing and significance of *time*. Economic decisions are always decisions in time, temporally bounded and having temporal referents. The complexities of time cannot be elided by the conception that our vision of tomorrow can be safely delimited by our knowledge of yesterday.

Let us imagine that a statement of probability is before us. This may be a statement that *in a large number of conceivable experiments* there is a well-attested reason to believe that *in a specified proportion of the total number of outcomes* a designatable result will emerge. In this sense, *statistical* probabilities have meaning and applicability in economic affairs, in life insurance mortality tables, for example. In general, the experiments to whose outcomes probabilities are attached must be seriable, or replicable, and no aspect of uniqueness should surround the experiment to prohibit its recall and subsequent reproduction. On the other hand, the statement of probability may purport to be a description of the likelihood that *in a single experiment,* or as a result of a *single and unique decision,* a designated possible result will emerge. In *that* sense, the statement of probability has no meaning.

The assignment of probabilities to *future* possible outcomes, either in the form of assumedly objective probability distributions or of subjectively assigned probability distributions, is actually an *assumption of knowledge.* It is this that makes the entire probability machinery inapplicable to decisions under uncertainty. For knowledge is the antithesis of uncertainty. It is the abolition of uncertainty (see Shackle, 1969, Ch. VII). The assignment of a probability distribution to possible outcomes involves the assertion that if the same event were to be repeated a large number of times, a designatable outcome would emerge in a prespecifiable proportion of instances. But such a replicability of experiments is precluded by the *unique* character of most economic decision situations. The taking of economic decisions frequently destroys forever the possibility of their being taken again. Decisions are in this sense "self-destructive."[1]

For probabilities to be assigned over a set of possible outcomes, the assumption must be made that the set is complete and exhaustively descriptive of the possibilities *without a residual hypothesis.* As a homely example due to Shackle, imagine that of six candidates for a job one is, on all the grounds we can contemplate, the most qualified for the position. We accordingly assign probabilities of success to each of the six candidates with this imagination in mind. The probabilities assigned sum to unity and we have, supposedly, a bona fide probability distribution of the outcome. Suppose now that a seventh candidate is introduced, and that he appears to possess much the same qualifications as five of the six previous candidates. Now when we introduce the seventh individual to the candidate set, we assign a probability distribution over the seven possible outcomes. But we still have the necessary summation of probabilities to unity only by taking away part of the probabilities already assigned to one or more of the other six. If we try to capture the uncertainty

---

[1] The arguments in this and the following sections are heavily dependent on the work of Shackle, who has developed, in numerous books and articles over the last three decades, a critique of probability theorizing and has constructed an alternative potential surprise decision apparatus. These have been subject to extensive evaluation and criticism. See Shackle (1969, Ch. XI) for Shackle's evaluation of some of his critics, the recent extensive critique by Ford (1983), and Vickers (1978, Ch. 8). See also footnote 2.

by treating the outcome variable in this way as a distributional variable, we are making the assignment of probabilities dependent on the number of possible outcomes in view even though the very meaning of probability assignment implies the assumption that the distribution encompasses an *exhaustive* specification of the set of possible outcomes.

We have supposed that the seventh individual possessed qualifications that were comparable with those of the other five and were again quite below those of our previous outstanding candidate. We therefore ask the telling question: How surprised would we *now* be if the outstanding candidate were awarded the job? Would we be less or more surprised than we would have been in the original situation? The introduction of the seventh candidate may make no difference at all to our contemplation of the outcome so far as the outstanding candidate is concerned. In the light of this, surely a means of handling uncertainty in decision-making situations needs to be devised that can take account of precisely this kind of possibility.

This need arises because of what we have identified previously as the uniqueness of decision situations. Let us ask by way of further illustration whether it would have been meaningful for Napoleon to have assigned a probability distribution to the outcome of the battle of Waterloo. We may answer in the negative on the grounds that if he won the battle, there would be no need to repeat it, and if he lost the battle, it would not be possible to fight it again. In many economic situations, in investment decisions in the firm, for example, the decision events are unique in the same sense as was Napoleon's situation. The taking of the decision forever changes the decision environment and the decision nexus beyond recall. For these reasons, it appears necessary to replace the distributional analysis of probability by an analysis that focuses on the *possibilities* of outcome magnitudes of *nondistributional* variables.

Potential-surprise function

Let us approach the decision-making problem from the opposite side from that on which probability thought forms are imagined to be applicable. By asking the decision maker to describe the probabilities he would assign to certain specifiable outcomes, we are asking him to base his judgment on degrees of *belief* in conceivable results. Let us instead envisage a procedure that attaches degrees of *disbelief* to possible outcomes. We may imagine that when confronted with a range of possible outcomes, the decision maker specifies, on an ordinal scale, the degree of *potential surprise* he feels *now*, at the decision moment, he would experience in the future if various outcomes were to occur. By focusing on degrees of disbelief in the description of possible outcomes, our argument will be protected against any attempt to transform it

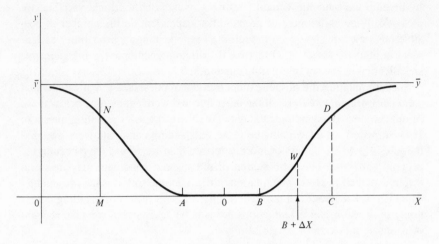

Figure 12.1

into an argument in probability. The logic of the following argument is that the potential-surprise function is in no sense transmutable into a probability density function (see Katzner, 1986).

Of course, the moment at which, in the future, the event that was previously in view *actually* occurs is different from the moment at which the decision is made on the basis of the contemplated *potential* surprise. No meaning can attach to the question of what surprise the decision maker *would* get *in the future* if a specified event occurred. He is concerned with the contemplation *now* of the *potential* surprise with which he contemplates the various possible outcomes of his decision.

To give definiteness to these ideas, let us consider the relationship described in Figure 12.1. The horizontal axis measures the values of an outcome variable X, which we can assume for the present to be money values, thus providing a continuous scale. In different applications they may be, for example, the money values of cash flows generated by an investment activity or the rates of return on assets. Outcome values to the right of the zero point in Figure 12.1 are understood to be positive, and those to the left will be negative.

The vertical axis of Figure 12.1 measures, on an ordinal scale defined on an arbitrary choice of origin and unit of measurement, the degree of potential surprise that the decision maker attaches to the various possible outcomes. To the possible outcome of $0C$, for example, is attached a potential surprise of CD. That magnitude will have been arrived at in answer to a question regarding the degree of disbelief with which the possibility of an outcome equal to

$0C$ was envisaged, or the degree to which, in his present state and manner of seeing things, the individual imagines he would be surprised to see the value $0C$ emerge. Proceeding in a similar fashion, it is possible to build up the entire curve $y = y(x)$ describing the potential surprise attached to the entire range of possible outcomes (see Vickers, 1978).

In contemplating the possible outcomes from a decision event, an individual will conceivably be able to specify a positive magnitude so large that he entertains an extremely high degree of disbelief in its possible occurrence. This may be so high that he does not regard the outcome to be possible at all. He regards it as perfectly *impossible*. A maximum degree of potential surprise is thus attached to that outcome magnitude. We have labeled that maximum potential surprise as $\bar{y}$ in Figure 12.1. Drawing a horizontal line at that ordinate, we have shown the potential-surprise curve as asymptotic to it in the easterly direction. Similarly, the loss outcome segment of the potential-surprise curve would be asymptotic to the maximum potential-surprise magnitude in the westerly direction.

The rates at which the respective positive and negative segments of the potential-surprise curve approach the asymptote will not necessarily be the same. The one side is not necessarily the mirror image of the other. Everything depends on the determinants of the decision maker's imaginative view of things at the unique decision moment at which the various outcome possibilities are contemplated. Moreover, the potential-surprise curve should perhaps in certain instances be truncated in the loss direction. Suppose, for example, that the X values represented wealth outcomes from an investment activity and that the magnitude M on the horizontal axis represented the individual's total wealth and therefore his maximum sustainable loss. In that event, the loss segment of the curve to the left of the point N, which is vertically above the maximum sustainable loss M, has no meaning. For decision-making purposes, the curve should be truncated at that point.

Consider now the segment AB on the X variable axis. Ignoring for the moment the remainder of the curve, imagine that in the decision event being contemplated the entire range of possible outcomes is described by a potential-surprise curve coinciding with the X axis throughout its length and terminating in A and B. It can then be said that the decision maker is attaching a zero potential surprise to all possible outcomes in this range. As he sees things, he would not be at all surprised if any outcome in the range AB occurred. For purposes of vocabulary, all outcomes in the range AB are conceived to be *perfectly possible* and have associated with them *zero potential surprise*.

Continuing to imagine a function that terminates at A and B, the individual will, we suggest, focus his attention on only the best and the worst possible outcomes the project offers. In reacting to the ability of this project or economic opportunity to arrest or grasp or command his attention, the individual will find his attention focused on the magnitudes A and B. These will be referred to as the *focus elements,* the focus loss and the focus gain of the project. For there is no point in an individual's being interested in the fact that an activity may bring a moderate fortune, say within the range of $0B$, if it is equally possible, or in this case perfectly possible, that it will bring a considerable fortune, $0B$. At the same time, there is no point in being concerned that the activity may result in moderate misfortune, say within the range of $0A$, if it is likewise perfectly possible that it will result in considerable misfortune, $0A$.

"When many different things are all equally and perfectly possible," Shackle observes, "it is the brilliant and the black extremes which hold our thoughts" (1969, p. 118; see also Shackle, 1970, Ch. 5). In the case in hand, then, we can characterize the *attention-arresting power* of the project in terms of its *focus elements* A and B. In more complex and realistic cases, it is perfectly conceivable that within such a range "zero potential surprise can be assigned to each of an unlimited number of rival, mutually exclusive [outcome] hypotheses all at once; any number of suggested answers to a question . . . can all be regarded . . . as perfectly possible. The same is true of any other degree of potential surprise. . . . Potential surprise is completely nondistributional" (Shackle, 1969, p. 70).

Suppose now that a project being contemplated differs from the one we have just considered in that its range of possible outcomes extends along the X axis to the right of B and also possibly to the left of A. Its potential-surprise curve can still be as shown in Figure 12.1, having an *inner range* of *perfectly possible* or *zero potential surprise* outcomes, but with the prospect also of other possible outcomes to which positive potential surprise is attached. Examine now the rightward segment of such a project's potential-surprise curve.

A slightly higher outcome than B, say $B + \Delta X$, may be conceived to be possible, but less than perfectly possible, and it may have associated with it a positive potential surprise indicated by the point W on the curve. As the level of possible outcome is higher, the degree of potential surprise will also become larger. Indeed, in view of the increasing degree of uncertainty surrounding the higher possible outcomes, and considering the fact that the possible outcomes become more shadowy in the decision maker's vision, the potential surprise may well increase for a time at an increasing rate. But for very high possible outcomes, for those, for example, in the range that is thought to be nearly impossible, the rate of increase in potential surprise will have slackened, and the potential-surprise curve will approach the asymptote $\bar{y}$. It follows that the rightward segment of the potential-surprise curve is likely to assume the elongated S form shown in Figure 12.1. A comparable argument can be applied to the S form of the leftward or loss segment of the potential-surprise curve also.

In the first of the projects we discussed, the project's *power to arrest and command the decision maker's attention* was encapsuled in the gain and loss *focus values B* and *A*. For the second project, as the contemplated possible outcome increases, say to $B + \Delta X$, the attractiveness of this value, or its power to grasp or focus the decision maker's attention, may outweigh the nonzero degree of potential surprise associated with it. Thus the focus element of the project may shift from B to W. Then whereas the first project commanded attention by virtue of its focus elements A and B, the second project commands attention by virtue of *its* focus elements A and W.

We can visualize in this way a cognitive and evaluative process in the mind of the decision maker whereby he marshalls together, with respect to a given project, both (i) the range of possible outcome elements associated with the project and (ii) the degree of uncertainty associated with each such element or subset of the total range of elements. If we assume that the decision maker is risk averse, to employ the parallel thought form we encountered in the theory of utility in Chapter 6, then he will be (1) attracted in a positive sense by higher possible money values of possible outcomes but (2) repelled by the higher degrees of potential surprise associated with them. A trade-off evolves in the decision maker's mind. He will want to choose projects or commit economic resources in such a way that if he is risk averse, he will have the prospect of realizing as high as possible a value outcome without the potential-surprise curve at such a point having risen too far above the X axis.

Investment decision criterion

We now recall that each potential-surprise curve that the decision maker confronts will refer to a specific investment project or other economic opportunity. If investment projects are in view, the decision maker will confront a nest or series of such potential-surprise curves, one for each project available for consideration.

In respect to each potential-surprise curve, the decision maker must confront all possible outcomes extending over the range over which the curve is defined, but he must regard these *not* as possible occurrences in a series of repetitive processes but as *rival* outcomes. Only one of them can eventuate, determined by the unique conjunction of forces that give rise to it. Not only are all of the possible outcomes rivals in this sense, but the decision situation in which the decision maker stands is unique in the sense in which we have explained its uniqueness before. It is unique in that it occurs at a unique point in historic time, in the fact that the decision environment, existentially and epistemologically, is therefore unique, and unique in the fact that the taking of the decision may destroy forever the possibility of its being taken, or even contemplated, again. But we can deduce a still firmer statement. As all of the possible outcomes of a given project over which its potential surprise function is defined are rival outcomes and only one of them can occur, no meaning at all could be attached to any kind of averaging of them, for no repetitive processes are available to give any rationale to such an averaging process. Potential surprise is completely nondistributional. No logical meaning can possibly attach to any such concept as the expected value or the variance of possible outcomes in such unique situations.

Consider now a potential-surprise function of the kind described in Figure 12.1 associated with a specific investment project A. We now describe on the outcome axis the possible net present values of the project. We concentrate separately on its positive, or gain, and its negative, or loss, segments. We wish to isolate, in a manner consistent with the basic development to this point, what we called *focus elements*, or magnitudes on the value outcome axis on which the decision maker can concentrate his attention for purposes of evaluating the project. On the gain side, for example, such an element may be the value magnitude associated with points W or D on the potential-surprise curve in Figure 12.1.

The focus element summarizes, as we observed in our development of the underlying potential-surprise function, the power of the investment project to arrest or command the decision maker's attention. Such an attention-arresting function, designated R in Equation (12.1), or what has been previously referred to as an attractiveness function (Vickers, 1978, p. 148), will be defined over the possible-outcome and potential-surprise magnitudes, x and y, respectively:

$$R = R(x, y) \tag{12.1}$$

In Figure 12.2 are shown the isoattractiveness contours implicit in the attractiveness function described in Equation (12.1), together with a potential-surprise curve. As will be indicated immediately, that focus element will exert the maximum attention-arresting power, or will provide the maximum attainable value of the attractiveness function, which establishes an equality between the slope of the isoattractiveness contour and the potential-surprise curve. The arrows in Figure 12.2 indicate the directions of increasing attracting power of possible focus points.

Given the relation between the potential-surprise and outcome values, $y = y(x)$, and recognizing that the potential-surprise function operates as a constraint on the possible values of the attractiveness function, or that the operative values of the latter function will be determined by coordinates that lie on the potential-surprise function, the attractiveness function becomes

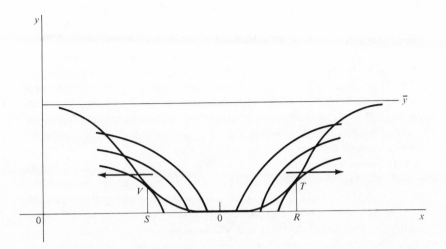

Figure 12.2

$$R = R[x, y(x)] \tag{12.2}$$

Taking R_1 and R_2 as the partial derivatives of the attractiveness function with respect to its first and second arguments, respectively, the attention-arresting power of a project is summarized in the following relations:

$$R_1 \gtrless 0 \quad \text{for } x \gtrless 0$$
$$R_2 < 0 \quad \text{for } 0 \leq y \leq \bar{y}, x \neq 0 \tag{12.3}$$

In determining the gain and loss focus elements, the decision maker will investigate the (x, y) coordinates that generate the maximum value of the R-function in each of the gain and loss directions, understanding, as has been noted, that the relevant coordinates will lie on the potential-surprise function. The decision maker's subjective reaction to possible outcomes and potential surprise summarized in Equations (12.1) and (12.3) therefore implies that the focus elements of the investment project under examination will be the points at which the subjective outcome-surprise trade-off implicit in Equation (12.1),

$$dy/dx = -R_1/R_2 \tag{12.4}$$

is equal to the corresponding trade-off defined in the potential-surprise function that is relevant to the project. That is,

$$\left. \frac{dy}{dx} \right|_{\text{PS}} = \left. \frac{dy}{dx} \right|_{R} \tag{12.5}$$

where the left-hand and right-hand sides of Equation (12.5) represent, respectively, the slope of the potential surprise function and the slope relation between the arguments of the attractiveness function. Such points occur at T and V in Figure 12.2, reflecting focus values of R and S on the x axis immediately below them. At those points, the highest attainable values of the R-function will be registered. No possible (x, y) point on the potential-surprise function would generate a higher power of attraction or attention-arresting power as summarized in the attractiveness function. The point of maximum attainable R-value, therefore, will describe the (x, y) coordinates on the potential-surprise function that serves as the focus element.

Corresponding arguments thus lead to the specification of focus elements on both the loss, or negative, and the gain, or positive, segments of the potential-surprise function. The focus values describe the projects that the decision maker will subject to particularly careful scrutiny in the course of making his investment decision. He will be interested in those projects that promise high favorable outcomes with low potential surprise and/or large possible losses or unfavorable outcomes with low potential surprise.

In his final project selection, the decision maker will be positively disposed to the high possibility, or low potential surprise, of large gains. Similarly, he will prefer not to invest in projects that hold out the prospect, with high possibility or low potential surprise, of large losses. In the example of the investment project, the loss could be visualized as negative net present values. We may therefore make use of the focus elements to establish an investment decision criterion in the following manner.

In relation to the investment project, we now possess four pieces of information or input data for the decision event. These are (i) the focus element on the gain side, which we shall refer to in the following argument as FG, or, in the case of project A, as FG_A; (ii) a comparable focus element on the loss side, FL_A; (iii) a potential-surprise magnitude associated with the focus gain value, PS_{GA}; and (iv) a potential surprise associated with the focus loss value, PS_{LA}. The potential-surprise curve for project A with which we are working may not extend into, or may not extend significantly far into, the loss segment. Economic conditions may be generally so favorable that the firm can expect, with a high degree of confidence, to realize a positive outcome, or at the worst virtually break even, on the project. In such a case, the loss segment of the potential-surprise curve may be virtually vertical at or near the zero point on the outcome axis. What we are here referring to as the loss region may therefore include small positive values.

The final investment decision leading to an acceptance or rejection of project A involves a subjective weighting in the mind of the decision maker of these four pieces of information. We may therefore conceptualize a Decision Index (DI) and stylize it as

$$DI_A = f(FG_A, PS_{GA}, FL_A, PS_{LA}) \tag{12.6}$$

When the decision index value relevant to the project has been determined, the investment criterion can be visualized as

$$DI \gtrless \theta \tag{12.7}$$

where θ describes a critical required level set by the firm. The project will be acceptable to the firm only if it has associated with it a Decision Index value no smaller than the prespecified critical level. This critical value may, of course, be zero. It will be set by the decision maker at a level that reflects his general aversion to uncertainty, as well as, in appropriate cases, the need to concentrate resources on investment projects that promise a rapid return cash inflow, or a low payback period. This may be desirable in situations, such as we encountered in the preceding chapter, where cash flows are highly desirable as a means of financing further investment outlays that facilitate the continued growth of the firm and promise highly attractive benefits in the longer run future.

The general form of the Decision Index function in Equation (12.6) can be further specified as follows. Writing f_i, $i = 1, \ldots, 4$, to refer to the partial derivatives, indicating the directions of change of the function value with respect to the four arguments in the order in which they are stated in Equation (12.6), we have

$$f_1 > 0, f_2 < 0, f_3 < 0, f_4 > 0 \tag{12.8}$$

This means that high focus gains are desirable, but that high potential surprises associated with them are undesirable. On the other hand, high focus losses are undesirable, but that undesirability will be modified if a high potential surprise is associated with their possible occurrence.

It is not possible to represent the four-dimensional Decision Index function geometrically, but an intuitive view of one of its planes can be seen in Figure 12.3. The figure shows the plane bounded by values of the first and the third arguments in the function described by Equation (12.6), given fixed values of the second and fourth arguments. Point A in the figure locates a pair of simultaneous observations from the focus gains and losses. We note that this point lies to the northwest of the curve 00, emanating from the origin of the plane. This curve might be understood as an indifference locus generated by the form of the Decision Index function, describing the manner in which, in the decision maker's mind, different combinations of possible gains and losses would contribute to the quantification of the Decision Index when the values of the remaining arguments are given. It is envisaged in Figure 12.3 that an indifference map may be deduced from the Decision Index function and drawn in a plane such as that indicated. The positive slope of the indifference curves

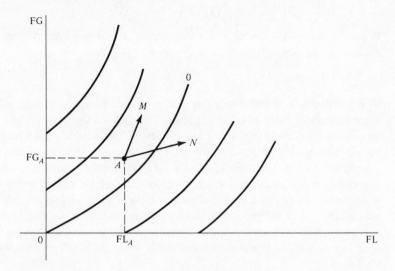

Figure 12.3

follows from the posited signs on the partial derivatives in (12.8). The convexity in the curves suggests that as higher focus loss regions are contemplated, it will be necessary to offset these, for any value of the Decision Index, by higher focus gain values, the magnitude of which increases at an increasing rate as contemplated losses increase. Gain and loss combinations lying to the southeast of the 00 indifference curve, which we may refer to as the origin indifference curve, would then be less desirable than not committing money capital to any investment at all. So far as this plane is concerned, it would be desirable, for effective investment decisions, to choose available investment projects whose gain–loss coordinates, such as those represented by the point A, lie as far as possible to the northwest of the origin indifference curve, 00.

In this way, it is possible to compare the desirability of different investment project opportunities and to rank them by the criterion of their Decision Index values. By this means, an adequately full attention can be paid to the characteristics of uniqueness surrounding each such project confronting the firm, to the uniqueness of the time point at which the decision is contemplated, and to the likely impact of a decision on the future structure and operating experience of the firm. It is not suggested, in other words, that the characteristics of uniqueness should be violated by the pretence, as is required by the alternative interpretation of the decision moment required by the probability calculus, that averages of potentially unique and rival outcomes can be meaningfully calculated. Nor is it suggested that meaning can attach to the average extent of the dispersion of such potentially unique outcomes around any such average value. The notion of potential surprise from which the Decision Index is derived is, we have seen, nondistributional.

Interpretation of economic value

It was supposed, in the preceding example of the project investment decision criterion, that the outcome axis in Figure 12.1 over which the potential-surprise function was defined could be taken to describe the net present value of the project. This implies that the firm first computes the possible net present values by employing the discounting procedures we outlined earlier and then describes the potential-surprise function over the values obtained. These actual computations would employ the basic valuation equation we took into account in the preceding chapter:

$$V = \sum_{t=1}^{n} S_t (1+m)^{-t} \tag{12.9}$$

In this equation, the discount factor is again taken as the effective marginal cost of obtaining money capital. We shall see below that the investment decision may be sensitive to the assumed possible values of the discount factor, and it will therefore be necessary for the firm to analyze its prospects and projects carefully in terms of a range of possible marginal costs of capital. Similarly, it will be necessary to assume ranges of values within which the periodic cash inflow, S_t in Equation (12.9), may fall. By such means, and by examining different possible combinations of periodic cash flows and money capital costs, it will be possible to build up a picture of the possible net economic values of the project over which the potential surprise function can be defined. Investment project selection can then proceed in the manner already indicated.

But an alternative application of the decision methodology may be made. Let us focus initially on the successive periodic cash inflows and consider any one particular element of the series. We may specify the range of possible outcomes within which we assume the value of this S_t may occur and then describe a potential-surprise function in the familiar manner for that S_t. In this way we may focus, in the same manner as previously, on the focus gain and the focus loss of the tth period's cash inflow. Of course, it may again be the case that for specific periods, or perhaps for all periods, the potential-surprise curves defined over the cash flows might not extend into, or not significantly far into, the loss region at all. The cash flows may be confidently expected to be positive.

By this means, we can specify the focus elements of *each* of the periodic elements of the cash flow stream. These focus values may be discounted back to the present by employing for this purpose the firm's marginal cost of money capital in the same manner as before. The successive periodic focus gains and losses should be discounted separately, in order to preserve the gain–loss distinctions we have worked with consistently in this approach to investment project evaluation. We thereby derive a present discounted value of focus gains that we can refer to as V_G, or V_{GA} in the case of project A. Similarly, we can derive a discounted value of the focus loss elements, referring to this as V_L, or again as V_{LA}. Referring to the magnitudes of the focus gain and loss elements of the possible tth period's cash flow as S_{tG} and S_{tL}, respectively, we have

$$V_G = \sum_t S_{tG}(1+m)^{-t} \tag{12.10}$$

and

$$V_L = \sum_t S_{tL}(1+m)^{-t} \tag{12.11}$$

At the same time as the focus elements of the successive periods' cash flows were specified to provide the basic data for the discounting or valuation procedure, the decision maker will have made subjective observations of the range of potential-surprise magnitudes associated with them. On this basis, it will be possible to specify also the potential-surprise magnitudes associated with the V_G and V_L values. In this way, the procedure will have provided the input values necessary to estimate the relevant value of the Decision Index. The only difference in the present case is that the first and the third arguments in the Decision Index function will now appear as the V_G and V_L values we have just derived. One further possible complication may, however, arise. It has to do with the possibility of what we shall refer to as investment project reversal. It can be envisaged briefly as follows.

The possibility of project reversal

Consider for this purpose the gain–loss plane of the Decision Index function as shown in Figure 12.3. In the present application of the project evaluation methodology, we may label the horizontal and vertical axes, respectively, as V_L and V_G. We again visualize the coordinates of project A in this gain–loss value plane.

Suppose now that a lower cost of money capital is assumed for purposes of discounting the periodic cash flow elements. This will have the effect of increasing both the V_G and the V_L values associated with the project. The resulting effect on the project evaluation, so far as it is representable in the amended plane of Figure 12.3, may be to move the coordinate point from A to, say, M. If that should occur, the capitalized value of the gain outcomes has increased to a greater degree than that of the loss outcomes. The project's attractiveness has improved, as the coordinate point has moved further to the northwest of the origin indifference curve. On the other hand, it is conceivable that a reduction in the cost of money capital may cause a larger increase in the discounted values of the loss elements than in those of the gain elements. In that case, the coordinate point in Figure 12.3 may move from A to N. If this should happen, the project will fall from the northwest to the southeast of the origin indifference curve, and it will no longer be attractive to the firm.

If the latter possibility should eventuate when a lower cost of money capital is assumed, the relation between investment expenditure and the cost of capital is running counter to that generally posited in neoclassical theory. Investment has become less, rather than more, attractive at lower costs of capital. The reason for this possibility lies in the different time shapes that may be assumed by the loss sequences and the gain sequences implicit in prospective cash flows. The possibility uncovers what became an intense ground of debate a decade ago under the name of "reswitching" and "capital reversal" in the theory of capital (see Shackle, 1969, pp. 238, 290; Harcourt, 1972).

Utility reappraised

Recalling the development of the preceding investment decision criterion, it would be an understandable inference to interpret the Decision Index as an implicit utility function defined over outcomes and potential surprise. Obviously, there is a *formal* similarity between the traditional utility function and the Decision Index, but the differences provide good ground for keeping the vocabulary quite distinct.

The utility function, or the expected utility function defined in Chapter 6 and applied to the equilibrium theory of financial asset prices and yields in Chapter 7, was defined over the moments, principally the mean and the variance, of the subjectively assigned probability distribution of a random variable. But in the potential-surprise analysis of this chapter, the probability underpinning has been abandoned completely in favor of a nondistributional variable approach. There is therefore no warrant for speaking of expectations and associated dispersions in a mathematical-statistical sense, and such a procedure has been deprived of legitimacy. Any trade-off that arises in this new way of looking at things necessarily has a different connotation and is embedded in a very different specification of variables.

The Decision Index, moreover, is tied uniquely to a specified decision moment in real historic time. At each point in time at which a decision is made, a new set of potential-surprise functions and a new Decision Index must be created, dislodging the old as events and attitudes are reshaped. Any notion of an intertemporally stable utility function comports best with a static view of decision situations and events, not with the dynamic evolution of affairs that belongs to the world of fact. Utility analysis and its associated vocabulary have meaningful reference only to the timeless and static constructs of the traditional theory that we have summarized in the preceding chapters.

A final note on probability

It may be imagined also that the potential-surprise curve can be regarded as essentially a probability distribution turned upside down and that all that has been said about potential surprise can be transformed into statements about probability. The suggestion may be encountered that the potential surprise attached to a possible outcome can be interpreted as unity minus the probability of its occurrence. But this would evince a failure to understand fully the decision apparatus we have proposed, and it would overlook some important and fundamental distinctions (see Shackle, 1969, Part II, Chs. 11, 12; Georgescu-Roegen, 1966, p. 260f. and Ch. 6; Katzner, 1986).

It should be borne in mind that we are dealing here with *potential* surprise, and this requires us to bring into our analysis all that has been said regarding the *uniqueness* of the decision event and the decision maker's stance at a unique point in the flow of time. *Potential* surprise refers to an individual's assessment of what he imagines *now,* at the decision point, would be the surprise he would feel in the future if a possible outcome were to occur. There is no logical meaning in the comparison between *surprise actually experienced* at one point in time and the *potential surprise* with which a possible outcome was contemplated at an anterior point in time. Each such temporal point has its own uniqueness. But more particularly, the transformation of potential surprise, based on degrees of disbelief, into probability, which is related, on the contrary, to degrees of belief, is prohibited in a large number of economic-financial decisions by the fact that the occurrence of decisions at temporally separate and discrete dates makes it logically impossible to regard the decision events as repetitive or replicable.

Consider the fact that our argument anchored the potential-surprise curve in the reality of *perfect possibility.* It would be well beyond our province to inquire into the psychological foundations that prepare an individual to take observable and describable attitudes to situations and possibilities and events. All that we have posited is that as the individual surveys the range of possible outcomes, he *is* able to say that there is a range of outcomes, a subset of the entire possibilities, such that he would *not be at all surprised* if any of them were to occur. Such an *inner range* need not be large. It may be quite small. The important thing is that, small or large, this is a range of outcomes that the decision maker regards as *perfectly possible* and to which, therefore, he attaches *zero potential surprise*.

To make probability transformations out of this would involve a gigantic leap. For what *probability* is to be taken as representing perfect *possibility?* Is it unity? But the analysis speaks of perfect *possibility* and *not* perfect *certainty*, for the whole tenor and motivation of the ideas is *un*certainty. Moreover, there is nothing to prevent our saying that any number of outcomes are perfectly possible, and therefore assigning to them all a zero potential surprise.

What is more, it is quite reasonable to assign perfect possibility to both a possible outcome and its contradictory. Inevitably this is involved when we invoke the *uniqueness* of the decision event, for from a given decision only one actual outcome can eventuate. What, then, would be the probability it might be wished to associate with our uncertainty concept of perfect possibility? In the light of what has been said, it cannot be unity. But then on what grounds is it possible to say that *any* designatable probability magnitude corresponds to perfect possibility? "Should we not rather say that there is *no* natural and self-justifying basis for a mapping of probability on possibility, and therefore, on potential surprise?" (Shackle, 1969, p. 71).

This does not deny that the decision maker's judgments as to possibility and potential surprise may arise in part out of objectively given frequency ratios described in historically generated data. Yet, regardless of information, fashions, and even the conventional reliance on the likelihood that the outcomes of tomorrow will be like the events of yesterday, it does *not* follow that potential surprise can be *mapped into* probability. A hypothesis may, from a probability point of view, be rendered more improbable merely by a change in an individual's knowledge as time passes and introduces additional hypotheses, even though the first hypothesis is *in itself* quite unaffected by such new knowledge. Against all such changes as these, however, potential surprise is invariant.

In connection with repetitive experiments, the idea of a probability distribution can find a haven. In such cases, the foundation postulate that financial theory deals with "choices among probability distributions" would have meaning. But this, we have argued, is simply not the case in large numbers of economic-financial decisions. The latter involve preponderantly unique decisions under uncertainty, and the "unsureness" that abounds cannot invoke the probability methods that sweep uncertainty away.

New knowledge does, however, appear as time passes. The experiences that time bequeaths and the actual surprises, delights, and disappointments, and regrets they administer shape our perceptions of things at succeeding decision moments. Our perceptions of the ranges of bounded possibilities may change, along with what history has taught us about the ways of anticipating different kinds of outcomes in different situations. Our ability to be surprised changes. Our understanding of our own potential surprise varies. The general structure of our expectation formation changes, though we realize that we never know more about the future. The future is forever unknown. It is unknowable. It is for that reason that we need an apparatus of thought with which to approach the task and responsibilities of decision making that acknowledges the realities of ignorance in which we inevitably stand.

Further applications and the place of economic judgment

The potential-surprise methodology has wider applications in the firm than simply to the capital investment expenditure decision we have examined. In the preceding chapter, the capital expenditure and the associated financing decisions were visualized in terms of a comparison between the cost of money capital and an expected rate of return on investment outlays. Though the discussion will not be extended at this stage, a potential-surprise function could equally well be described over a range of possible rate-of-return outcomes and the methodology could be implemented on lines parallel to the foregoing.

The potential-surprise function may be described also over the possible rate-of-return outcomes or the possible economic values that can be realized from holding a portfolio of assets. The argument is not necessarily applicable only to the single-project or single-asset choice situation we have so far envisaged. The economics and the mechanics of asset diversification assumed a prominent place, of course, in the equilibrium asset market theory we examined in Part II. The most acute difficulty with it, however, is that it is grounded in the assumption that rates of return on assets can be properly treated as random variables describable by assigned probability distributions. We have discussed at some length the serious epistemological difficulties in imagining that the unknown and unknowable future can be corraled and its uncertainties defined away in this fashion. Moreover, the firms whose securities are assumed to generate the rates of return, as we observed at the beginning of our argument in Chapter 1, are not able to be treated as stable, unchanging, event-generating mechanisms. Firms change, grow, decay, and die. Their operating, financing, and general economic structures change over time. There does not therefore appear solid and secure reason to treat their periodic rates of return as random variables in a statistically manipulable sense.

But individuals do hold, to varying degrees, portfolios of assets, and firms do invest in different asset forms, with a view to spreading risks and taking advantage of presumed or anticipated benefits of diversification. It might be agreed that the logic by which such diversification is grounded in probability assignments is defective. But there do remain reasons why investors diversify, such, for example, as the possession of specific information, hunches, guesses, or a willingness to rely on the positivist notion that yesterday's outcomes will in general be repeated again tomorrow or a readiness to imagine that historic distributions will continue to describe the future.

Given that this is so, it is a straightforward matter to envisage the returns and benefits that any number of possible portfolios of assets might generate and to describe potential-surprise functions over them. From that point, a choice between portfolios may be contemplated in now familiar ways. Derived data descriptive of each of the portfolios may be brought into the Decision Index and their relative attractiveness compared.

The strength of the analysis we have proposed lies to a significant degree in the place it accords to economic judgment in decision problems in the firm. Rather than assuming away the uncertainties for what they are and where they really exist, or reducing them to certainties or certainty-equivalents by stochastic reduction methods where the calculus of distributional variables cannot properly apply, the real-world decision maker's responsibility has been identified and provided with a logically robust framework of analysis for dealing with it. Judgments need not partake of the mathematical precision that might appear to inhere in the analysis as it has been presented. The main conclusion is that judgments involving comparisons between economic alternatives have to be made, and a quite simple and straightforward modus operandi for making them has been proposed.[2]

[2] The foundations of decision making under conditions of uncertainty have become the subject of an extensive literature. On the proposals of Shackle, on whose scheme of analysis we have presented a variation in the foregoing, see the evaluation and critique in Ozga (1965, Ch. 7), Carter and Ford (1972), and Georgescu-Roegen (1966). In this literature, particular note might be taken of those proposals that, like our foregoing argument, suggest alternatives to probabilistic reductionism. See Ozga (1965, p. 263f.) for relevant comments on Savage's notion of minimum subjective loss (Savage, 1951), Hurwicz's index of pessimism and optimism (Hurwicz, 1972), Fellner's theory of safety margins (Fellner, 1960), and Roy's theory of minimum chance of disaster or what has become widely known as his safety first argument (Roy, 1952). Elton and Gruber (1984, p. 222f.) present a highly interesting reconciliation of Roy's safety first argument with the mean–variance theory of asset selection that we considered in Part II. This kinship stems from Roy's use of observed frequency distributions of rates of return and the application of Tchebycheff's theorem on probabilities based upon them.

References

Amey, L. R. 1973. *Readings in Managerial Decision.* London: Longmans.

Archer, S. H., Choate, G. M., and Racette, G. 1983. *Financial Management,* 2nd ed. New York: Wiley.

Arditti, F. D., and Levy, H. 1977. "Portfolio Efficiency Analysis in Three Moments: The Multiperiod Case." *In* Levy, H., and Sarnat, M. (eds.), *Financial Decision Making Under Uncertainty.* New York: Academic, pp. 137–50.

Arrow, K. J. 1971. *Essays in the Theory of Risk-Bearing.* Chicago: Markham.

Barges, A. 1963. *The Effect of Capital Structure on the Cost of Capital: A Test and Evaluation of the Modigliani and Miller Propositions.* Englewood Cliffs, NJ: Prentice-Hall.

Baumol, W. J. 1952. "The Transactions Demand for Cash: An Inventory Theoretic Approach." *Quarterly Journal of Economics* 66: 545–56.

——— 1959. *Business Behavior, Value and Growth.* New York: Macmillan.

Baumol, W. J., and Malkiel, B. G. 1967. "The Firm's Optimal Debt-Equity Combination and the Cost of Capital." *Quarterly Journal of Economics* 81: 547–78.

Bausor, R. 1982. "Time and the Structure of Economic Analysis." *Journal of Post Keynesian Economics* 5: 163–79.

——— 1984. "Toward a Historically Dynamic Economics: Examples and Illustrations." *Journal of Post Keynesian Economics* 6: 360–76.

Bernoulli, D. 1968. "Exposition of a New Theory on the Measurement of Risk." *In* Page, A. N. (ed.), *Utility Theory: A Book of Readings.* New York: Wiley, pp. 199–214.

Bierman, H. Jr., and Hass, J. E. 1973. *An Introduction to Managerial Finance.* New York: Norton.

Black, F. 1972. "Capital Market Equilibrium with Restricted Borrowing." *Journal of Business* 45: 444–55.

Boulding, K. E. 1950. *A Reconstruction of Economics.* New York: Wiley.

——— 1966. *Economic Analysis,* 4th ed. New York: Harper & Row.

Brealey, R., and Myers, S. 1984. *Principles of Corporate Finance,* 2nd ed. New York: McGraw-Hill.

Buchanan, N. S. 1940. *The Economics of Corporate Enterprise.* New York: Henry Holt.

Carter, C. F., and Ford, J. L. (eds.). 1972. *Uncertainty and Expectations in Economics: Essays in Honor of G. L. S. Shackle.* Oxford: Blackwell.

Chamberlin, E. H. 1933. *The Theory of Monopolistic Competition.* Cambridge, MA: Harvard University Press.

232

Coats, A. W. (ed.). 1983. *Methodological Controversy in Economics: Historical Essays in Honor of T. W. Hutchison.* Greenwich, CT: JAI.

Coddington, A. 1983. *Keynesian Economics: The Search for First Principles.* London: Allen & Unwin.

Copeland, T. E., and Weston, J. F. 1983. *Financial Theory and Corporate Policy,* 2nd ed. Reading, MA: Addison-Wesley.

Davidson, P. 1965. "Keynes's Finance Motive." *Oxford Economic Papers* 17: 47–65.

   1978. *Money and the Real World,* 2nd ed. London: Macmillan.

Durand, D. 1952. "Cost of Debt and Equity Funds for Business: Trends and Problems in Measurement." *In Conference on Research in Business Finance.* New York: National Bureau of Economic Research, pp. 215–47.

Eichner, A. S. 1976. *The Megacorp and Oligopoly, Micro Foundations of Macro Dynamics.* Cambridge: Cambridge University Press.

   1985. *Toward a New Economics: Essays in Post Keynesian and Institutionalist Theory.* Armonk, NY: Sharpe.

Elton, E. J., and Gruber, M. J. 1984. *Modern Portfolio Theory and Investment Analysis,* 2nd ed. New York: Wiley.

Fama, E. F., and Miller, M. 1972. *The Theory of Finance.* New York: Holt, Rinehart *American Economic Review* 68: 272–84.

Fama, E. F., and Miller, M. 1972. *The Theory of Finance.* New York: Holt, Rinehart and Winston.

Fellner, W. 1960. *Competition Among the Few.* New York: Kelley.

Ford, J. L. 1983. *Choice, Expectation and Uncertainty: An Appraisal of G. L. S. Shackle's Theory.* Totowa, NJ: Barnes & Noble.

Friedman, M., and Savage, L. J. 1968. "The Utility Analysis of Choice Involving Risk." *In* Page, A. N. (ed.). *Utility Theory: A Book of Readings.* New York: Wiley, pp. 234–68.

Friend, I., and Bicksler, J. (eds.). 1977. *Risk and Return in Finance.* Cambridge, MA: Ballinger.

Gabor, A., and Pearce, I. F. 1952. "A New Approach to the Theory of the Firm." *Oxford Economic Papers* 4: 252–65.

   1958. "The Place of Money Capital in the Theory of Production." *Quarterly Journal of Economics* 72: 537–57.

Georgescu-Roegen, N. 1966. *Analytical Economics.* Cambridge, MA: Harvard University Press.

Gordon, M. J. 1962. *The Investment, Financing, and Valuation of the Corporation.* Homewood, IL: Irwin.

Gordon, M. J., and Shapiro, E. 1956. "Capital Investment Analysis: The Required Rate of Return." *Management Science* 3: 102–10.

Hahn, F. H. 1970. "Some Adjustment Problems." *Econometrica* 38: 1–17.

   1971. "Equilibrium with Transactions Costs." *Econometrica* 39: 417–39.

Hahn, F. H., and Brechling, F. P. R. (eds.). 1965. *The Theory of Interest Rates.* London: Macmillan.

Haley, C. W., and Schall, L.D. 1973. *The Theory of Financial Decisions.* New York: McGraw-Hill.

Hamada, R. S. 1969. "Portfolio Analysis, Market Equilibrium and Corporation Finance." *Journal of Finance* 24: 13–31.

Harcourt, G. C. 1972. *Some Cambridge Controversies in the Theory of Capital.* Cambridge: Cambridge University Press.

Harris, L. 1981. *Monetary Theory.* New York: McGraw-Hill.

Harris, S. E. 1947. *The New Economics.* London: Dennis Dobson.

Henderson, J. M., and Quandt, R. E. 1971. *Microeconomic Theory: A Mathematical Approach,* 2nd ed. New York: McGraw-Hill.

Herendeen, J. B. 1975. *The Economics of the Corporate Economy.* New York: Dunellen.

Hey, J. D. 1979. *Uncertainty in Microeconomics.* Oxford: Martin Robertson.

Hicks, J. 1946. *Value and Capital,* 2nd ed. Oxford: Clarendon.

1967. "The Pure Theory of Portfolio Selection." *In Hicks' Collected Essays, Critical Essays in Monetary Theory.* Oxford: Clarendon, pp. 103–25.

1976. "Some Questions of Time in Economics." In Tang, A. M., Westfield, F. M., and Worley, J. S. (eds.), *Evolution, Welfare, and Time in Economics: Essays in Honor of Nicholas Georgescu-Roegen.* Lexington, MA: Lexington Books, pp. 135–51.

1979. *Causality in Economics.* New York: Basic Books.

Hirshleifer, J., and Riley, J. G. 1979. "The Analytics of Uncertainty and Information: An Expository Survey." *Journal of Economic Literature* 17: 1375–1421.

Hurwicz, L. 1972. *Optimality Criteria for Decision Making under Ignorance.* Cowles Commission Discussion Paper, *Statistics* 370. Reproduced in amended form in Arrow, K. J., and Hurwicz, L., "An Optimality Criterion for Decision Making under Ignorance." *In* Carter, C. F., and Ford, J. L. (eds.). *Uncertainty and Expectations in Economics: Essays in Honor of G. L. S. Shackle.* Oxford: Blackwell, pp. 1–11.

Hutchison, T. W. 1937. "Expectations and Rational Conduct." *Zeitschrift fur Nationalokonomie* 8: 636–53.

1960. *The Significance and Basic Postulates of Economic Theory,* 2nd ed. New York: Kelley.

1978. *On Revolutions and Progress in Economic Knowledge.* Cambridge: Cambridge University Press.

Jensen, M. C. (ed.). 1972. *Studies in the Theory of Capital Markets.* New York: Praeger.

Kalecki, M. 1937. "The Principle of Increasing Risk." *Economica* 4: 440–47.

Katzner, D. W. 1986. "Potential Surprise, Potential Confirmation, and Probability." *Journal of Post Keynesian Economics* 9: 58–78.

Keynes, J. M. 1936. *The General Theory of Employment, Interest and Money.* London: Macmillan.

1937. "The General Theory of Employment." *Quarterly Journal of Economics* 51: 209–23. Reprinted in Harris, S. E., *The New Economics.* London: Dennis Dobson, pp. 181–93.

Knight, F. H. 1933. *Risk, Uncertainty, and Profit.* Boston: Houghton Mifflin, London School of Economics Reprint.

Koopmans, T. C. 1957. *Three Essays on the State of Economic Science.* New York: McGraw-Hill.

Lachmann, L. M. 1956. *Capital and Its Structure.* London: G. Bell, London School of Economics Reprint.

1959. "Professor Shackle and the Economic Significance of Time." *Metroeconomica* 11: 64–73.

Lange, O. 1936. "The Place of Interest in the Theory of Production." *Review of Economic Studies* 3: 159–92.

Levy, H., and Sarnat, M. (eds.). 1977. *Financial Decision Making under Uncertainty.* New York: Academic.

Lintner, J. 1965. "The Valuation of Risk Assets and the Selection of Risky Investments in Stock Portfolios and Capital Budgets." *Review of Economics and Statistics* 47: 13–37.

1969. "An Aggregation of Investors' Diverse Judgment and Preferences in Purely Competitive Securities Markets." *Journal of Financial and Quantitative Analysis* 4: 347–400.

Littlechild, S. C. 1979. "Radical Subjectivism or Radical Subversion." *In* Rizzo, M. J. (ed.), *Time, Uncertainty, and Disequilibrium,* Lexington, MA: Lexington Books, pp. 32–49.

Loasby, B. J. 1971. "Hypothesis and Paradigm in the Theory of the Firm." *Economic Journal* 81: 863–85.

1976. *Choice, Complexity and Ignorance.* Cambridge: Cambridge University Press.

Lorie, J. H., and Savage, L. J. 1955. "Three Problems in Rationing Capital." *Journal of Business* 28: 229–39.

Luce, R. D., and Raiffa, H. 1957. *Games and Decisions.* New York: Wiley.

Markowitz, H. M. 1952. "Portfolio Selection." *Journal of Finance* 7: 77–91.

1959. *Portfolio Selection: Efficient Diversification of Investments.* New York: Wiley, for the Cowles Foundation for Research in Economics.

Marris, R. 1964. *The Economic Theory of Managerial Capitalism.* London: Macmillan.

Marshall, A. 1920. *Principles of Economics,* 8th ed. London: Macmillan.

Miller, M. H., and Orr, D. 1966. "A Model of Demand for Money by Firms." *Quarterly Journal of Economics* 80: 413–35.

Minsky, H. P. 1975. *John Maynard Keynes.* New York: Columbia University Press.

Modigliani, F., and Miller, M. H. 1958. "The Cost of Capital, Corporate Finance and the Theory of Investment." *American Economic Review* 48: 261–97.

Mossin, J. 1972. *Pricing Theory and Its Implications for Corporate Investment Decisions.* Morristown, NJ: General Learning.

1973. *Theory of Financial Markets.* Englewood Cliffs, NJ: Prentice-Hall.

Nickell, S. J. 1978. *The Investment Decisions of Firms.* Cambridge: Cambridge University Press.

O'Driscoll, G. P., Jr., and Rizzo, M. J. 1985. *The Economics of Time and Ignorance.* Oxford: Blackwell.

Ozga, S. A. 1965. *Expectations in Economic Theory.* Chicago: Aldine.

Page, A. N. (ed.). 1968. *Utility Theory: A Book of Readings.* New York: Wiley.

Patinkin, D. 1965. *Money, Interest, and Prices,* 2nd ed. New York: Harper & Row.

Penrose, E. 1959. *The Theory of the Growth of the Firm.* Oxford: Blackwell.

Pratt, J. W. 1964. "Risk Aversion in the Small and in the Large." *Econometrica* 32: 122–36.

Rizzo, M. J. (ed.). 1979. *Time, Uncertainty, and Disequilibrium.* Lexington, MA: Lexington Books.

Robbins, L. 1935. *An Essay on the Nature and Significance of Economic Science,* 2nd ed. London: Macmillan.

Robertson, D. H. 1940. "Mr. Keynes and the Rate of Interest." *In* Robertson, D. H. (ed.), *Essays in Monetary Theory.* London: P. S. King, pp. 1–38.

Robichek, A. A., and Myers, S. C. 1965. *Optimal Financing Decisions.* Englewood Cliffs, NJ: Prentice-Hall.

Robinson, J. 1969. *Economics of Imperfect Competition,* 2nd ed. London: Macmillan.
   1974. *History versus Equilibrium.* London: Thames Polytechnic.

Ross, S. A. 1976. "The Arbitrage Theory of Capital Asset Pricing." *Journal of Economic Theory* 13: 341–60.
   1977. "Return, Risk, and Arbitrage." *In* Friend, I., and Bicksler, J. (eds.), *Risk and Return in Finance.* Cambridge, MA: Ballinger, pp. 189–218.
   1978. "The Current Status of the Capital Asset Pricing Model (CAPM)." *Journal of Finance* 33: 885–902.

Roy, A. D. 1952. "Safety First and the Holding of Assets." *Econometrica* 20: 431–49.

Sandmo, A. 1971. "On the Theory of the Competitive Firm under Price Uncertainty." *American Economic Review* 61: 65–73.

Savage, L. J. 1951. "The Theory of Statistical Decisions." *Journal of the American Statistical Association* 46: 55–67.

Shackle, G. L. S. 1967. *The Years of High Theory.* Cambridge: Cambridge University Press.
   1969. *Decision, Order and Time in Human Affairs.* Cambridge: Cambridge University Press.
   1970. *Expectations, Enterprise and Profit: Theory of the Firm.* Chicago, IL: Aldine.
   1972. *Epistemics and Economics.* Cambridge: Cambridge University Press.
   1974. *Keynesian Kaleidics.* Edinburgh: Edinburgh University Press.
   1979. "Imagination, Formalism, and Choice." *In* Rizzo, M. J. (ed.), *Time, Uncertainty, and Disequilibrium.* Lexington, MA: Lexington Books, pp. 19–31.
   1983. "The Bounds of Unknowledge." In Wiseman, J. (ed.), *Beyond Positive Economics?* New York: St. Martin's, pp. 28–37.

Sharpe, W. F. 1963. "A Simplified Model for Portfolio Analysis." *Management Science* 9: 277–93.
   1964. "Capital Asset Prices: A Theory of Market Equilibrium under Conditions of Risk." *Journal of Finance* 19: 425–42.
   1970. *Portfolio Theory and Capital Markets.* New York: McGraw-Hill.

Smith, V. L. 1959. "The Theory of Investment and Production." *Quarterly Journal of Economics* 73: 61–87.

1961. *Investment and Production: A Study in the Theory of Capital-Using Enterprise.* Cambridge, MA: Harvard University Press.

Solomon, E. 1956. "The Arithmetic of Capital Budgeting." *Journal of Business* 29: 124–29.

Sraffa, P. 1926. "The Laws of Return under Competitive Conditions." *Economic Journal* 36: 535–50.

Stigler, G. 1950. "The Development of Utility Theory." *Journal of Political Economy* 58: 307–27, 373–96. Reprinted in Stigler, G. 1965. *Essays in the History of Economics.* Chicago, IL: University of Chicago Press, pp. 66–155.

Tang, A. M., Westfield, O. M., and Worley, J. S. (eds.). 1976. *Evolution, Welfare, and Time in Economics: Essays in Honor of Nicholas Georgescu-Roegen.* Lexington, MA: Lexington Books.

Tobin, J. 1958. "Liquidity Preference as Behavior Towards Risk." *Review of Economic Studies* 25: 65–86.

1965. "The Theory of Portfolio Selection." In Hahn, F. H., and Brechling, F. P. R. (eds.), *The Theory of Interest Rates.* London: Macmillan, pp. 3–51.

Turnovsky, S. J. 1970. "Financial Structure and the Theory of Production." *Journal of Finance* 25: 1061–80.

Vickers, D. 1966. "Profitability and Reinvestment Rates, A Note on the Gordon Paradox." *Journal of Business* 39: 366–70.

1968. *The Theory of the Firm: Production, Capital, and Finance.* New York: McGraw-Hill.

1970. "The Cost of Capital and the Structure of the Firm." *Journal of Finance* 25: 35–46. Reprinted in Amey, L. R. (ed.), *Readings in Managerial Decision.* London: Longmans, pp. 87–99.

1975. "Finance, and False Trading in Non-Tâtonnement Markets." *Australian Economic Papers* 14: 171–86.

1977. "Financial Theory of the Firm." *In* Weintraub, S. (ed.), *Modern Economic Thought.* Philadelphia: University of Pennsylvania Press, pp. 203–15.

1978. *Financial Markets in the Capitalist Process.* Philadelphia: University of Pennsylvania Press.

1981. "Real Time and the Choice-Decision Point." *Journal of Post Keynesian Economics* 3: 545–51.

1983. "Formalism, Finance, and Decisions in Real Economic Time." *In* Coats, A. W. (ed.), *Methodological Controversy in Economics: Historical Essays in Honor of T. W. Hutchison.* Greenwich, CT: JAI, pp. 247–63.

1984. "The Uncertainty About Uncertainty." *Eastern Economic Journal* 10: 71–77.

1985a. *Money, Banking, and the Macroeconomy.* Englewood Cliffs, NJ: Prentice-Hall.

1985b. "On Relational Structures and Non-Equilibrium in Economic Theory." *Eastern Economic Journal* 11: 384–403.

1986. "Time, Ignorance, Surprise, and Economic Decisions." *Journal of Post Keynesian Economics* 9: 48–57.

von Neumann, J., and Morgenstern, O. 1953. *The Theory of Games and Economic Behavior,* 3rd ed. Princeton, NJ: Princeton University Press.

238   References

1968. "The Notion of Utility." *In* Page, A. N. (ed.), *Utility Theory: A Book of Readings*. New York: Wiley, pp. 215–33.

Walras, L. 1953. *Elements of Pure Economics*, translated by W. Jaffee. Homewood, IL: Irwin, American Economic Association.

Weintraub, E. R. 1979. *Microfoundations, The Compatibility of Microeconomics and Macroeconomics*. Cambridge: Cambridge University Press.

Weintraub, S. 1949. *Price Theory*. New York: Pitman.

(ed.). 1977. *Modern Economic Thought*. Philadelphia: University of Pennsylvania Press.

Weiss, N. 1984. "Capital Markets, Output, and the Demand for Inputs under Uncertainty." *Eastern Economic Journal* 10: 51–70.

Williams, J. B. 1965. *The Theory of Investment Value*. New York: Kelley.

Wiseman, J. (ed.). 1983. *Beyond Positive Economics?* New York: St. Martin's.

Wood, A. 1975. *A Theory of Profit*. Cambridge: Cambridge University Press.

Index

absolute risk aversion, 117–18
see also relative risk aversion
accept-or-reject decision, 47, 222–3
accounts receivable, 27, 45, 61, 66
allocation, 108
Amey, L. R., 232
arbitrage, 149, 172
mechanism, 166–8, 170, 174–5
Arbitrage Pricing Theory, 149
Archer, S. H., 180
Arditti, F. D., 134
Arrow, K. J., 107, 118, 134
asset market theory, 133, 200, 230
see also financial asset market
asset portfolio, 23, 103
attention arresting power, 219, 220–2
attractiveness function, 220–2
see also iso-attractiveness contours
Average Surplus Cash Flow, 204
axioms of choice, 109, 119, 124
completeness, 119
complexity, 121
continuity, 120, 123
monotonicity, 121
substitutability, 120
transitivity, 119

balance sheet, 9–10, 22, 24, 66
analysis, 24–8, 37–8
homeostasis of, 27–8, 37
see also income statement
Barges, A., 161
Baumol, W. J., 10, 14, 165
Bausor, R., 6, 17
belief, 215
Bernoulli, D., 108
beta coefficient, 146–9, 154, 155, 182
see also market beta
Bicksler, J., 233
Bierman, H., 134, 172
Black, F., 148
book value, 24, 161
Boulding, K. E., 22, 23, 27–8, 37
break-even probability, 125, 126
Brealey, R., 10, 31, 134, 165, 180, 182, 183, 199

Brechling, F. P. R., 233
Buchanan, N. S., 14

capital, 22
budget, 197, 199, 204, 208
consumption, 24
see also depreciation
expenditure, 205, 208
factor, 13, 23, 191–2
issues, 45, 199, 200
marginal productivity, 192
market, 50, 199, 204, 209–10
see also financial asset market
mobility, 34–5
structure, 15, 169, 170, 172, 184
surplus, 26
see also debt capital, equity capital, money capital, real capital
capital gains tax, 168, 184, 198
capitalization, 28
of equity income, 38–40, 60–1, 74, 156, 175
rate, 60–1, 74, 78, 80, 136, 164
capitalized value, 64, 175, 226–7
Capital Market Line, 142, 144, 150, 200
capital reversal, 227
Carter, C. F., 231
cash flow, 10, 28, 43–4
internally generated, 197, 204, 205, 207–8
marginal, 204, 208
sequences, 187
certainty-equivalents, 16, 212, 231
certificates of deposit, 11
Chamberlin, E., 4, 6
Choate, G. M., 180
choice, 7, 17, 108
see also axioms of choice
criteria, 108
decision moment, 7
objects of, 109, 110
see also stochastic objects of choice
theory of, 19, 108, 138
Coats, A. W., 233
Coddington, A., 23
coherence, 195